# SUICIDE IN NAZI GERMANY

The suicides of Hitler, Goebbels, Bormann, Himmler, and later Goering at the end of World War II were only the most prominent in a suicide epidemic that has no historical parallel and that can tell us much about the Third Reich's peculiar self-destructiveness and the depths of Nazi fanaticism.

Looking at the suicides of both Nazis and ordinary people in Germany from the end of World War I until the end of World War II, Christian Goeschel shows how suicides among different population groups, including supporters, opponents, and victims of the regime, responded to the social, cultural, economic, and political context of the time. Richly grounded in gripping and previously unpublished source material *Suicide in Nazi Germany* offers a new perspective on the central social and political crises of the era, from revolution, economic collapse, and the rise of the Nazis, to Germany's total defeat in 1945.

# SUICIDE IN NAZI GERMANY

CHRISTIAN GOESCHEL

OXFORD
UNIVERSITY PRESS

## OXFORD
### UNIVERSITY PRESS

Great Clarendon Street, Oxford, OX2 6DP,
United Kingdom

Oxford University Press is a department of the University of Oxford.
It furthers the University's objective of excellence in research, scholarship,
and education by publishing worldwide. Oxford is a registered trade mark of
Oxford University Press in the UK and in certain other countries

First published 2009
First published in paperback 2015

Published in the United States of America by Oxford University Press
198 Madison Avenue, New York, NY 10016, United States of America

British Library Cataloguing in Publication Data
Data available

Library of Congress Cataloging in Publication Data
Data available

ISBN 978–0–19–953256–8 (Hbk.)
ISBN 978–0–19–960611–5 (Pbk.)

# Contents

# *Acknowledgements*

It is a great pleasure to thank all those who have supported my work for this book. I should like to thank the Arts and Humanities Research Board, the Allen, Meak and Read Scholarship, and the Cambridge European Trust for funding my research at Cambridge. I am also grateful to the Sir John Plumb Charitable Trust and the German History Society for financing various research trips to the archives. The Cambridge University Prince Consort Studentship, the Kurt Hahn Trust, the Institute of Historical Research's Scouloudi Fellowship, the Charles H Revson Fellowship at the United States Holocaust Memorial Museum, and, above all, my parents provided crucial extra support.

I should like to thank the many librarians and archivists in Britain, Germany, and the United States who have supplied me with material for this book. Without their expert advice, I could not have written it. My work has benefited in many ways from discussions with other scholars. I was fortunate enough to be a member of the Cambridge Modern European History Workshop and Richard J Evans's Cambridge Workshop on Modern German History where some of the ideas presented here first took shape. At an early stage of my research, Hans Medick and Andreas Bähr invited me to give a paper at a very stimulating conference at Erfurt University, where I received invaluable advice. Hartmut Kaelble and Wolfgang Hardtwig kindly invited me to their colloquia at Berlin's Humboldt University which provided lots of useful feedback. In Berlin, I also had many productive conversations with Monica Black and Molly Loberg who both read early versions of some of the material presented here. Monica organized a very useful panel discussion at the German Studies Association, where I benefited from Frank Biess's commentary. Jeffrey Herf invited me to his research seminar at the University of Maryland which provided lots of food for thought. In Washington, DC, I had very fruitful exchanges with my colleagues at the Center for

Advanced Holocaust Studies. In California, I enjoyed discussing my work at Claremont McKenna College and the Lessons and Legacies Conference. In England, I received very constructive feedback at the Oxford Modern German History Seminar, the Modern German History Seminar at the Institute of Historical Research and the Holocaust Workshop at Royal Holloway.

Earlier versions of Chapters 3 and 5 have appeared as articles, and I thank the editors and readers for their stimulating feedback: 'Suicides of German Jews in the Third Reich', in *German History*, 25 (2007), 22–45; 'Suicide at the End of the Third Reich', in *Journal of Contemporary History*, 41 (2006), 153–73.

Without the generous support of many other scholars, I could not have written this book. I should like to thank Richard Bessel for all his help and support at an early stage of my research. I also owe special thanks to Moritz Föllmer for many fruitful discussions over the years. I have benefited enormously from stimulating conversations with Darcy Buerkle, Zoë Waxman, Hubertus Jahn, Dan Magilow, and Jonathan Petropoulos. Dan kindly helped me translate some of the quotations and Jonathan assisted me in approaching this publisher.

Other friends and colleagues too have read earlier versions of some or all of this material. I am extremely grateful to Geoffrey Giles, Emanuel Heisenberg, Maximilian Horster, Susan Morrissey, Mark Offord, and Nick Stargardt. Chris Clark and Sir Ian Kershaw gave me the most generous and helpful feedback on an earlier draft of this work, and I am deeply grateful to them.

Over the last few years, I have greatly enjoyed the privilege of working with Nikolaus Wachsmann in the stimulating and supportive atmosphere of Birkbeck College's School of History, Classics and Archaeology. My colleagues Sean Brady, Lucy Riall, and Nikolaus Wachsmann all read my manuscript and did much to improve it. Catharine Edwards made some excellent suggestions on the introduction. I also owe particular thanks to my students at Birkbeck College who have helped me shape my ideas about the history of the Third Reich. I am deeply indebted to my brother Joachim for his expert help with the statistics at the end of this book. Christopher Wheeler and his team at Oxford University Press have been enthusiastic supporters of this project, and Jeremy Langworthy has been an exemplary copy-editor.

Most of all, I have to thank Richard J Evans for all his help and support. His comments on various drafts were always to the point and his advice could not have been more generous.

CG
London

# List of Tables

# List of Figures

# List of Abbreviations

| | |
|---|---|
| ADW | Archiv des Diakonischen Werks, Berlin-Dahlem |
| BAB | Bundesarchiv, Berlin |
| DNVP | Deutschnationale Volkspartei (German National People's Party) |
| EZAB | Evangelisches Zentralarchiv, Berlin |
| GStA | Geheimes Staatsarchiv Preußischer Kulturbesitz, Berlin-Dahlem |
| IWM | Imperial War Museum, London |
| KPD | Kommunistische Partei Deutschlands (German Communist Party) |
| LAB | Landesarchiv, Berlin |
| NSDAP | Nationalsozialistische Deutsche Arbeiterpartei (National Socialist German Workers' Party) |
| PRO | Public Record Office, Kew |
| RSHA | Reichssicherheitshauptamt (Reich Security Head Office) |
| SA | Sturmabteilung (Storm troopers) |
| SD | Sicherheitsdienst (Security Service) |
| SS | Schutzstaffel (Protection Squad) |
| SPD | Sozialdemokratische Partei Deutschlands (German Social Democratic Party) |
| StA | Staatsarchiv |
| WL | Wiener Library, London |

# Note to the reader

Under German law governing personal data and records, individuals' identities are to be protected during their lifetime and for a certain period after their deaths. Relatives of individual suicides must also be protected, of course. This regulation creates some problems for any historian. I have therefore decided to abbreviate the last names of individual suicides, unless their cases have been published before.

Important suicide statistics are presented in a statistical appendix.

# Introduction

## I

Most people know that the Third Reich ended in an orgy of self-immolation, with the suicides of Hitler and Eva Braun, Goebbels and his wife, Himmler, later on Göring, and many other leading Nazis. But few know very much about how these events fitted into the wider pattern of self-destruction in Nazi Germany. Were they startlingly unexpected, or did they form the culmination of broader and deeper trends in ideology and behaviour? This book aims to provide an answer to this question, examining suicide in Germany between 1918 until 1945, from the end of the First World War till the end of the Second World War.

Suicide is the 'most private and impenetrable of human acts', as the historian Richard Cobb declared in 1978.[1] It can serve as the ultimate way out of emotional, social, or economic problems that appear insoluble. Modern society generally relates suicide to illness, thereby dismissing suicides' motivations as pathological; but this way of thinking deprives suicides of the 'potential of ethical choice and reflexivity'.[2] It furthermore suggests that any historical analysis of suicide would be meaningless because the decision to kill oneself is ultimately the product of timeless frailties. But in the late nineteenth century, the French sociologist Emile Durkheim disputed this view.

Durkheim saw suicide as the result of socially determined structures. Suicide results from the individual's lack of integration with society. Durkheim was concerned mainly with the extent of modernity's destructive and chaotic impact on civilized society.[3] His study of suicide stands in the tradition of 'moral statistics', a nineteenth-century genre that sought to uncover broad patterns of human behaviour over time. Their genesis reflected political and cultural developments of the mid- to late nineteenth century, a time when governments, concerned with social policy, became increasingly interested in birth and death rates, crime levels, and similar statistical phenomena. From the 1870s onwards, state institutions increasingly saw suicide statistics as correlated with the moral well-being of society.[4] Durkheim conceived of three main types of self-destruction: egoistic, altruistic, and anomic suicide. Egoistic suicide resulted from a lack of social integration, altruistic suicide stemmed from people's desire to die for the cause of society, and anomic suicide resulted from a complete turnover of norms and values.[5] All of these categories are relevant to the present study, but anomie is particularly useful because it can explain suicide as a historical event. Moreover, contemporaries used a notion corresponding to the concept of anomie (though not the term itself) to interpret their experiences of modernity and the reversal of norms and values which in their view prompted suicide. A number of historians have adopted Durkheim's ideas. In a brief, but nevertheless thought-provoking, section of his study of English pre-industrial society, Peter Laslett applied Durkheim's theory of suicide in a way typical of 1960s and 1970s historiography. Laslett held that 'suicide [was] the most usual index of social demoralization...marking the relationship between personal discipline and social survival'.[6] The historian Olive Anderson's monograph on suicide in Victorian and Edwardian England concentrates overwhelmingly on statistics and relies on Durkheim's positivist and social-scientific approach, taking into account differences of generations, gender, and class to explain different suicide patterns.[7]

Yet the medievalist historian Alexander Murray notes that 'the concepts of suicide and statistics are from one angle as remote as two concepts can be'.[8] The structuralist model blames social factors for suicidal acts. Because of its exclusive focus on the social dimension of suicide, this model largely disregards individual motivations for self-destruction, neglecting the freedom of action of the individual.

Suicide statistics do offer 'a visible, tangible indication of that of which it is an extreme instance', but they leave out the individual.[9] We therefore need a multi-faceted methodology to study suicide in Weimar and Nazi Germany, one that places emphasis on both the individual and society by studying both statistics and documents pertaining to individual suicides.

In their work on suicide in early modern England, Michael MacDonald and Terence Murphy take a different approach towards suicide. They emphasize the cultural and subjective aspects of suicide, which are largely absent from Durkheim and Anderson's accounts. MacDonald and Murphy find it unhelpful to calculate a suicide rate and engage in quantitative approaches towards suicide. Instead they focus on the changing cultural and social meanings of suicide in early modern England, ultimately taking suicide as a case study for cultural change.[10] MacDonald and Murphy's approach reminds us to pay attention to the textual construction of suicide and of the changing cultural assumptions underlying suicide statistics. MacDonald and Murphy's approach is therefore helpful. It is possible to reconstruct from the context at least a tentative view of motives as well as justifications.

Yet suicide is not merely culturally constructed. It is an action that takes place in material reality. Statistics represent the quantitative extent of suicide, and we have to take them into account, regardless of their inherent culturally determined flaws. One historian pointedly comments: 'We should be denying historians their calling if we believed all recorded events were detached from some objective reality.'[11]

In 1967, the sociologist Jack D Douglas suggested that there were serious flaws in Durkheim's statistical approach to suicide. Suicide rates reflect the discourses and values underlying them, which are the main influence on the reporting of suicides as such.[12] Some suicide statistics compiled in Nazi Germany classified suicide motives, but these broad typologies of suicide motives were a direct result of Nazi thinking on suicide, which policemen and statisticians imposed on individual suicides.

And it is certainly the case that not all suicides were reported to the statistic-compiling authorities nor do attempted suicides always find their way into statistics. As the early modern historian David Lederer argues, the claim that Protestant areas carry a much higher suicide rate than Catholic regions is an assumption that has turned into a cultural stereotype. There is indeed a very strong taboo on suicide in Catholicism, which treats it as a mortal sin. There was considerable pressure on doctors and policemen in Catholic regions to record suicides as accidents, as Friedrich Zahn, the President of the Bavarian Statistical Office, complained in 1932.[13] So religion is likely to impact upon the accuracy of the statistics.

Like all historical statistics, suicide statistics have an indubitable margin of error. Yet this does not mean they are meaningless or worthless. Thus in Weimar and Nazi Germany, suicide rates correlated in various ways with broader trends, for example with unemployment rates. It is surely safe, therefore, to conclude that they are not wholly inaccurate. Statistical evidence from both national and regional levels by age and sex reflects in rationally explicable ways the different patterns in rural and urban, as well as Protestant and Catholic areas and over time.

So we need to combine both schools, the statistical and the cultural, to understand suicide in Nazi Germany. We need to analyse the private dimension of suicide to shed light on the existential and emotional problems that drove individual suicides into this form of extreme behaviour. Yet suicide took place within a special social and political context and we need to disregard the entrenched frontlines and consider both the individual and the social aspects of suicide.[14] We need to analyse what was written on suicide and to undertake a critical reading of the documents left by suicides, including suicide notes. Suicide statistics were published within particular conceptual frames, thereby shaping the categories and perceptions of contemporaries. They helped to shape a popular notion of the social sphere and even the causes of suicide. Thus as well as interpreting suicide levels as indicators of social and political developments, this book also studies the way in which contemporaries perceived them.

This book brings the individual back into history. It is informed by the genre of the 'microstudy', such as Richard J Evans's work on narratives of crime and punishment in nineteenth-century Germany. Historians working on deviant behaviour in the 1960s and 1970s tended to be largely concerned with the macro-level and the broader statistical level, since they were trying to link their findings to large-scale developments such as industrialization and secularization. Evans concludes, with some justification, that in this research 'the human dimension tended to disappear beneath a mountain of statistics' in books that were hardly readable. To avoid the pitfalls of an exclusively statistical study, this book also studies individual experiences and suicide discourses.[15]

There are, therefore, three different ways of approaching the study of suicide: the discursive, the social, and the individual. These are not simply different methods that should be juxtaposed to each other. Rather, there is an interpenetration of all three. In Weimar and Nazi Germany suicide featured very prominently in political, societal, cultural, and medical debates. This book therefore discusses changes and continuities in suicide discourse. But suicide is not simply a discourse; we also need to pay attention to practice. Suicide itself is a practice, as are the various regulatory mechanisms of state and church institutions. Studying suicide as a practice helps us overcome the self-referentiality of discursive approaches and to recover an element of individual agency.[16]

Why did people commit suicide in Nazi Germany? Can we ever answer this question?[17] All we have are contemporary descriptions and discourses, broad correlated socio-economic trends, the wider context, and, if available, suicide notes. All of these sources do tell us a great deal about representations of and subjective views on suicide. Individual suicides will have had different reasons for killing themselves, of course. This book identifies some common patterns in suicide motives, examining their continuities and discontinuities in Weimar and Nazi Germany. Did men's reasons for committing suicide differ from women's suicide motives? Male suicides had a higher profile than female suicides in Weimar and Nazi Germany and elsewhere in modern Europe, and male suicide rates were higher than female ones. This monograph takes up the recent interest in gender. In particular, it sheds light on changing ideals of masculinity through a study of suicide. For men, masculinity was both an internalized value and a social status with a set of roles and expectations. Failure to live up to these expectations was an important trigger for killing oneself.[18]

While it will never be possible to discover beyond any doubt the ultimate reasons why people killed themselves, farewell missives allow one to attempt at least a plausible interpretation of suicide motives. At the same time, the Nazis often gave deliberate misrepresentations of fact in order to conceal murders as suicide. So we need to bear in mind the crucial difference between the representation of suicide on the one hand and its material reality on the other.

Suicide has, of course, different meanings in different societies. To give an example, many people persecuted by the Nazis killed themselves. Are these deaths to be seen as suicides? Is any act of death by one's own hand suicide, even if it is subject to external control and impositions? Or is it more useful to restrict the definition of suicide to acts of intentional self-destruction committed autonomously in sound mind and with the clear intent of death at a specific time? This book considers both facets of suicide.[19]

## II

These very complex methodological issues help explain why very little has been written on suicide in the Third Reich. Furthermore, sources are scattered in archives across Germany. The first works on suicide in this period were therefore not very solidly grounded in archival-based research. In 1953, the left-wing author Günther Weisenborn published his pioneering survey of what he called 'the resistance movement of the German people' against the Nazis. In it, Weisenborn argued that suicide could sometimes be an act of political resistance in Nazi Germany. He declared: 'Apart from suicide, under some circumstances a powerful act of resistance, for example when someone killed himself in the Gestapo prison, there were many forms of opposition.'[20] But suicide in the Third Reich was not only an act of political dissent, as we will see. The first scholarly attempt to get to grips with suicide in that period were two articles written by Susanne Hahn and Christina Schröder, two Marxist historians of science, who argued that suicide became an essential part of what they called 'the fascist concept of the extermination of useless life'.[21] But they did not provide any evidence beyond a few selected Nazi pamphlets and did not argue their points, making their study inconclusive.

Ursula Baumann offers a short account of suicide in Nazi Germany in a monograph that focuses overwhelmingly on the nineteenth century. Baumann offers worthwhile compilations of suicide statistics as well as a very detailed account of the contemporary academic literature on suicide. However, she fails to contextualize her findings with the available secondary literature on the nature of the Third Reich and barely engages with the flourishing English-speaking literature on the history of suicide more generally, which is too rich and diverse to be ignored with impunity. Her main interest lies in suicide discourse and in the transformation of the right to die by one's own hand. Her work thereby risks reducing suicide to mere representation and discourse. So her approach has serious limitations in terms of explaining the social and political dimension of suicide in Weimar and Nazi Germany.[22]

This book goes beyond the earlier historiography and uses a wide range of sources. National suicide statistics are only accessible until 1939. Regional and local statistics are available for the war years, however, and will, therefore, also feature in the present book. There is also a wide range of printed sources, both academic and popular, giving insights into contemporary perceptions of suicide. Many academics published on suicide in the 1920s and the 1930s. However, academic studies tend to reflect elite views. In his 1995 study of suicide in 'Western culture',

Georges Minois, for example, implies that historical change only occurs among the elites and that common, everyday suicide was largely immune to historical influences until the top-down diffusion of enlightenment ideas and secularism during and after the eighteenth century. Yet it is difficult to see how this apparently helps us understand the mass society and culture of the first half of the twentieth century.[23] Newspapers shaped popular views on suicide. Religious ideas on suicide still played a significant role, especially in rural areas. Political parties, especially the Nazis, also held strong views on suicide, which they regularly used in their propaganda until the downfall of the Third Reich.

Archival evidence for this book covers both rural and urban, and Catholic and Protestant areas. Unpublished documents from Hamburg, Berlin, the Protestant region around Darmstadt, the Catholic region around Würzburg in Lower Franconia, and also from the Catholic Rhineland, Silesia and East Prussia feature in this book. Sources on rural suicides are sparse, as patterns of suicide in the countryside changed very slowly. Even the economic crises that affected rural Germany in the 1920s and early 1930s, a major factor behind suicides in the countryside, were not new in principle nor in their emotional impact on individuals.

A unique collection of suicide notes and police investigations will be presented throughout this book. Criminal police and legal files yield information on the personal background of suicides and often contain interrogation information from relatives, which in turn tell us a lot about how ordinary people viewed suicide. This collection was compiled by the famous chief of the Berlin homicide squad in the 1920s and 1930s, Ernst Gennat. It contains a remarkable collection of suicide notes from 1901 until 1945, allowing close insights into the mentalities of suicides. These sources also reveal state interventions in cases of suicide, and show how suicide was policed in Weimar and Nazi Germany. A closer look at the subjectivity of these suicide notes adds a new dimension to the history of everyday life in Weimar and Nazi Germany.[24] Suicide notes are, of course, often written under great mental stress. Yet people who write a farewell letter, whether they address it to state institutions, such as the police or the welfare office, or to relatives, usually intend to ascribe one particular meaning to their suicide. Studying suicide notes as the final communication between suicide and society, therefore, helps us to study the circumstances under which people took their lives.

# III

This book engages with various significant aspects of suicide in the Third Reich. It starts with an examination of the crucial Weimar background and looks at suicide in Germany between the defeat of 1918 and the Nazi takeover of power. Suicide levels increased dramatically in the short-lived Weimar Republic; social dislocation seems to have prompted ordinary people to commit suicide, even if not in the numbers that some contemporaries claimed. The Nazis in particular associated rising suicide levels with the defeat of 1918 and Germany's purported political and socio-economic misery. How accurate was this claim? The book then shifts to suicide from the Nazi seizure of power until the outbreak of the war. The Nazis suppressed public knowledge and discussion of suicide, although suicide levels remained high in comparison to other countries; Nazi terror and persecution prompted many to kill themselves. German-Jewish suicides during the Third Reich happened within the context of Nazi racial policies and deserve particular consideration in a separate chapter. These suicides can be seen as the last attempts to keep one's dignity and agency amidst the devastation of the final solution. Farewell missives offer a unique contemporary view on German-Jewish reactions to Nazi persecution. A discussion of suicides in the Third Reich at war follows. During the Second World War, the Third Reich increased its terror, and some people saw suicide as the only way out. Powerful case studies of suicides during this time shed new light on a key debate in recent historiography, namely the extent to which German society as a whole had developed an ideological commitment to the Nazis. The radical Nazi pursuit of war and the Allied bombings affected everyday lives to a greater extent than other events before. Military suicides and suicides within the German resistance against the Nazis feature in this chapter too. Finally, this book looks at suicide at the end of the Third Reich. It traces the origins of suicides at that time in a general feeling among Germans that everything was coming to an end. It analyses its background with reference to Nazi propaganda, the Nazi cult of death, and the Allied occupation of Germany. Death, destruction, and heroic self-sacrifice, the willingness to commit suicide for Germany, were key Nazi concepts especially during the Second World War.[25] Were the suicides of top Nazi leaders altogether surprising if one takes into account recent studies of the nature of the Nazi system of rule? The conclusion briefly looks at post-war Germany's suicide levels and concludes by offering a new approach towards the history of the Third Reich. This book, then, is about the phenomenon of suicide in Germany from the end of the First World War until the downfall of the Third Reich and its individual and statistical resonance, as well as about societal and political views of it.

# I

# The Weimar Background

## I

On 27 December 1918, just a few weeks after Germany's defeat, the scientist Richard Semon shot himself, wrapped in a German Imperial flag, in his Munich study. He was allegedly depressed by the German defeat.[1] Justifying one's suicide with reference to the defeat of 1918 was common among nationalist men in the war's immediate aftermath, reflecting despair at Germany's failure. In a similar case, Karl, the older brother of Baldur von Schirach, the later leader of the Hitler Youth, shot himself in November 1918. Allegedly, as Baldur von Schirach wrote in his autobiography in which he tried to justify why he became a Nazi, Karl committed suicide because he did not want to 'survive Germany's misfortune'.[2] For these suicides, the German defeat, the revolution of 1918, and the shift from a largely authoritarian monarchy to a seemingly chaotic republic amounted to a vast upheaval of traditional norms and values. Their known world had ceased to exist. Here was suicide presented as an act of patriotism, reflecting the military tradition of shooting oneself to maintain one's honour.

After 1918, contemporaries generally believed that times of general uncertainty, political disorder, and socio-economic hardship inevitably led to rising suicide levels. This obsession with rising suicide rates helped undermine the stability of the Weimar Republic. The Weimar background is crucial to an understanding of Nazi attitudes towards suicide in the Third Reich. The Nazis and other extremist political parties attacked the Weimar Republic by pointing to the high suicide rates. But not only extremist parties shared the belief that Weimar Germany was doomed with record suicide levels. Popular newspapers and ordinary people increasingly shared this notion. In order to understand how this assumption gradually turned into a mantra, we need to begin with a brief analysis of suicide levels and their contemporary perceptions. Then we will turn to various discourses on suicide and finally to individual acts of suicide.

At the turn of the century, newspapers began to link suicide with urbanization and modernization. Newspaper articles on suicide had carried headlines such as 'Tragedy in the Big City' or 'Defeated in the Struggle for Survival'.[3] Many thought that the defeat and revolution of 1918 and the Versailles Treaty had overthrown the existing order.

Observers pointed to rising suicide levels from the mid-1920s onwards. 'Our country has been hit by an alarming suicide epidemic, which has reached a climax that has to be stopped by every means ... This is yet another representation of the enormously tragic fate of the German *Volk*.'[4] Thus the Catholic *Kölner Tageblatt* claimed on 17 November 1925. Generally, contemporary observers not only blamed the defeat of 1918, the inflation and the Versailles Treaty for the increasing suicide levels, but also the impact of modernity and secularization.

Things were getting worse and suicide rates rose. The following 1925 article in *Der Berliner Westen*, a local paper, was typical:

> In greater Berlin ... the terrible suicide epidemic ... is consistently causing casualties ... and it can be safely assumed that our people have not yet become so brutalized and indifferent, despite war and bloodshed, mass murder, and revolution that voluntary death does not move people and genuine philanthropists to help ... Misery is great, and voluntary death persists. Each hour of failure makes us guilty, since other people's suffering, even if caused by themselves, is a concern for everyone ...[5]

Acts of suicide should thus have prompted other Germans to help each other and strengthen their sense of community to prevent others from killing themselves. The statistics, however, suggested that this did not happen or, if it did, it did not work. Suicide rates carried on rising. The general rise, however, concealed wide variations between different age groups, and within these, between men and women.

During the First World War, the suicide rate dropped. According to Durkheim, wars have a lower suicide rate, since almost everyone is drawn into the war effort. This mobilization prompts a higher degree of social integration.[6] Some argued that during the war, the state authorities in charge of registering suicides did not have the necessary staff resources to do so adequately. Writing in 1940, at a time when many Germans glorified the experience of the First World War, the psychiatrist Hans W Gruhle dismissed this claim and commended the 'great communal experience' of the war.[7] Of course, during the war, front-line soldiers could easily commit suicide by exposing themselves to enemy fire, and such cases would not be recorded as suicide. This might offer a partial explanation as to why suicide levels fell during the war. Nevertheless, the rise from 1917 to 1919 and then 1921 is still striking, but we cannot say with complete certainty that the war alone really led to lower suicide levels.

A detailed study of suicide compiled by the municipal statistical office of Frankfurt am Main in 1932 revealed that suicide had become a more common way of dying since the end of the First World War. In 1913, only 1.15 per cent of all deaths in Germany had been suicides. But in 1931, 2.5 per cent of all deaths were suicides. August Busch, the author of this study, explained this rise with reference to a drop in other causes of death, such as tuberculosis, in the city, so that the usefulness of this particular measure is questionable.[8]

Female levels were much lower than male levels. However, throughout the Weimar years, female suicide rates were much higher than they had been in 1913. Male rates only began to rise significantly above pre-war levels in the final years of the Republic, despite a slight jump in 1926. More than 2 million young men had died on the battlefields and in the trenches, so elderly people, generally more prone to commit suicide than young people, formed a higher proportion of the general population.[9] With the deaths of so many young men, the surplus of women in the population increased.

The unemployed were more likely to kill themselves than others, many commentators thought.[10] In particular, unemployed men, especially fathers of families, were more likely to commit suicide than single women without a job. For men with families, unemployment did not just mean the simple loss of earnings. It had much wider social ramifications. Jobless fathers of families felt unable to fulfil their role as breadwinners for their families. Such men thought that they had failed to conform to social expectations about what it meant to be a man.[11] In this devastating situation, many men committed suicide. Since the winter of 1925–6, unemployment figures had been rising, and for the rest of its existence, the Weimar Republic suffered from high unemployment. From 1929 millions of Germans were unemployed. The existing system of support could not cope, not even after crisis relief (*Krisenunterstützung*) for those ineligible for unemployment relief (*Erwerbslosenfürsorge*) was introduced in 1926. Most of the long-term unemployed thus had to rely on welfare relief, paid by local authorities, which was substantially lower than unemployment benefits. These cuts in welfare provision created a feeling of hopelessness and despair and prompted, as we will see, many welfare recipients to threaten to commit suicide. Victimization was a widespread feeling in Weimar Germany. Ordinary people saw themselves as victims of insufficient welfare provisions and the political and economic uncertainty, while their need for welfare support constantly rose at the same time.[12]

Of course, unemployment alone does not explain suicidal behaviour.[13] Nevertheless, it seems obvious that it must have been a factor in the rising suicide rates of the late 1920s and early 1930s. In 1932, the medical doctor Karl Freudenberg argued that the overall suicide rate had not increased since 1918 as a result of the inflation and mass unemployment, but rather because of the different age structure, with more elderly people living in Germany, and a lower birth rate.[14] Freudenberg commented on the suicide rate among the male population of employment age: 'Despite the especially adverse conditions, the suicide rate is thus hardly higher than in 1913 ... This should prove that the main reasons for suicide do not lie in the environment.'[15] A breakdown of suicide levels by age and sex surely invalidates this argument.

The following statistical analysis presents a broad survey of the quantitative extent of suicide in Weimar Germany. It furthermore enables us to identify potential distortions of suicide rates by commentators like Freudenberg and their reasons for deliberate misinterpretations of suicide rates. While conceding that many suicides were due to economic problems, an article in the liberal *Berliner Tageblatt* on 29 January 1932 concluded, based on a recent survey by the Berlin Statistical Office, that 'these tragic reactions to a desperate economic situation have not increased so much in the years of crisis as is commonly assumed'.[16] A closer analysis of suicide by age and sex yields some further conclusions. The more advanced the age, the higher the suicide rate.[17] Suicide rates among young women did not increase significantly under the Weimar Republic: indeed they even fell slightly down to 1924. Although female suicide rates were higher than they had been before the war, they did not seem to be much affected by the ups and downs of the Weimar economy, except perhaps at the very end.[18]

Among 15- to 30-year-olds, both male and female rates were relatively consistent with pre-war levels. The lack of increasing rates among 15- to 30-year olds may conceal an increase among those in the twenties (a more precise generational breakdown is unfortunately not available). Rates were generally very low among adolescents. Young men's energies may have been galvanised up to 1923 by crime and street violence in a general context in which political activity was on the rise among the young, although they probably did not affect a majority of them.

The increase in suicide levels in 1924 among young men was most probably due to the deflationary economic reforms that had brought the inflation to an end and the resulting sharp rise in unemployment. It became suddenly much more difficult to find a job.[19] Men of working age had a higher suicide rate in 1924 and thereafter because of unemployment. Women's suicide rates were higher in the 15- to 30- age bracket during the inflation, when women's domestic role of finding food and shopping had come under considerable pressure, and jumped in 1923 when this role became almost impossible to fulfil. In 1924, the economic deflation and the consequent rise in unemployment for men coupled with the mass dismissal of female 'double-earners' had an almost equally severe effect. The great majority of young women still worked and earned wages only before they got married, so this age-group was especially vulnerable. Rising levels of suicide towards the end of the Republic may well have reflected rising female unemployment levels.[20]

Suicide rates in the age group 30–60, where most men were working, or expected to work, and most women were bringing up children, or were engaged in the part-time, casual labour market, or both, were somewhat higher among those aged 30–60 than among 15- to 30-year olds in the early 1920s but became a great deal higher during the Great Depression. Rates among men rose in 1924, levelling off in 1926–7, and after a small decline, increased again from 1929 onwards. This correlates neatly with the rise in unemployment during the post-inflationary stabilization, the years of relative prosperity from 1925 to 1928, and the sharp rise in unemployment from 1929. The mass unemployment from 1929 until 1932 is clearly behind the rise in rates among 30- to 60-year olds. So huge was unemployment that older dependants were now suffering too. Suicide rates of males at working age were substantially lower than in 1913 until the mass unemployment of the Great Depression in 1930. From 1924 to 1931, suicide rates of females at working age were much higher than in 1913 due to the rise in female employment and subsequent unemployment. Suicide rates also increased among women of working age, reflecting female employment patterns and a new understanding of gender roles. The female unemployment rate rose, though not as sharply as among men, during the Great Depression.[21] This was also a difficult time for housewives, with the husband or father often unemployed, and economic crisis hitting the household.

Suicide rates in the age bracket 60–70 were generally two to three times higher than those in the age group 30–60; the gap narrowed during the Great Depression but was still substantial. The same pattern, though less marked than among the younger age groups, is noticeable here too, namely a decline in the 'good years' of the Weimar economy and a rise during the Great Depression. The same factors were probably at work here too — unemployment and living standards. Many of the people behind these statistics (those 65 and younger) were still of working age and were hit by unemployment, perhaps more severely than younger people as companies tended to make elderly, rather than young people, redundant. Women were hit particularly hard. Female pensioners were affected badly by the inflation of 1923, when many lost their assets and during the Great Depression when the government cut pensions.

Among those aged 70 and above, where almost everybody was a pensioner or a dependant, suicide rates rose sharply during the inflation. This rise most probably reflected the severe economic difficulties this caused for these people, with savings and pensions losing all value. The suicide rate here in 1923 was extraordinarily high among men in particular. Here too there was a decline in the mid-1920s and then a rise in the Great Depression years, though by no means as striking as that of the inflation.

There was also a religious divide of German suicide rates. In Bavaria, largely Protestant areas such as Middle Franconia had substantially higher rates than Catholic ones such as Upper Bavaria. Probably trying to prevent people from comparing Bavarian suicide levels to others, the Bavarian Statistical Office did not publish suicide rates, but only absolute numbers. This makes a comparison to other *Länder* impossible. Some comparative material is available in the national statistics however. Protestant Saxony's suicide rates were almost twice as high as Catholic Bavaria's. Saxony was one of the most densely populated and most heavily industrialized German states and had traditionally carried very high suicide rates.[22] Gruhle's monograph on suicide offers some revealing numbers for Bavaria. From 1919 until 1921, there were 19.6 suicides per 100,000 of the population in Middle Franconia, similar to national levels. Only 27.01 per cent of the Mid-Franconian population was Catholic. In Upper Bavaria, with a

91.06 per cent Catholic population, on the other hand, there were only 16.8 suicides per 100,000 at the same time. Presumably, Munich suicides made up the largest proportion of Upper Bavarian suicides. Indeed, in 1922, 136 of the 251 Upper Bavarian suicides took place in Munich. Contemporaries saw big cities, as noted earlier, as creating a suicidal environment.[23] Furthermore, Gruhle noted: 'In the countryside, it is much easier to conceal suicides and to pretend accidents and illness, while in cities, the statistical registration of suicide is more exact.'[24]

Were Catholic suicide rates generally lower than Protestant rates? In Baden, a confessionally mixed area (38.2 per cent of Badeners were Protestant and 58.4 per cent Catholic), the average suicide rate for the years 1927 to 1935 was 31.2 per 100,000 for Protestants and a mere 18 for Catholics. Protestant levels broadly reflected the national average, while Catholic rates were substantially below it.[25] Protestant areas thus carried higher suicide rates than Catholic areas. The Catholic proscription against suicide was so strong that it either prevented Catholics from killing themselves or prompted relatives and doctors to conceal suicides.

Rural areas generally displayed lower suicide rates than towns. In the rural Buchen district of Baden, the average suicide rate for the years 1926 to 1935 was 10.3 per 100,000. The corresponding rate for the heavily industrialized and urban Mannheim district was 32.7.[26] Gruhle analysed suicides in Prussian towns and concluded that the denser the population, the greater the suicide levels. In 1924, Berlin's suicide rate was 45.4, while the average Prussian town with a population of 15,000 to 20,000 inhabitants had an average suicide rate of 22 per 100,000.[27] This rate still exceeded rural suicide rates. Gruhle blamed cities for causing higher suicide rates because of 'industrialization, more conflict and the dissolution of traditional milieus (church) and … dubious, morally unstable persons'.[28] His statement reflected the anti-modern and anti-urban sentiment many contemporary observers shared, above all if they were writing in the Third Reich like Gruhle. Yet suicide rates were higher in towns than in villages. In villages, religious affiliations were generally greater than in cities, which might have prevented people from killing themselves.[29]

Official suicide levels rose in the Weimar Republic. Amidst the ubiquity of public suicide discourses (discussed below), authorities may well have been more inclined to report suicides than they had been before 1918. However, the available evidence suggests that Weimar authorities largely used the same bureaucratic practices when compiling suicide rates as they had done in Imperial Germany.[30] The increase was therefore a real one. Female suicide levels rose considerably. Socio-economic factors clearly did matter. Suicide statistics reflected these changes, which affected people's everyday lives. This rather detailed statistical analysis has identified broader motivations for suicide like socio-economic change and unemployment. Yet these statistics hardly shed light on people's personal motivations for killing themselves.

# II

How did contemporaries deal with the problem of suicide and how did they interpret the statistics? Did these contemporary views on suicide have any bearing on actual individual suicides? The 1924 official government statistics, published by the Reich Statistical Office, claimed 'that suicide is first and foremost caused by insanity, neuropathy and physical illness. Thus ... the frequency of suicide is only to some extent due to changing socio-economic circumstances.'[31] In Weimar Germany, Social Darwinist views had widespread currency among the medical and criminological professions. Doctors such as Freudenberg often blamed inherited moral and physical weaknesses rather than socio-economic factors for the increase in suicide rates. These ideas date back to the late-nineteenth century when Social Darwinists such as the Italian psychiatrist Enrico Morselli argued that suicide was 'an effect of the struggle for existence and of human selection, which works according to the laws of evolution'.[32] Elite views had gradually shifted. Rather than condemning suicide as a crime against oneself and against the supreme authority of God over life and death, suicide was widely coming to be seen as a biological and hereditarian problem. Not all Weimar commentators shared this diagnosis, of course, and many continued to see suicide as a socially determined problem.[33]

In an article published in 1926, for example, Karl Freudenberg was forced to concede that the suicide rate of men aged over 70 years had risen considerably during the inflation of 1923 'because of assets that had withered away'.[34] Socio-economic factors could thus not be entirely dismissed. Another contemporary observer opined:

> It is not ... the working class who ... had to cope with little or no means at all in all these years, that has the strongest tendency to suicide, but the middle

class, which has seen better days, but was then suddenly impoverished by war, revolution and inflation and now has to face nothingness with no means and no work.[35]

Although this view was widely shared among the middle classes at the time, there is no evidence that proportionally more middle-class people than workers committed suicide. A study of files held by the Berlin First Aid Office (*Rettungsamt*) on suicide and attempted suicide between April 1923 and March 1927 noted that suicides among the working class were much more likely to be registered by the police or the *Rettungsamt* than suicides among the middle or upper classes. Among higher echelons of society, relatives usually called private doctors to avoid the stigmatization of having a suicide in one's family.[36] Working-class pensioners with no assets or extra income other than their pension found themselves in total poverty. But the middle classes usually did not lose everything during the inflation. Middle-class people lost money invested in war bonds, but those who had borrowed some money before the inflation were now able to repay their debts for virtually nothing. In many cases, these two situations affected the same person.[37] So the incomes of the middle classes were not destroyed and there seems no socio-economic reason why their suicide rates should have been high.

Class determined the way in which people killed themselves, some observers claimed. Taking an average count for the years from 1924 until 1931, 37 per cent of manual workers and craftsmen who killed themselves in Frankfurt during this time hanged themselves, while 40 per cent of white-collar workers and civil servants who committed suicide during the same period shot themselves.[38] In Berlin, working-class suicides tended to gas themselves, according to the Berlin First Aid Office's files on suicide and attempted suicide.[39] In Kiel, between 1919 and 1921, male suicides tended to kill themselves by hanging and shooting, while most female suicides gassed or drowned themselves.[40] Many male suicides still had guns from the war, of course; and shooting oneself left one with almost no chance of survival and had very masculine connotations. Female suicides, on the other hand, preferred methods of suicide that still left them with a slight chance of survival, such as drowning themselves or slitting their wrists. Women were less determined to die than men, a contemporary male doctor claimed, and were therefore inclined to use 'soft' means of suicide.[41] Means of suicide were thus gender-specific as were murder methods.[42]

The terminology people used also reflected contemporary attitudes towards suicide. In German, there are at least two words for suicide. A distinction is made between *Freitod* (voluntary death) and *Selbstmord* (self-murder). *Freitod* has positive connotations, suggesting that the act of suicide is rational and voluntary. *Selbstmord* implies negative associations with murder or homicide. In 1933, the philologist Karl Baumann traced the origins of *Selbstmord* in the Christian taboo placed on suicide, evoking the idea that only God was allowed to decide between life and death. In contrast, *Freitod*, a term first used by the Austrian philosopher Fritz Mauthner in 1906, was a secular term.[43] In 1911, Mauthner had declared: 'Against the older term, which suggests criminal law, I prefer the new, if not entirely neutral, expression *Freitod* because so-called 'self-murder' is indeed not an unnatural death.'[44] Karl Baumann declared that *Freitod* was 'an almost symbolical expression of the complete secularization of religious and moral culture',[45] and that it had been previously used in a different form, yet with a somewhat similar intention, by leading proponents of Social Darwinism such as Ernst Haeckel. In 1905, Haeckel had declared, brushing aside any Christian concerns:

> Voluntary death through which man brings his unbearable suffering to an end is in fact an act of redemption. Therefore, one should designate this act, which is also carried out with [the precepts of] reason, as self-redemption (*Autolyse*) and view it with the sincerest sense of Christan charity. We should not stigmatize it with the hypocritical scorn of our rotten morality.[46]

This adoption of the concept of voluntary death by Social Darwinists would lead one to expect that the Nazis, generally believing in a vulgarized form of Social Darwinism, preferred *Freitod*. This was not so, however. Quoting a speech Hitler gave at the inaugural session of the Nazi charity (*Winter-hilfswerk*) campaign in the October 1934, Baumann suggested that Hitler had denounced the notion of *Freitod* as the result of Jewish degeneracy. Commenting on suicide in the Weimar Republic Hitler insisted: 'These irresponsible Jewish authors of this age described this abjectly as *Freitod*.'[47]

In the Weimar Republic, the social democrats preferred *Freitod*, reflecting their generally secular ideology. The term was thus not necessarily Social Darwinistic. It was also an affirmation of agency, reason, and freedom. Leo Rosenthal, a social democratic writer, declared in 1924:

> We socialists subscribe to the view that we bear within ourselves our own destinies and that we are the masters and judges over our own lives. For us,

therefore, there is only one way to adjudicate the question whether one may consciously seek out voluntary death. The inalienable right to bring one's existence to a voluntary end belongs to any person who cannot be helped by other means.[48]

In an opinion poll which Karl Baumann took in late 1932, Paul Löbe, SPD president of the Reichstag until 1932, also argued in favour of the word *Freitod*.[49] The usage of the various terms for suicide was divided along ideological lines. Those arguing for an anti-individualist notion of the body—such as the Nazis, the churches and the communists—dismissed *Freitod*, while those in favour of individualism welcomed it. Karl Baumann conceded that despite its ideological implications, *Freitod* gained more widespread currency in the Weimar years. The press, including the liberal *Frankfurter Zeitung*, the *Vossische Zeitung*, as well as the communist *Rote Fahne*, and the socialist *Vorwärts* used *Selbstmord* and *Freitod* as synonyms.[50] Thus, in their everyday use, the two notions became blurred in the 1920s and 1930s.

# III

Politicians and political commentators referred to suicide to illustrate the ostensible decline of morality in the Weimar Republic. This could take various forms. Looking back at the purportedly chaotic Weimar Republic in a 1935 publication, the right-wing commentator Roderich von Ungern-Sternberg blamed 'rising expectations' and 'the lack of endurance' of the German population in times of crisis for the increasing suicide levels. He accused the feminist movement and its demands for female emancipation of being behind the rise in female suicides: 'The rising frequency of suicide among women does not reflect well on the modern women's movement.'[51] Another observer blamed 'seduction, which is much more widespread these days' for the increased suicide rate among young women, reflecting a widespread concern amongst conservatives about the freer sexual mores of the roaring twenties.[52] An article in the *Deutsche Zeitung* in May 1931 blamed the 'German suicide misery' (*Deutsches Selbstmordelend*) on the Brüning government's welfare cuts by Emergency Decree. The article warned: 'The coming years will probably yield still further increases in suicide rates, brought on by the expanding economic privation.'[53] Supporters of the Weimar Republic, on the other hand, tended to reject any connection with suicide rates. The social democratic *Abend* declared in 1931: 'Even now one can by no means speak of a suicide epidemic.'[54] Many commentators perceived Weimar Germany as an inherently suicidal environment irrespective of statistics. Commentators used suicide rates to attack trends of Weimar society, politics and culture they did not like—such as female emancipation. They were able to point to rising suicide rates as evidence for their claim that things were getting worse.

On the Left, writers predictably blamed suicides on the capitalist system. In Josef Maria Frank's novel *Unus multorum* (One of many), published in 1925 by the SPD-owned Dietz publishing house, an unemployed and impoverished artist kills himself in Berlin by jumping into the river Spree near the Museum Island. A rich banker, on his way to a restaurant, sees the man on the bridge, gets out of his car, and is handed a suicide note addressed 'To the last man who has seen me alive', before the suicide takes his fatal leap. Reading this letter at the restaurant, the banker learns that he himself was to blame for the suicide, since he had refused to give a loan to the artist. When he tells his friends at the restaurant, the suicide's girlfriend overhears this and shoots him in revenge. For Frank, suicide was clearly a result of the increasing social problems of the Weimar Republic, for which he blamed the capitalists.[55] Unemployment also figured in filmic representations of suicide. In *Kuhle Wampe* (1931/2), a film for which Bertolt Brecht wrote the script, suicide was portrayed as the last way out for unemployed workers. The first scene entitled 'One unemployed less' (*Ein Arbeitsloser weniger*) begins with a man jumping out of a window to his death. It is not the individual that is to blame for his suicide in this film, but society more generally and capitalist exploitation in particular.[56]

Newspapers from across the political spectrum also ran headlines on the allegedly direct relationship between unemployment and suicide. The communist *Welt am Abend*, owned by Willi Münzenberg, widely known as 'the Red Millionaire',[57] reported suicides on an almost daily basis from the late 1920s onwards, reflecting the upsurge in unemployment and the increasingly hostile attitude of the more and more Stalinist KPD towards the Weimar Republic. It had already made the point on 12 July 1924 in an article 'On Suicide, Unemployment and Hunger', published as the post-inflation cutbacks were taking a grip and suicide rates among men of working age were rising.[58] On 14 January 1931, the front page story of the *Welt am Abend* was on 'Suicide at the Labour Exchange'. An unemployed man had swallowed some cyanide at the Spandau labour office, for which the *Welt am Abend* blamed 'chicanery by the authorities'. This perception was widespread among the communists and the many unemployed men who, at the end of the Weimar Republic, were the main supporters of the KPD.[59] On 31 March 1932, the headline ran: '12 suicides within 30 hours. Causes: deprivation, fear of dismissal, hunger'. The sensationalist article culminated in the claim that the KPD would eliminate the problem of suicides, which were, in the vast majority, motivated by economic deprivation:

> Hardly an hour passes any longer without someone in Berlin taking his life. Yesterday, out of desperation, seven people voluntarily left this world, including married couples, an unemployed engineer, and an eighteen-year-old girl. By late this morning, five additional suicides had already been reported. Thus in less than thirty hours, there were no fewer than eleven suicides in the nation's capital … Suicide levels increase, as does the misery, since suicides result mostly as a consequence of the politics of the lesser of two evils, of emergency decrees, downsizing, and mass-unemployment. Today and tomorrow, welfare support for the poorest of the poor is being cut, even as rents rise. The time has come for everyone to use the upcoming elections to put an end to this situation.[60]

Continuing its attack on the Weimar Republic and capitalism, the same newspaper claimed on 30 May 1932:

> The gruesome figures are incriminating … Over the last four months, 683 people in Berlin brought their lives to an end. 18,000 people within 365 days. This means that every day in the Germany of emergency decrees, roughly 60 people throw their lives away. But suicide is not the answer. Only the struggle of the working people following the example of the Soviet Union can bring bread and work for all.[61]

While 18,625 suicides were indeed officially recorded in Germany in 1931,[62] the paper's claim that this meant an average of 60 suicides per day was rounded up for effect (in fact, the daily average was only 51). But this propagandistic use of suicide statistics continued nonetheless after Franz von Papen's right-wing cabinet cut state pensions in early July 1932.[63] Three people killed themselves almost immediately as the *Welt am Abend* claimed.[64] Only a Stalinist regime could solve Germany's problems, declared the paper. It is impossible to verify the implicit claim that the Soviet Union had a lower suicide rate than capitalist states, since the Soviets refused to publish their suicide rates, following the assertion that Communism had overcome the problem of suicide.[65] The *Welt am Abend* wanted to appeal to its readers with reference to a general suicidal atmosphere, symbolizing perhaps also the KPD's view that capitalism was self-destructing in an orgy of violence and despair.

KPD politicians took a similar view on suicide, particularly after the communist leadership had decided in 1929 to use the Reichstag as a stage for denouncing the Weimar Republic, its democratic system of government, and its main supporters, the social democrats.[66] In a Reichstag debate on the problems of the German economy on 18 June 1929, the communist deputy Ende insisted:

> The issue is not the misery of your economy … but the desperate state of the proletariat, of whom millions are unemployed. Perhaps you even know that here in Berlin, a suicide occurs every five hours. But it is not a suicide whereby a person simply throws his life away, but rather suicide day by day, hour by hour, that arises directly out of the privation of the proletariat.[67]

Ende referred to Berlin's suicide levels to denounce the Weimar Republic's legitimacy. However, his implicit calculations that there were around 1,800 suicides in Berlin per annum were rounded up for effect, with only 1,481 officially recorded suicides for 1928.[68] On 28 June 1929, the Reichstag debated the further cutting of unemployment benefits. ('Crisis benefits' a new and substantially lower form of welfare benefit than 'unemployment support' had already been introduced in 1926 amidst rising unemployment and declining state income in the wake of the Great Depression.) During the debate, the communist deputy Maddalena claimed that an unemployed man had tried to kill himself in the visitors' gallery of the Reichstag in protest against the government's plans to reduce unemployment benefits. The non-communist press did not report this case. The communists claimed that bourgeois and socialist newspapers fully supported the plans to reduce welfare payments.[69]

The KPD's party organ, the *Rote Fahne*, reported suicides in particularly graphic detail. On 4 January 1933, it ran a story on a 35-year-old unemployed man, Arthur Müller, from Leipzig, who threw himself on the track of the Berlin underground at the busy Friedrichstadt interchange during the evening rush hour, allegedly leaving a suicide note saying: 'I did what I did because of hunger.'[70] Implicitly blaming the political order of the Weimar Republic for the increase in suicide levels, the communists contributed to the weakening of the legitimacy of the Weimar Republic.

# IV

The press thus played a key role in encouraging a widespread interest in suicide and political parties made capital out of it. Already before the First World War, newspapers had regularly reported suicides and had associated them with life in the city and modernity. Not only political papers, whose circulation numbers were declining in the late Weimar years, but tabloids and broadsheets also ran regular reports on suicide. Newspapers that supported the Weimar Republic, such as the *Frankfurter Zeitung*, the *Berliner Morgenpost*, Berlin's best-selling paper owned by the Ullstein family, and the *Berliner Tageblatt*, published by the liberal Mosse family, were generally more cautious and denied that there was a direct relationship between the Weimar Republic and suicide; nevertheless the Mosse and Ullstein papers ran sensationalist stories on suicides. Suicide featured so prominently in newspapers because it still aroused associations of something forbidden and was therefore morbidly fascinating, even among urban people. Suicides provided sensational 'human interest' stories to go along with murders and other crimes of passion.[71]

The press devoted a growing number of columns and inches to suicide towards the end of the Weimar Republic, in line with the widespread perception of living through hard times of record unemployment and political chaos. By winter 1930/31 there were more than five million unemployed, and in 1932, this number was to rise to six million.[72]

The *8 Uhr-Abendblatt*, a tabloid published by the Mosse family, ran a headline story on the 'Suicide of a whole family because of unemployment' in May 1932. After being sacked from his job as a business clerk, a father had opened the gas pipe, and his wife and ten-year-old daughter died together with him.[73] Infanticide, murder and suicide of fathers of families due to unemployment featured quite prominently in newspapers of the time, not least because of their rather emotionally manipulative appeal. On 24 September 1929, the journalist Gabriele Tergit published a story in the local section of the liberal *Berliner Tageblatt* about a 35-year-old former teacher turned farmer from Mecklenburg who had incurred debts of 3,000 Mark. This allegedly prompted him to kill himself and his six-year-old daughter with an overdose of Veronal pills and gas in his sister's flat in Berlin, taking advantage of the anonymity of the big city. The father had decided to kill his daughter allegedly because: 'The child was so much like

me and that's why I wanted to take her along. I didn't want her to have
to go around forever tainted by the fact that her father killed himself.' But
he and his daughter survived, since neighbours, smelling gas, had alerted
the police and the fire service at the last moment. Accusing him of the
attempted murder of his daughter, a Berlin court, taking into account a fate
that must have been quite common at a time of increasing unemployment
and socio-economic deprivation, sentenced him to one and a half years
in prison.[74] So the nexus between suicide and unemployment, even if
mythically exaggerated, had a tangible impact on the public perception
of suicide. Suicide was the most radical expression of the failure of man's
traditional role as *pater familias* amidst the socio-economic deprivation of
the late Weimar years.

Suicides caused by problems in people's love lives also featured in
newspapers. Articles reflected a fascination with romantic love and suicide
pacts in which couples ended their lives together. In such stories, it was
the man who killed his wife or girlfriend. He was then forced to kill
himself, since otherwise he would have been charged with murder, which
still carried the death penalty.[75] On 26 April 1932, the *8 Uhr-Abendblatt*
reported a 'Double suicide with champagne' (*Doppelselbstmord bei Sekt*)
in Berlin's Grunewald forest. The 20-year-old Richard Rath, son of a
hotel owner, and the 18-year-old Hanna Röhl, daughter of an accountant,
killed themselves after their parents had forbidden them to meet.[76] Most
famously, perhaps, the so-called *Steglitzer Schülertragödie* in June 1927
dominated newspaper headlines in June 1927 and February 1928. Paul
Krantz, a student taking his university entrance examination, was accused
of murdering his friend Günther Scheller, with whom he had concocted
a 'suicide pact' while drunk at a party at Scheller's house in Steglitz, a
fashionable district to the south of Berlin, on 28 June 1927. Scheller shot
his friend Hans Stephan and then himself, while Paul Krantz, in love with
Scheller's sister Hilde, did not follow the agreement and failed to turn
the gun on himself. Accused of murder, he was tried before the Moabit
criminal court. He was acquitted in February 1928. This case, reflecting
the life of the Berlin *jeunesse dorée* and adolescents' experiences of romantic
love, dominated the headlines during the time of the trial, overshadowing
the political crisis within the centre-right Reich government.[77]

For the Nazis, this case was emblematic of the Weimar Republic's
'asphalt culture' and the loose sexual mores among the youth. An article
in the *Völkischer Beobachter*, the Nazi daily, blamed the corrupting influence

of the Jewish 'spirit of the Kurfürstendamm'. Only a Nazi regime could create a new, healthy 'German youth', thereby preventing 'suicides among youths resulting from moral depression'.[78]

The press also reported some politically motivated suicides. On 24 February 1931, the 28-year-old unemployed and homeless shop assistant, Alois Broll, from Upper Silesia appeared at the official residence of Reich President Hindenburg in the Wilhelmstraße in Berlin, carrying a briefcase with official letters rejecting his claims for welfare payments. Challenged by a policeman in the anteroom to Hindenburg's office, Broll suddenly produced a pistol with which he wanted to shoot himself, and put his finger on the trigger. The policeman managed to seize the weapon and arrest Broll. According to a report in the *Vossische Zeitung*, Broll had not planned to shoot Hindenburg, but had rather wanted to speak to him, since he had been unable to find a job in Berlin. The communist *Berlin am Morgen*, emphasized Broll's misery, which almost inevitably drove him into suicide. The article declared:

> The investigation revealed circumstances typical of a man unemployed for years... Since 1923 he has had no steady work. He has compensation claims against the Reich. But the Oppeln district governor (*Regierungspräsident*) rejected all of his petitions. The situation at home has been dismal too, in that his father is retired and his brothers have also been without work or income for a long time ... In this dire situation, Broll decided to go to Berlin to make known to representatives of the Reich government his opinions about the injustice done to him. He appears in fact to have been obsessed with the naïve belief of such a possibility existing... After he arrived in Berlin, Broll allegedly sought out the Reich Chancellery but by accident went instead into the office of the Reich President. Here, he explained his case to a criminal police officer. When he was once more turned away, he wanted to end it all. Broll emphatically denies that he intended to shoot the Reich President. His act is the act of a desperate scatterbrain who cannot comprehend that the state will not help him. If he could comprehend the 'Why' then his battle and the means he would choose would be different.

In the end, Broll was sentenced to six weeks in gaol, for illegal possession of a gun. Reflecting broader suicide discourses of the time, which blamed individual degeneracy rather than socio-economic factors for suicide, the judge insisted: 'According to the medical report, one must in the case of the accused account for the possibility of a psychopathic fit, with the result that he must be viewed as... mentally inferior.' Hindenburg's State Secretary, Otto Meissner, probably embarrassed by the media attention lavished on the case, commented that Hindenburg would accept this verdict.[79] Media and politicians conveyed the impression of a suicidal climate in the late Weimar Republic. A performative incident such as the one in Hindenburg's palace seems to be a reflection of that atmosphere. The fascination of the late Weimar public with suicide, which newspapers, either explicitly or implicitly, closely associated with what they saw as the political and socio-economic instability of the Weimar Republic thus contributed to the general lack of legitimacy of the first German democracy.

Not surprisingly perhaps, the Nazis used propaganda similar to that of the communists to denounce the Weimar Republic. On 15 January 1931, *Der Angriff*, a Berlin Nazi newspaper, edited by Joseph Goebbels, reported the suicide of Walter Bürkner, a 27-year-old unemployed SA man. *Der Angriff* declared:

> Now he personally felt the Young misery [a reference to the 1929 Young Plan] which is burdening our Fatherland even harder than previously. He became withdrawn, unhappy about himself, and he was suffering increasingly from ... mental depression—until he just could not go on and took his own life which had become a torture.[80]

The object of *Der Angriff*'s attack was not the capitalist system, but the Young Plan of 1929, an international agreement to reduce and reschedule Germany's reparations payments to the Allies in recompense for the damage caused to these countries by German aggression and occupation in the First World War. The Nazis had vehemently opposed the plan, arguing that reparations caused severe economic hardship and should be stopped altogether.[81] A similar report in the *Völkischer Beobachter* of 15 April 1932 claimed that 'The Young deprivation (*Elend*) drives a couple with its three children into death.' A closer reading of the article shows that the family father, the 44-year-old businessman Karl Lehnert from Munich, had actually been tried for fraud at court. Nevertheless, the *Völkischer Beobachter* stereotypically insisted that 'hard economic difficulties' had been the main motive for the father gassing his wife and children and himself.[82]

Top Nazis directly blamed the Weimar 'system' for suicide. In a speech on foreign policy at a party rally on 13 July 1928, Hitler declared: 'Today we are confronted with the following fact: Germany has 62 million people who live on 460,000 square kilometres. They cannot feed themselves. The consequence is that, on the one hand, hunger and desperation rage and, on the other, that 20–60,000 suicides take place every year.'[83] This was a crude Social Darwinist view that saw the conquest of *Lebensraum* in the east as the solution to Germany's problems. In 1927, only 15,974 suicides had been officially recorded in Germany.[84] Hitler thus considerably exaggerated suicide levels on this occasion. After coming to power, Hitler claimed in an interview with a British journalist on 18 October 1933: 'Thanks to the Versailles Peace Treaty, it was the case up to now that, on average, 20,000 people voluntarily took their lives each year because of misery and despair.'[85] This was nearer the true figure: in 1932, the climax of suicide levels in Weimar Germany, 18,934 suicides had been officially recorded.[86] Like the communists, Hitler claimed that suicide was an inevitable result of adverse social and political conditions. These anti-liberal views on suicide helped to discredit the legitimacy of the Weimar Republic among communist and Nazi supporters. Suicide became a propagandistic lever across political divides, and a routine signifier of Weimar misery.

# V

Suicide was the subject of discussion not only in politics and the media, but also among the churches. The Protestant and Catholic churches placed great emphasis on prevention. The leading national proponent of suicide prevention was the Protestant pastor Gerhard Füllkrug (1870–1948), one of the directors of the Central Committee of the Inner Mission, the Protestant church's welfare organization.[87] In two monographs published in the Weimar years, he complained about the 'crowd of antisocial elements' threatening society. In general agreement with Social Darwinist principles, he also saw the principle of the 'struggle for the survival of the fittest' as one of the main reasons for the increasing suicide rate after the end of the First World War. Füllkrug suggested the re-criminalization of suicide and a strengthening of societal cohesion by promoting a revival of religion. He thought that the suicide problem was directly linked to what many observers since Durkheim had seen as a radical individualization of society.[88] The decline of religious belief and practice was a key factor in his view. Without giving credible evidence, Füllkrug claimed that 'Schleswig-Holstein boasts the lowest numbers of attendance at the Eucharist and, accordingly, a very high suicide rate.'[89] His crusade against suicide had begun before the outbreak of war in 1914. For Füllkrug, as a pastor, suicide was a sin and he exaggerated the problem of suicide to gain public attention for the

issue. In April 1925, he gave a paper at the Dresden congress of the Inner
Mission on 'The Fight against Suicide'. Without actually referring to any
films which, at least until the late 1920s hardly thematized suicide, Füllkrug
believed it necessary to close down cinemas. It was only natural that 'from
these popular places of entertainment, there stems a widely corrupting
influence on a wide range of people and ... movies are propaganda for
suicide'.[90]

Deeply conservative and nationalist officials of the Inner Mission, which
became one of the central pillars of the welfare system of the Weimar
state amidst the increasing social deprivation and mass unemployment
of the late 1920s, perceived suicide as a curse of modernism and the
socially and culturally chaotic post-war years.[91] Not only did Füllkrug
lament suicide, he also tried to prevent suicidal people from killing
themselves. William Booth's 'Anti-Suicide Bureau', founded under the
auspices of the Salvation Army in London in 1907, had pioneered suicide
prevention, offering completely confidential advice to potential suicides.
Confidentiality was crucial, given that suicide was still a criminal offence in
England and Wales until 1961.[92] In Berlin, the Protestant church founded
a similar institution, the Suicide Counselling Service (Selbstmordseelsorge)
in 1910.[93]

But this would not do, Füllkrug thought. A stronger institution for
suicide prevention was urgently needed amidst the record suicide levels
allegedly caused by the German defeat and the inflation. In 1925, Füllkrug
therefore set up the Permanent Commission for the Observation and
Prevention of the Suicide Question (Ständige Kommission zur Beobachtung
und Verhütung der Selbstmordfrage) in Berlin-Dahlem, based at the Inner
Mission's Central Committee (Centralausschuß für Innere Mission). Füllkrug's
anti-suicide commission consisted of deputies of the Berlin City Council,
the Catholic and Jewish welfare organizations, the Salvation Army, the
Berlin Welfare Office, and the Berlin Police President, following the
pulling-together in March 1921 of various welfare organizations under a
nation-wide umbrella organization.[94]

The collaboration between state and church was close in the field of
suicide prevention. While suicide had been decriminalized in the German
states in the wake of the Enlightenment, state authorities felt responsible
for preventing people from killing themselves, amidst the widespread
perception of rising suicide levels after 1918.[95] State intervention could
take on very practical forms. Writing on the role of the police in suicide

prevention, the Catholic policeman M Julier from Augsburg argued in
*Caritas*, the trade journal of the Catholic Church's welfare organization,
that 'the observation of river banks is also a way to prevent suicidal persons
from taking the final step'.[96] This reflected contemporary ideas of policemen
about the surveillance of public places by both police and public as a means
of crime and suicide prevention.[97]

   More generally, the discourse of the people's community, in which
the life, not of the individual but of the community, mattered, became
gradually more important in the Weimar years.[98] Berlin's deputy police
president, Bernhard Weiss, ordered his policemen to write down the names
and addresses of all people who had attempted suicide and refer them either
to Füllkrug's anti-suicide commission, or to the welfare office for help.[99]
A draft letter to be distributed to those hospitalized for a suicide attempt,
written very euphemistically, read:

> Sorry for writing these lines to you concerning the event which took you to
> hospital. There must have been very serious reasons which led you to this
> step. But according to my conviction, such a throwing away of one's own
> life would only make sense if man really found rest in his grave from all his
> sorrowful thoughts, anxieties and concerns … Who knows whether even the
> worst thing will be overcome in due course, whether the worst illness will
> be defeated and the sun of life will shine again?[100]

In penning this letter, Füllkrug only referred implicitly to religious ideas,
perhaps since he knew that religion had lost much of its appeal in a big
city like Berlin.[101] Rather ironically in the light of his statement on movies
causing suicides, Füllkrug designed a slide show in 1928 to be used during
his lecture tours across Germany. The show neatly summarized the views
he had already presented in his two books.[102] In the slide show, Füllkrug
drew an alarmist picture of suicide in Germany, which he described as a
'national disease' (*Volkskrankheit*) that had hit Germany particularly hard
after the defeat of 1918. Lumping together unemployment, the Dawes
Plan (an earlier version of the Young Plan) and increasing secularization,
Füllkrug insisted:

> The misery of the Fatherland broke the heart of many men. We see an
> explanation for the steady rise of the suicide rate even above that of 1913
> in the continuously increasing economic misery … in unemployment, in the
> impact of the Dawes plan, but also in the growing secularization of almost all
> groups of our *Volk*.[103]

Füllkrug implicitly argued that the collapse of the traditional male role as a breadwinner amidst mass unemployment would almost inevitably cause suicides. There is no evidence that the Dawes plan (1924), which saw the rescheduling of German reparations payments over a longer time span, prompted more people to kill themselves than before: economic deflation was a more likely general cause of the rise in suicide rates at this time. What mattered more to contemporaries than a precise statistical breakdown of suicide levels was the impression of living through hard times, reinforced by people like Füllkrug; a situation which many thought led unavoidably to higher suicide numbers.

Catholics also started a campaign against suicide, led by the journalist Hans Rost. A debate developed between representatives of the Protestant and Catholic churches, focusing on the question of which faith was better at preventing people from killing themselves. This reflected a wider dispute between the Protestant and Catholic welfare organizations that was going on in the late 1920s.[104] Rost had already argued in 1905 that Catholics were less prone to commit suicide than Protestants. Indeed, as noted earlier, statistics support this view, although suicide statistics of Catholic regions were probably gross underestimates due to the Catholic ban on suicide. By contrasting the traditionally high suicide levels of Protestant Saxony with the relatively low ones of Catholic Spain, Rost insisted that 'the impact of confessions on suicide is everywhere a positive one for Catholicism'.[105]

The Catholic Rost effectively agreed with the Protestant Füllkrug that modernity was one of the core reasons for suicide. Rost also introduced anti-Semitic overtones into the debate on suicide. He argued:

> The basic problem is the increasing irreligiousness, the lack of humility and submission and a hedonism that is going beyond any sensible extent. Social democracy, the liberal and, not to mention, Jewish *Weltanschauung* have moved the centre of gravity of being to this life. The masses of people are told that the hereafter is a popish swindle and that pleasure is the only aim of life that is worth pursuing.[106]

An official from the Protestant *Oberkirchenrat* attacked Rost in 1928 in an internal memorandum. He declared:

> He [Rost] is known in professional circles as a tendentious statistician: from controversial statistics he only chooses with great care and cunning what is advantageous to the Catholic population. He ignores contradicting results (eg

from criminal statistics); the same applies to all results of confessional statistics, which portray the Catholic population as being backward in any respect. All refutations have no impact on him. Dr Rost just selects everything from the rich literature on the current subject (frequency of suicide) that suits him ...[107]

Apart from editing a bibliography of suicide, a standard work to this day, Rost founded an international periodical devoted to suicide research and prevention in 1932.[108] Using medical analogies, Rost likened the fight against suicide to attempts to cure tuberculosis and cancer. He claimed that states suffering from the 'terribly harsh dictates of the Peace' and an alleged suppression of Christianity, such as Germany, Hungary and Czechoslovakia, displayed particularly high suicide rates.[109] (Rost deliberately failed to mention that Hungary and Bohemia-Moravia, both largely Catholic, had already shown very high suicide levels before the First World War. This inconvenient fact would have undermined his own hypothesis that Catholic countries displayed lower suicide rates than Protestant ones.) Rost's views on suicide must have been influential, since he gave a broadcast on the Bavarian Radio on 14 November 1931. The defeat of 1918 had caused the increased suicide levels, Rost insisted. Suicide was less of a social than a moral problem, for which secularization and urbanization were to blame. Similarly to Füllkrug, Rost blamed newspapers, 'cinemas, some theatres and other entertainment venues', and, perhaps surprisingly, Schopenhauer's philosophy (with which very few listeners can have been familiar) for driving people, especially youths, into suicide.[110] For people like Füllkrug and Rost, the root of the suicide problem was thus modernity, especially the allegedly destructive impact of mass culture and secularization, exacerbated after 1918 by what they considered to be an immoral cultural, social, and political chaos which included the breakdown of traditional gender roles. Many members of welfare organizations and the German middle classes shared this view.

Rost and Füllkrug's views were not undisputed, however. The Hamburg psychiatrist Richard Detlev Loewenberg attacked Füllkrug and Rost's claims in a study of suicide in Hamburg. Blaming psychological disorders for suicide, he declared: 'It is thus really no longer sufficient ... to go over these problems with reference to ... the lure of the big city versus simple country life or the evil curse of unbelief, which make people become desperate ...'[111] Reflecting his general concern about suicide rates, Füllkrug persuaded the members of his commission to announce a prose competition on suicide on 1 May 1926. He had secured the Prussian Welfare Ministry's sponsorship. The Ministry was itself concerned about suicide levels and allocated the considerable sum of 1,000 Reichsmark for the 'purposes of hygienic popular education' (*für Zwecke der hygienischen Volksbelehrung*).[112] The competition was advertised nationally and received many entries. Füllkrug wrote to famous authors of the time and asked them to act as prize judges and assess the literary quality of the entries. Thus on 5 March 1926 he wrote to the novelist and popular historian Ricarda Huch and invited her to sit on the prize panel; she politely declined.[113] Walter von Molo, a right-wing author, agreed to sit on the panel but later came to the harsh conclusion, in literary terms at least, that 'the result [was] catastrophic'.[114]

Many of the entries were manifestly quite motivated by Füllkrug's lofty purpose. One contributor, for example, wrote:

> You had this year announced an essay prize competition concerning a story ... The story narrates the case of a maid whose savings are taken away from her by a gallant cheat ... [She] wants to die in this collapse of money and love. The moral point of this work is how she is dissuaded from her decision by looking at her old savings book and her plan to make up for this setback by new work and saving more.[115]

As this plot summary suggests, suicide, thanks to coverage in the mass media and traditional assumptions shared by many people, was primarily associated with apolitical popular clichés, such as betrayed love and a loss of money. The prize panel found the entries' quality so poor that they announced a new competition in July 1927. This received no fewer than 186 entries, reflecting suicide's public significance. The winning entry, entitled 'Night on the Bridge', by Maria Kohn, has survived in the files. Its plot, featuring an unemployed and lonely man standing on a bridge, prepared to jump into his death, was far from original. But it did manage to combine Weimar Germany's problems with a somewhat overdrawn religious element. After jumping into the river, the man is saved by a young boy's dog.[116] The prize panel found this quite appealing.

Rather than entering short stories into the competition, however, many correspondents, usually men, simply asked Füllkrug for money and threatened to kill themselves if he did not comply with their request, thereby using the religious taboo on suicide as a means of blackmailing the Inner Mission. These letters are a remarkably rich source, even if the intentions they state were not genuine. Most of the correspondents were not necessarily church-going Christians; in fact, many probably wrote to Füllkrug because they had seen his anti-suicide commission mentioned in the press. On 25 May 1926, for example, the 25-year-old Richard M from Plauen described his sorrows and threatened that he was 'ready to take [his] life if [he] did not find some direct help by the end of this week'. He had embezzled 1,000 Reichsmark because he did not know what to do on a monthly income of 180 Reichsmark. He warned Füllkrug not to tell his 'parents, bosses, or the authorities', and thought that the Inner Mission might be able to help. Needless to say, Füllkrug and the anti-suicide commission had neither the will nor the means to pay M's debts.[117]

Social conditions had an impact on people, whatever the statistics. Erich S, a former clerk at the Siemens factory in Berlin, got in touch with Füllkrug in April 1930 to complain about his fate. Having worked for Siemens from 1906 until 1925, he had been made redundant in 1925 and 'could not stand his life after about five years of being unemployed'. Rather curtly, Füllkrug recommended him to get in touch with the Protestant Central Welfare Office in Berlin and refused to correspond with Siemens on his behalf.[118] Pastors from across Germany started forwarding their correspondence with suicidal men to Füllkrug because they did not know how to cope with the suicide problem. In April 1930 pastor Hartmann from Rheine, a small town in Westphalia, wrote to Füllkrug. Karl L, a failed businessman, whom pastor Hartmann 'had known for some years', had previously complained to Hartmann that he had only had five hot meals since 29 December 1929 and that he could only afford to eat bread. He had asked Hartmann for some money to get a new business started, namely producing canned chicken, and threatened to kill himself if he did not get any money, since 'the horrible circumstances of the past four months had often driven [him] into greatest despair, but the hope for some improvement had always prevented [him] from the last step'.[119]

Despite his widely publicized stance on suicide prevention, Füllkrug usually did not take these threats seriously. When people threatened that they would commit suicide unless he helped them out with money, Füllkrug filed their begging letters, annotated with the statement 'Wants some money', as he did with a letter from Hermann L from Bad Kreuznach on 17 April 1930. Born in 1898, L had served in the trenches of the Western Front, where he was wounded. Because the inflation had ruined his father's estate, L claimed, he had had to drop out of university in 1927.

Now he asked Füllkrug for a loan of 8,000 Reichsmark to save what was left of his father's farm. He threatened to kill himself, and reminded Füllkrug of the 'French statesman who had spoken of Germany as being overpopulated, and who could not show any other way out than starving them'. Füllkrug politely replied on 25 April 1930 that his commission only dealt with cases from Berlin.[120] L directly linked his personal fate with the rather desolate state of Germany, as his reference to the French statesman, probably Clemenceau, reveals; his views here showed some congruence with those of the Nazis.

Füllkrug not only refused to respond to these suicide threats; he also turned away suicidal men who approached him directly at the anti-suicide commission's offices. In September 1930, amidst rising unemployment and suicide levels, Fritz Reppo, a reporter for the *Welt am Morgen*, wrote a very sarcastic and devastating undercover report on the way in which Füllkrug and the Protestant Church dealt with suicidal people. Reppo, dressed in rags, pretended to be tired of life and unemployed. He called on various Protestant welfare organizations in Berlin. Reppo first went to Füllkrug's office in the leafy Dahlem suburb 'where the extremely wealthy businessmen from the city live'. Füllkrug's wife answered the door and snapped at him that Füllkrug was not in. Reppo did not ask her for any money, and pretended that he simply wanted to have a conversation. Füllkrug's wife, far from being generous and helpful, offered Reppo some sausage sandwiches and 20 pfennigs. She then told him to go away. He should 'trust in God's mercy', she added, before referring Reppo to the local Welfare Office. Reppo then went to the Berlin City Mission. Here, a pastor accused him of 'complaining like an old woman'. This dismissal had been common since the First World War when doctors and welfare officials had been accusing soldiers seeking help of hysteria in order to reject their claims for support.[121] Being dismissed as an 'old woman' undermined the confidence of unemployed men genuinely contemplating suicide in their male status as breadwinners. The pastor offered Reppo a two-night stay at the City Mission. Reppo decided to try his luck at the City Mission in Moabit, a working-class district. Here, a pastor boasted that he would go begging if he were in Reppo's situation. Finally, he sent Reppo away, giving him a meagre 50 pfennigs. Predictably, Reppo concluded that 'Christian welfare' was totally useless.[122]

Füllkrug was not particularly helpful either to veterans whose benefit claims had been rejected. Hermann E, a man from Sorau in Silesia, wrote to Füllkrug on 22 April 1930. E did not threaten to kill himself. He insisted that most suicides were due to what he called the current 'dispute over pensions'. After Füllkrug had politely told him that he could not provide any help, E wrote another, this time more aggressive letter, in which he accused the president of the Reichsbank, Dr Hjalmar Schacht, who had resigned from his office in 1930, of being corrupt:

> It is not the sick and unemployed who are the biggest 'welfare recipients' and cause a burden for the economy, but gentlemen like Dr Schacht who has secured 50,000 Reichsmark for himself per annum or a golden handshake worth 1.5 million. I and my 5 children receive a disability pension of 965 Reichsmark per year, and for this, I have had to pay my contribution week by week for the last 20 years...[123]

The *Reichsbund der Kriegsbeschädigten*, the SPD's organization for those who had been wounded in the war, also drew an alarmist picture of suicide to counter the attempts of the Brüning government to cut down veterans' pensions. In February 1931, the *Reichsbund* blamed the government for suicides among veterans. For war veterans facing impoverishment, suicide was the last way out, declared the *Reichsbund*, implying that poverty undermined the war veterans' status as men. Allegedly, 49 members had killed themselves in the second quarter of 1931 alone. And in July 1931, the *Reichsbund*'s journal reprinted a suicide note that had reportedly been written by a veteran who had been severely wounded in the war. The letter read:

> I just want to tell you what is happening to me. I've gone through a lot. I was in the war, started by the money-grubbers. My hand was hurt, I was hit twice in the shoulder and once in the head... I worked from morning until night, and the only thing I have to show for it are debts. I asked the veterans' office to guarantee a mortgage... I told them that if they couldn't help, my family and I simply couldn't live any longer... The office I asked told me that they couldn't do anything... I've had enough. I would have done this on the 20th, only I didn't have a gun, and I want my family's end to be quick and painless. We learned that in the war. I was always a good father and took care of my family... And it's just because I don't want my family to have to live in poverty that I'm taking them with me. Maybe my action will help other disabled veterans... Long live the world revolution.

After sending off this letter to a friend, the author is said to have shot his wife and three children, before turning the gun on himself. Even though we cannot be sure if this suicide note was genuine, it reflected the feeling of many veterans that the Brüning government had let them down. Under these circumstances, killing one's family and then committing suicide seemed the only way out for this particular veteran.[124] Here was suicide presented again as the last way out for impoverished fathers of families.

In another remarkable case in 1930, Füllkrug wrote a stern reply to the 25-year-old Otto U who had complained about his inability to marry because of his lack of money and threatened to kill himself. Füllkrug sternly retorted:

> If you read all of the letters which we received over the last few days, following a newspaper report on our work against suicide, you would no longer consider your situation as difficult. Thousands of fathers of families are unemployed these days...You, on the other hand, have a job, and are making 31 Reichsmark per week...In our opinion you do not have any reason for giving up the will to live. Every man has to cope with problems, and a healthy young man should take up the fight of life with joy and courage. Perhaps it would be worthwhile for you to have a serious word with your pastor.[125]

Füllkrug's reference to many people being worse off than U was, many contemporaries felt, a reaction all too typical of Weimar welfare organizations to requests made by people in need. Whether or not Füllkrug's correspondents seriously considered suicide as a way out of their problems probably matters less than the fact that they threatened to. Suicide was a particularly apt theme, since in the popular imagination it was still associated with breaking a taboo due to the traditional religious ban on suicide, upheld since the early Middle Ages. Using suicide as a threat was, many people evidently thought, especially useful in shocking church officials like Füllkrug. For people in urban settings, the religious taboo probably mattered less than it did for rural people, but suicide continued to arouse associations of something disreputable, even at a time when newspapers were full of reports on suicide.

Füllkrug was not the only recipient of fraudulent suicide letters. On 4 March 1931, Ernst W, the owner of a pen factory in Vienna, left two letters near the Royal Palace in Berlin, one ostensibly written by a Baron and another one by a girl, together with a hat and a chest, and a photograph of Mussolini. A street sweeper found the box and passed it on to the police. A letter attached to the box promised 1,000 Reichsmark to the finder. In the suicide note, which W had penned himself, a Baron takes his farewell from life after receiving a letter from the girl brushing him off.

Leading the investigation, the head of the Berlin homicide squad, Ernst Gennat concluded on 5 March 1931 that this was the work of W, who had previously played similar pranks elsewhere in Germany. Back in Vienna, W was interrogated by the Austrian Security Service (*Sicherheits-Bureau*) on 9 March 1931. He explained that he had been motivated by a desire to seek the German judiciary's attention. In 1912, a Dresden court had sentenced him to three years in prison for fraud (he had been using the name Henckel von Donnersmarck), and his attempts at rehabilitation by the Dresden court had so far been without any success.[126]

Newspapers reported the unusual find. The *Berliner Börsen-Kurier* quickly got the point and thought that W was just attention-seeking. The *BZ am Mittag* mentioned that the finder would receive 1,000 Reichsmark.[127] This prompted Anni M, a young woman from Berlin who had read an article about the find in a newspaper, to write to Gennat, requesting that he should give her the money. She wanted to marry soon, she said, and she and her family 'were also hit hard by the current economic situation'.[128] The promise of money was a deception, too. The quick response of newspaper readers, and the fact that people used suicide to seek attention, again shows the significance of suicide to Weimar people. On 25 March 1931, after losing her job, Helene B, a 31-year-old worker at the Sarotti chocolate factory, wrote a letter to the Berlin criminal police. She explained that she would commit suicide: 'The undersigned takes the liberty to let it be known that I have committed suicide, please say hello to my dead parents. Otherwise, just a final greeting from Helene B, born 13 March 1898 in Hanover-Döhren, who attended school in Tempelhof. It came to this because of lovesickness and unemployment.'[129] B was clearly suffering from some kind of mental illness. It is not entirely clear whether she killed herself, but the fact that she wrote a suicide note, which took up public clichés about suicide from the press, is revealing insofar as it confirms the great impact of newspapers on people's perception and interpretation of suicide.

On 1 April 1932, along with his colleagues, Füllkrug was forced to resign from the Central Committee of the Inner Mission in the wake of a slush funds scandal, which would have almost led to the Inner Mission's bankruptcy. This scandal also prompted a crisis of public confidence in the Inner Mission at a time when many people already distrusted the German welfare system more generally. By deliberately blaming the post-war order for suicide, Füllkrug and others had contributed to the undermining of the

Weimar Republic's legitimacy, right from its beginning.[130] The medical doctor and economist Hans Harmsen, perhaps more famous as an eugenicist and champion of racial hygienics and birth control,[131] took over Füllkrug's position as chairman of what was now known as 'Help for those Tired of Life' (*Hilfe für Lebensmüde*) on 10 February 1933, just after the Nazis had come to power on 30 January 1933.[132]

Füllkrug and the Inner Mission never really accepted the Weimar Republic and welcomed the Nazi takeover in 1933.[133] Still under Füllkrug's auspices, the anti-suicide commission drafted a leaflet in 1933, which was to be distributed on the streets. It portrayed suicide as a phenomenon of the Weimar years, now past. The authors blamed 'the terrible forces that overcame our people and Fatherland and against which we were defenceless' and 'Versailles, inflation and unemployment' for the 'more than 200,000 people' Germany had lost through suicide in the Weimar years. The leaflet went on to complain about the lack of 'community' and the 'active help of our national comrades' in the Weimar years, and promised that there would not be any suicides in the Third Reich.[134]

The anti-suicide commission met irregularly after 1933. In one of the final sessions on 9 June 1937 the Berlin City Mission's deputy bluntly emphasized that most suicides no longer stemmed from economic problems such as unemployment which the Nazis had allegedly solved.[135] There is no evidence of meetings of the commission after 1937, which suggests that the commission ceased to exist. Füllkrug, who had remained on the board of the anti-suicide commission, and others, claimed that the Nazis had successfully combated suicide, so there was, by implication, nothing left for them to do.

# VI

People not only threatened suicide in letters to welfare institutions, they also frequently wrote farewell missives before actually killing themselves. We have access to these documents from an unparalleled collection of investigation files compiled by the homicide squad of the Berlin criminal police, founded in 1926, and led by the detective superintendent Ernst Gennat, an enormously overweight man with an incurable craving for cake. These files shed light on the ways in which ordinary people represented their suicides.[136] What was the impact of the public debates on suicide, discussed above, on individual suicides in the mass society of Weimar Germany where most people read newspapers on a daily basis?

In the Weimar Republic, policemen and criminologists were increasingly concerned with a typology of criminality and scientific explanations for deviant behaviour that saw criminals as inherently degenerate and incorrigible types. In the light of economic deprivation, social decline, and mass unemployment, many thought that suicide and criminality went hand in hand with each other. This view was shared in police circles, too. In 1927, a professor of criminology declared in a periodical read by criminal police members: 'The specific circumstances of a particular suicide are so strange that the preparation and the carrying out of the act itself must cast doubt upon the suicide's mental health.'[137]

Following calls from criminologists who had demanded a more efficient and rational system of classifying and identifying criminals, Gennat compiled a systematic central index of murder and suicide.[138] An internal memorandum of 1928 stipulated that investigating policemen must pay close attention to suicide, since in many cases it was not entirely clear at first glance whether the dead person had fallen victim to a murderer. The criminal police, particularly Gennat's homicide squad (*Morddezernat*), took a keen interest in suicide, amidst a widespread perception of rising suicide levels. This prompted Gennat to start collecting the suicide notes which he and his men had found during their investigations of suicides. Once the police had established that someone's death had not been caused by another person (*Fremdeinwirken*), the criminal police usually closed the case. One of the most professionalized and technically well-equipped criminal police forces in Europe at the time, the Berlin homicide squad was well-known in Berlin and elsewhere in Germany. Newspapers often asked readers to report any relevant clues to the police.[139]

Policemen often found it very difficult to establish whether the cause of death had been murder or suicide. This prompted an officer to give detailed practical advice for policemen on the beat in 1922:

> If a policeman on patrol is called to [investigate the death of] a hanged person, he should first of all cut off the noose. If the person can still be revived, the policeman should attempt to resuscitate him if he knows how to do so properly. Otherwise, a doctor is to be called. If the hanged person is male, there is a clear way to establish whether he committed suicide or was murdered, even if he is of an advanced age. The officer need only open the man's pants. If there is a fresh emission of semen on the shirt, one

undoubtedly has a case of suicide, whereas if the person was murdered, one
will find excretion, the consequence of fear.[140]

While the accuracy of this advice remains doubtful, the fact that such tips
were circulated among ordinary policemen suggests that the Weimar police
were concerned with distinguishing suicide from murder.

One theme, parents killing their children before taking their own lives,
featured quite regularly in suicide investigations and, as we have seen, in
newspaper reports on suicide in the Weimar years because the murder
of children was particularly shocking. There was a notable gap between
police investigations and press accounts of suicides. Newspapers often
misrepresented someone's ostensible suicide motives to contribute to their
respective political agenda.

Take the case of Klara Engwicht, a 33-year-old cleaner from a Berlin
working-class neighbourhood. On 25 March 1932, Good Friday, Engwicht
strangled her three children aged between two and six years before hanging
herself. In an article entitled 'Welfare Recipient Goes into Death with
3 Children' the communist daily *Die Rote Fahne* emphasized Engwicht's
proletarian lifestyle and went on to describe her house as 'typical proletarian
accommodation'. Unable to pay her rent for three months, she was facing
eviction from her flat. On top of that, she had become pregnant again.
Inflating this case to an ideological battle, the article accused the social
democratic *Vorwärts* of having lied about Engwicht allegedly receiving
sufficient money from the welfare office.[141] The article blamed those 'who
are responsible for today's circumstances' for her death, and reduced suicide
to a pre-determined act devoid of any personal motivations by claiming
that 'life had already been taken from the woman before she took it
from herself and her children'.[142] In contrast to this orthodox communist
view, the *Berliner Morgenpost*, Berlin's best-selling paper from the liberal
Ullstein house, delivered a much more sober and realistic account, which
confirmed that Engwicht had indeed received decent welfare payments.
The *Berliner Morgenpost* emphasized the fact that her new lover had left
her after promising to marry her as Engwicht's main suicide motive. The
*Morgenpost* also mentioned her alcoholism, and the fact that she treated her
children very badly even before she murdered them.[143]

The communists distorted their accounts of the Engwicht case for
political purposes. The police found out that Engwicht had indeed been
pregnant and that she had been carrying on various sexual relationships.

The plumber Walter C, her neighbour, testified that he knew this for sure, since the walls were very thin in their apartment block. He also told the police that Engwicht had wanted to marry him, but he had refused since he did not find her attractive. After confirming that 'Miss Engwicht had been supported sufficiently by the authorities', he claimed that she had 'recently beaten her children quite often, sometimes even at night'. At times she had been working as a prostitute; and recently, C testified, Engwicht had told another neighbour that she wanted to commit suicide, but did not tell him why. It quickly turned out that Engwicht's current lover, Gustav G, had something to do with the case, as Ida S, another neighbour, testified. Engwicht had planned to marry G, the father of the child with which she was pregnant, but G's mother had allegedly banned this, since she found Engwicht's lifestyle immoral. G, an unemployed fraudster, had allegedly already planned to marry Engwicht in October 1931 but had had to put this off, allegedly since he was so poor that he could not afford any appropriate clothes for the wedding. He had only recently been released from prison. In addition, his mother had replied to a letter from Engwicht in which she had evidently broached the topic of marrying him, in scathing terms:

Dear Frau Engwicht!

I have to reply to your letter that it is not good to sleep with a man if one is not married yet and that I do not have any use for you, since my son will definitely get another one without children.

Best wishes, Frau G.

The police concluded that Engwicht had indeed murdered her children and killed herself, chiefly because of G's broken promise. They did not mention her alleged financial problems.[144]

How did ordinary people react to suicides? And how did the police determine whether a death had been due to murder or suicide? Most of the suicides investigated by the Berlin homicide squad took place in working-class milieus, reflecting a traditional pattern of criminal police work. In December 1932, a local policeman had found the 27-year-old telegraph worker Willi W gassed in his flat in the Lichtenberg working-class district. Initially, the policeman assumed that W had committed suicide. Nevertheless, following the regulations, the policeman referred the case to Gennat's homicide squad, prompting a furious letter from Gennat to the man in charge of the Lichtenberg police precinct. Gennat doubted whether W had committed suicide and complained that policemen must be more careful when examining similar cases. In the past, local policemen had not bothered to investigate suicides properly and had failed to compile reports. Gennat insisted: 'I am not at all in favour of producing too much paperwork. However, even theft of a rabbit and other trivial thefts are usually reported in much more detail than suicides.'[145]

Convinced that W's death had been suspicious, Gennat interrogated W's widow on 29 December. In the dramatic interrogation, Frau W explained her miserable domestic situation in which she seems to have been the main breadwinner:

> I have always said, so much rent, and I'm even working and then my husband gave me 8 mark for household expenses and then he always went out drinking and so then I opened the gas valve. People want their money, and I'm not supposed to talk about money matters with my husband and then what else can I say? I can't do anything more, like work; I can't just wipe out our debts. Everything was going down the drain and we worked so hard and then he cheats on me behind my back.

Although she had a part-time job, their combined debts amounted to the enormous sum of 800 Reichsmark. Only when she had some money to spare did she insert coins into the slot meter for gas. Otherwise the couple were without heating and cooking facilities. Gennat tried to calm Frau W down and commended her for telling him the truth: 'That is the best thing you could do. You are showing some remorse.'[146]

The case also had a political dimension, since W was a Nazi, while his wife intended to vote for the communists. Frau W's mother testified in support of her daughter and confirmed that Herr W had indeed betrayed and mistreated his wife, allegedly telling her: 'I will get you to obey me.' Gennat showed some sympathy for Frau W, but nevertheless concluded that she had gassed her husband 'in a state of thoroughly righteous indignation and embitterment, caused by her husband's behaviour'.[147] Wrapping up the case, Gennat insisted that local policemen must carry out investigations more thoroughly. Gennat attached so much significance to the W case that he continued to try to track down the policeman who had been responsible in the first instance for the inaccurate reporting of the case until March 1933, when Gennat closed the file by concluding that he was going to use the case as teaching material.[148] Other murders went unnoticed by the police and were misclassified as suicides. To obtain more reliable statistics,

Gennat had already told his detectives to be more careful when filling out data sheets required for every suicide.[149]

While Frau W did her best to disguise murder as suicide, some suicides, particularly from the middle class, tried to conceal the fact that they had killed themselves. Middle-class Germans, perhaps less secularized than the working class, were more likely to conceal their suicide and make it seem like a murder to avoid the stigma still attached with suicide. Families of those whose deaths had been officially recognized as suicide were not eligible to receive any payment from life-insurance companies, if they had subscribed to one.

On 21 July 1931 the former Yugoslav Honorary General Consul in Berlin Dr Ernst Barckhausen was found shot dead in the study of his house in the expensive Tiergarten district. During the Great Depression, Barckhausen had lost both his money and his position as consul. Nevertheless he tried to keep up his reputation as an influential and respectable man, boasting, for instance, that he was personally acquainted with the ex-Kaiser. Indeed, Barckhausen had been the representative of German business in Yugoslavia and had also been in charge of negotiating German reparations payments to Yugoslavia. In desperation, having accrued a massive debt of more than 100,000 Reichsmark, Barckhausen decided to cheat on his car insurance. He sank his car, a blue Graham-Paige, in the River Elbe, and told his insurers that someone had stolen it. Unfortunately, however, someone found the automobile in the River Elbe on 10 July 1931. On 12 July 1931, Barckhausen received the news that his car had been found. Aware that the police would prosecute him, thus destroying his social reputation, he decided to kill himself.[150]

Life insurance companies were increasingly anxious about rising suicide levels at this time. In 1930, according to one source, ten per cent of their overall payments to relatives of people who had died were paid to the dependants of suicides. Many companies thus decided to introduce a waiting period (*Karenzzeit*), stipulating that a payment could only be made to suicide's relatives if the insurance policy had been taken out at least two years previously. Most companies extended this period to five years in 1932, reflecting the rise in claims for suicides.[151] If the waiting period had not yet elapsed, life-insurance companies usually only made full payment of the sum insured to relatives of suicides who were officially classified as mentally ill at the time of the deed (an interesting parallel to the traditional church policy that dictated that only those suicides who had been insane at the time of killing themselves were eligible for a funeral). Those who had taken out life insurance overwhelmingly belonged to the 'better-off classes', one expert claimed in 1934. Many such people, the expert went on, later killed themselves 'to find a desirable way out of their morally and economically life-threatening situation'.[152] According to a contemporary newspaper article, self-employed middle-class professionals were more vulnerable to economic change and thus to suicide in the case of bankruptcy.[153]

Barckhausen had insured his own life for the enormous sum of 200,000 Reichsmark. He was anxious that the sum should go to his family after his death, thus enabling them to pay off the debt. So he decided to arrange his suicide to look as if he had been murdered. Having set up the scene to look as if he had fallen victim to an armed robbery, Barckhausen was found dead, sitting behind his desk, where he had been writing a letter. He had forgotten to take the cap off his pen. Also, he had used his own revolver for blowing out his brains. Barckhausen's wallet had been found at a sorting office (he had left it in a public postbox so as to create the impression that he had been killed by a robber who had walked away with his money after shooting him). The criminal police attributed wider significance to this case and concluded: 'In the history of crime, there have always been so-called "borderline cases". Suicides have with outstanding skill been able to deceive people into believing that criminal circumstances surrounded their deaths.'[154] The *Vossische Zeitung* went further and interpreted this case as 'a unique example of a pretended murder, but also as a staggering document of human entanglement and guilt'. The newspaper put his death into the context of the increasing economic depression affecting Germany, and noted that it had coincided with the collapse of the *Darmstädter und Nationalbank (Danatbank)* on 13 July 1931, which almost led to the total collapse of banking in Germany.[155] The psychiatrist Richard Detlev Loewenberg did indeed reveal an increased incidence of suicide in Hamburg in the week of the crash of the *Danatbank*. From 13 July until 18 July, 17 suicides were registered in Hamburg. In the previous week, only five suicides had been reported, and in the week following, there were 12 cases. For Loewenberg and many others, these figures proved that adverse economic conditions directly caused suicides.[156]

In many cases, as in Barckhausen's, it was difficult for the criminal police to establish whether a death had been due to murder or suicide. Investigations often continued to rely on the interrogation of eyewitnesses. Social prejudices and clichés about suicide held by the criminal police and the public certainly also played a great role in determining whether a given death was classified as murder or suicide. Towards the end of the Weimar Republic, individual cases of suicide became increasingly politicized by the media as individual suicides within the ranks of the Nazis and the communists concerned the criminal police especially in the later Weimar years which saw increasing hostilities between the two parties. On 30 September 1930, the 23-year-old baker Franz G was found shot dead in his parents' flat in Herschelstraße in North Charlottenburg. Heavily politicized, people in this overwhelmingly working-class district fought their political enemies over the domination of their neighbourhoods. Particularly towards the end of the Weimar Republic, political violence turned almost into a civil war.[157] G, an active member of the Nazi party and a storm trooper, had been fighting the communist *Roter Frontkämpferbund* and had been arrested several times in 1927 and in 1929 for beating up communists who, in turn, had also attacked him. Assuming that G had been killed by the communists, the criminal police interrogated people from G's neighbourhood. On the night of 29 September 1930, the police established, G had shown up at two pubs, probably SA *Sturmlokale*, typical hang-outs for unemployed storm troopers. The landlord and an SA officer had evicted him, since he had been extremely drunk. On his way home, he had been overheard saying, 'If the Third Reich doesn't come about soon, I will finish myself off.'[158]

G's motivation may not have been entirely political. The businessman Heinrich K, G's SA leader (*Sturmführer*), testified that G's father had contacted him directly after G's death and asked him how much money he would get from the storm troopers' life insurance company, now that his son had died (the storm troopers had been offering their own insurance to members, as did trade unions and left-wing political parties).[159] K then accused G's father, formerly a social democrat, of his son's murder. (G's father claimed that he had been a member of the SPD 'merely for monetary reasons' to get promoted as a street cleaner.) Presumably K did not want the insurance fund to have to pay out, either because it would deplete it, or because G's father was not somebody he wanted to get the money. Three storm troopers would testify, K claimed, that G had already threatened to kill his son; to discredit him further, the storm troopers asserted that G's father was beating his daughter. Interrogated by the criminal police on 4 October, G's father explained that he had never had 'significant political arguments' with his son. He was anxious that his sons might get hurt during street fights, and asserted that he had only complained 'that they went out in public too often and took part in processions. And of course that they hung out on the street and in the pubs until 3 or 4 in the morning.' The police concluded that K's allegations were politically motivated and without foundation. G had clearly killed himself. Here, suicide had been politicized in a particularly direct way in the context of political conflict in the locality.[160]

Similar cases happened elsewhere in the politically turbulent final years of the Weimar Republic. In Silesia, local storm troopers fought the communists and the social democrats, among others, in a particularly brutal way in the wake of the July 1932 Reichstag elections, which had failed to bring the Nazis into power. The radical SA terror campaign of August 1932 nevertheless led to a crisis within the Nazi movement between those in favour of political violence and others advocating a tactic of 'legality'.[161] This atmosphere created a tendency to assume that almost any death of a politically active individual must be a political murder.

On 30 August 1932, the *Völkischer Beobachter* reported that the 26-year-old storm trooper Franz Rosemann had been run over by a train near Liegnitz. The Nazi newspaper insisted that communists had shot him, though not fatally, near the railway. The article claimed that Rosemann had been trying to run away from his would-be killers at the time when the train hit him. 'There was not the least evidence for suicide' in this case, declared the paper. The Nazis threatened to 'take the necessary steps', that is to retaliate against the alleged communist killers, since the 'political police had been satisfied with the assumption that it had been suicide'. Nevertheless, the investigation of the state prosecutor at the Breslau *Sondergericht*, a special court established to combat political unrest, reached a fundamentally different verdict. Rosemann had not in fact been killed by the communists, but had killed himself, as a railway guard who had witnessed his death testified. Rosemann had also been suffering from lovesickness, as his father told the police.[162] The Nazis' accusations against the communists were totally untenable in this case. After the Nazi seizure of power, Nazi lawyers went through the legal files of Nazis who had allegedly suffered from political 'persecution' in the Weimar years in order to reward their relatives and put their names on a list of fallen heroes. Rosemann, however, was not included in this list, and the Nazis accepted the view that he had killed himself.[163] Paradoxically, while both Nazis and communists emphasized and even exaggerated the prevalence of real suicide in the crisis-ridden final years of the Weimar Republic, they were only too often unwilling to believe it when it affected one of their own.

# VII

Most suicides did not think of politics when they penned their farewell missives. Did public debates on suicide have any impact on them? The Berlin criminal police under Gennat began collecting suicide notes in 1926, ranging from the blackly comic to the utterly tragic. Bureaucratic interest in the phenomenon of suicide grew in the mid-1920s. In a draft of the new German penal code (never actually implemented), incitement to suicide was to be penalized, so Gennat thought that the material might also be relevant to the Reichstag's penal-code reform commission (*Strafrechtskommission*).[164] These missives allow us to reconstruct ordinary people's attitudes towards suicide. Given the uncertainties about their statistical repetitiveness and the often idiosyncratic style and contents of the notes, it makes sense, rather than analysing the suicide notes in a quantitative-systematic way, to use them as qualitative evidence.[165]

Writing about the 'self-evidentiality of many suicide notes', one historian concludes that they reflect 'the basic structure of human freedom'.[166] However, only very few, if any, historical documents are 'self-evident', and merely reprinting them without contextualizing them is not sufficient. Suicide notes do in fact have the ability to tell us something about the social, economic and even political context within which they were penned. Farewell missives are the suicide's last means of communication. As we have seen, relatively few suicides leave notes, which are, of course, often written under great mental stress. However, those who write a farewell letter, be it to the police, the welfare office or to their relatives usually want to emphasize a particular suicide motive. Suicide notes thus offer a microcosm of the existential circumstances under which people took their lives. The ways in which people represented their suicides can be put into a historical context, which illuminates the circumstances of a suicide, alongside the main motive the suicide wanted to emphasize. As for the police, they took their own view of the circumstances, appending a brief note on the motivation for each case in the file with a red pencil. These files yield relatively little, if any, biographical information on the individuals presented here. Yet individual suicides are recoverable from these files, even without much background information about the individual suicides and their hopes and expectations.

In some cases, people who planned to commit suicide sent a note directly to the police in which they proposed arrangements for the disposal of their bodies. Probably only in Germany did suicides assist the police in this way. Most of them were from the working class and were too poor to have life insurance. Some wanted to ensure that friends and relatives were not accused of homicide, others wanted to protest against social conditions. Take the case of the 20-year-old chauffeur Ordulf Thomas, who shot himself in the Grunewald forest in 1928. Mocking the public media obsession with suicide, Thomas wrote a startlingly ironic letter to the local police office on the day before his death, detailing where the police could find his corpse:

> For the rest, I ask you to refrain from putting any entertaining notes in the newspaper. You will certainly be interested in the motives that prompted me to take this step—so I'll satisfy your curiosity. Simply for a change. Life was too boring for me, and I wanted to convince myself of the existence of the 'Beyond'. I couldn't care less what you do with my remains. As far as I'm concerned you can put me on the Victory Column. So, that should do, and I wish you much pleasure with my cadaver.[167]

While it is hard to say whether there was a literary influence here, Thomas's suicide note made fun of the public obsession with suicide and the genre of suicide notes, and mocked the romanticization of suicide in reports that attributed it to disappointment in love. His request not to be mentioned in the press, which the police observed, shows how some suicides tried to keep their death private, from whatever motives.

Emotional problems featured in many farewell missives. Oskar S, a 24-year-old unemployed waiter from the working-class Neukölln district wrote on a scrap of paper, still stained with his own blood in the archive eighty years later, to his girlfriend on 4 April 1926: 'Dear Winnie! I couldn't go on. Thanks for everything. My body hurts, why.' On the reverse, he continued: 'Long live life. Thank you, my dear parents, for everything. But I'm finished.'[168] Somewhat apologetically, Oskar anticipated that his relatives might be gravely offended by his suicide. He ended by expressing his love for his girlfriend and family.

On the other hand, some suicides used their final statement to express hatred, as did Hermann L to his daughter on 8 July 1926:

> When you find this note, do whatever you want, because I'm not coming back. I'm sick of you acting like an animal. It always reminds me of earlier times. You have no idea what a bitch your mother was. My disgust drove me away from her. Farewell and try to become a human being, *otherwise you'll perish, too.* Best wishes. Your Father.[169]

Here was suicide presented as a kind of revenge, designed to cause feelings of guilt and shame in the surviving next-of-kin.

Some suicides made explicit political statements in their final communications, probably hoping that their suicide notes would be noticed by the press. The Italian citizen Antonio S was found hanged on 1 June 1927 in a goods train near the station of Sagehorn in Lower Saxony. There are no further details available on S, probably a political refugee from Italy. In his suicide note, translated by the police, he protested against the Fascist regime:

> Persecuted and hunted like an animal, I had to leave my country in order not to lose my freedom. It was very hard for me to bring about my own death, but it's far better than being executed in the *Mussolini gaol*, because I am a political dissenter! Cheers to all decent people who do not violate their fellow citizens even when their politics are different.

It seems likely that S was facing extradition proceedings, and did not see any way out for himself other than suicide. The police tried to contact his relatives, but conceded on 20 September 1927 that 'the investigations in Milan were inconclusive'.[170]

Count Ernst von L, a lawyer, wrote his own very patriotic obituary instead of leaving a suicide note to his family before shooting himself in 1927 in his flat in Spandau:

> In accordance with his inner disposition, he remained to his core a loner. His heart was not tied to things of the ephemeral world. So outstanding

was his character that whatever the situation, he would not allow himself to go around flattering people, be they his superiors or others, at work or away from it. Toadying and pussyfooting were for him as good as having no character at all. His unabashed directness in dealing with his fellow men made him quite a few enemies... He was a German to his very core and a monarchist, an unflinching and avid confessor of his faith, a fanatical devotee of Bismarck and last but not least one whose hatred of the French nation was unmatched.[171]

While it is not entirely obvious what had prompted his suicide, it is clear that he completely identified himself and his status as an ex-soldier with the fate of the German nation.

Material problems, especially unemployment, served as a primary motive in many suicide notes, as one might expect from the statistical evidence. Fifty-nine-year-old chauffeur Wilhelm S's suicide note, written before he gassed himself on 9 September 1932 in his flat in the Friedenau garden suburb of Berlin, reads like a short autobiography and as a self-justification vis-à-vis the police. A war veteran, S had had marriage problems and, to make things worse, was now unemployed. He accused his wife of having destroyed his life, and, by implication, causing his suicide. It seems as if he would have been quite pleased if she had got into trouble with the police. S declared:

I must unfortunately leave behind this last missive, because I cannot live any longer and so I must depart from life. I have indeed done my duty. I have been married since 27 December 1900. As early as 1903 I had already been alerted to the fact that she would make me unhappy. And so it continued year after year. Then the war came. I returned and it all started. Her siblings were with her and had a bad influence on her and moved from one place to the next. I moved to Manteuffelstrasse 19 in Tempelhof and then things really went awry. They both got on each other ['s nerves]. She said the woman is making you unhappy, that was Wilhelm S and Emma S, nee L. Luise S was there, too. I complained that this should be kept a private matter, but it went to police station 178. Any of her siblings could have done it. [They] brought the whole matter to the attention of the Supreme Administrative Court (Oberverwaltungsgericht) at Hardenbergstr. 31. Everything is a mess. I had to take my wife to Buch [a Berlin mental asylum], but she was released. While my wife was in the mental asylum, I had to live with my daughter Else who did not make much money. She left on 1 May, packed up her stuff and [left me] some pennies. I used them [up] on the street but that wasn't enough for her so now my wife is taking everything over to her son who wouldn't even offer her a glass of water. He cannot eat and throws everything into the dustbin. Willi S lives at Bahnstr 9 and now I have the pain. Now I'm unemployed, it's even worse now, getting worse. I could put down more thoughts. Phone Dönhoff 9127, Kommandantenstr 18, signed Willi S, chauffeur. I was inclined to set everything on fire, but I felt sorry for the neighbours.[172]

Here, in this confused but powerful note, was suicide in rage and despair, triggered by economic misery and problems with his family.

Ordinary people sometimes asked the police not to pass on any inform-ation about their suicide. The 53-year-old bank clerk Johannes L, who gassed himself in his flat in the Barn District of Berlin on 22 July 1931, specifically requested that the press must not be informed; the police would be able to draw an 'appropriate donation' from his estate if they kept the matter quiet. According to the police, he was suffering from paralysis of the legs. Writing a suicide note to the local police office's head, L explained that the police should know 'that this is not a crime when someone finds me dead in my bed'. He also requested not to be taken to a morgue, but directly to the cemetery, in a coffin, which was ready for him. If true, this reveals that L had meticulously planned his suicide beforehand.[173]

Unemployment, despair and lost love were common motives for ordinary Berliners to justify their suicides. The case of the 25-year-old butcher, Hermann J from Glogau in Silesia, who shot himself in a hotel room in Berlin on 15 February 1931, is quite revealing in this regard. Leaving three suicide notes (one to his girlfriend, another one to his family and another one to relatives who had put him up in Berlin), J particularly emphasized his unemployment. In a letter to his family, he declared:

> You'll be surprised to get this letter from me. Since I still haven't found work and I don't know where to go, I've decided to end it all. If I'd just found work, then everything would have been fine, but maybe that's just the way things were to be. You wouldn't believe just how horrible the job outlook is. I tried so very hard, but in vain. And I really can't ask my brother-in-law to keep feeding me here month after month. He did so much for me. He's helped me out since November with food and lodging. And so I ask you to give my things and some money to Fritz. Otherwise I don't know what else to write so I'll stop here. Best wishes ... Farewell.

Taking this explanation for granted, the criminal police laconically com-mented that the 'motive of the suicide [was] unemployment and economic misery'.[174] Male unemployment and male suicide were thought to be causally related to each other, and the police did not bother to investigate this suicide further. Many suicides justified their deaths with reference to an unbearable combination of highly personal and socio-economic causes, although some emphasized solely private matters. They saw no way out of a political, emotional or practical crisis: they were alone, abandoned or persecuted by their country, or their family. Suicide notes not only linked the suicide to his or her own environment; they also documented in more ways than one the suicide's final rupture from it.

# VIII

In Weimar Germany, suicide statistics and the mass media helped to shape wider social and political representations of suicide. Suicide was widely associated with the political and socio-economic problems of the time, which many observers directly related to the defeat of 1918, the Versailles Treaty, the capitalist system, reparations, or modernity. For people from different classes and generations, suicide served as a focal point for their own beliefs and ideologies. In the public sphere, including newspapers, suicide, together with other manifestations of deviance such as crime and murder, entered the agenda as a focal point for conflicting ideologies. The churches, concerned with the implications of modernity, blamed secularization, urbanization, and the alleged atomization of society for the ostensible increase in suicide levels—which they considerably exaggerated. This prompted parts of the German public to relate Weimar society to a reversal of traditional, pre-1918 norms and values: an anomie prompting many suicides.[175]

Political parties, especially those on the radical fringes of the political spectrum, like the Nazis and the communists, blamed the political and economic order for rising suicide levels. Ordinary people tended to justify their suicides with direct reference to the political and socio-economic difficulties of the time, and, of course, mentioned personal and emotional motivations, including the collapse of traditional gender roles for men. Some were very much aware of the ways in which suicide was discussed in public. People wrote lengthy justifications in their suicide notes either addressed to the state authorities or to their own families. Many still saw suicide as a disreputable, highly extreme, last resort for one's problems with which, by common agreement, other institutions, such as the church and welfare agencies, could no longer cope. Yet at the same time, thanks to the impact of sensationalist newspaper stories, ordinary people began to accept that suicide was a mass phenomenon prompted by political and socio-economic disorder.

There was an interchange between personal suicide discourse and public suicide discourse, especially in the common emphasis of unemployment in the later years of the Weimar Republic. The political and socio-economic crisis of the Weimar years impacted upon individuals to the extent that many committed suicide in despair. The public and private representations of suicide overlapped, making it impossible to differentiate sharply between suicide as a discourse and the socio-psychological causes of suicide. Unresolved tensions therefore remain between these two levels. By 1933, suicide on an unprecedented scale had come to symbolize for many the disastrous, crisis-ridden epoch of Weimar. On coming to power in 1933, the Nazis promised to banish all this. Would they banish suicide too?

# 2

# Suicide under the Swastika, 1933–1939

## I

Under the Weimar Republic, Hitler and the Nazis had conflated cases of suicide with the German defeat of 1918, the Versailles Treaty, and the Weimar 'system'. Denouncing the Versailles Treaty, the reparations payments, and the economic problems of the Weimar years in his Reichstag speech on foreign policy on 17 May 1933, Hitler, now chancellor, ranted: 'Since the signing of this treaty ... 224,900 people, men, women, elderly people, and children have voluntarily taken their lives almost exclusively because of misery and deprivation!'[1] The figure quoted by Hitler was almost accurate. Between 1918 and 1933, 214,409 suicides had been officially recorded in Germany.[2] In July 1933, Julius Streicher's rabidly anti-Semitic newspaper *Der Stürmer*, widely sold and displayed in advertising boxes across Germany, blamed the Jews for the First World War and for the '220,000' suicides between 1918 and 1933. The paper insisted: 'Eighteen million war dead and 220,000 dead after the war. *Alljuda* is to blame! Even if the entire Jewish race disappeared from this planet, the grave crimes it has committed would still not be atoned.'[3] Hitler thought that most suicides were due to social and political despair caused by the Versailles Treaty and implicitly by the lack of living space. The economic misery caused by reparations allegedly increased suicide rates, while the Nazis' ostensible ending of unemployment reduced them. The alleged strengthening of the people's community through Nazi rule, according to Hitler, should have resulted in a decline of the number of suicides. Indeed, in his speech commemorating the anniversary of the Munich beerhall putsch on 8 November 1939, Hitler commended himself and the Nazi party for having overcome the 'times of the great unemployment and of the incredible suicides in Germany'.[4]

Predictably, other commentators followed Hitler's views on suicide. In 1938, Kurt Helpap, a medical doctor working at a Berlin hospital named after the Nazi martyr Horst Wessel, brushed aside claims that suicide could any more be a way of escaping from economic hardship: the Nazis claimed to have abolished this, and indeed, there was hardly any official unemployment by this time. If suicide was a selfish act, so it was now overcome by the Nazis as individualism was overcome. Helpap declared: 'There are only very few morally legitimate reasons for this action.'[5] Writing in 1940, the medical doctor Albrecht Graf zu Münster, a Nazi since 1929, claimed that due to the strengthening of the racial body (*Volkskörper*) a further increase in the suicide rate was highly unlikely. Münster blamed suicide on 'economic misery', which, as Hitler had already pointed out, allegedly did not exist in the Third Reich. According to Münster, the state was now able to 'exclude completely worthless elements from reproduction' through new legislation such as the Law for the Prevention of Hereditarily Ill Offspring of 1933, which allowed for the forced sterilization of the 'congenitally ill', or the notorious Nuremberg laws of 1935 which criminalized sexual relationships between Jews and non-Jews. Münster did not claim that all suicides had been mentally ill, since this would have made it difficult for him to explain the high suicide levels in Germany after the First World War.[6] The entry on suicide in a leading German encyclopaedia from 1942 followed the general Nazi line. While the religious condemnation of suicide, especially the Catholic one, had not helped reduce the number of suicides, so the entry declared, National Socialism was anxious to promote 'racial and eugenic health' and create 'life-circumstances based upon the principle of the people's community' to prevent suicides.[7]

The Nazi negation of individual freedom together with the strong emphasis on the interests of the racial body manifested itself not only in academic and popular discourses, but also in practical legal and adminis-trative initiatives of various parts of the Nazi regime. Almost immediately after coming to power, the Nazis set up a commission for the long-planned reform of the German penal code. The commission was not under the auspices of the Reichstag, as similar commissions had been in Imperial and Weimar Germany. It was chaired, in a typically authoritarian manner, by the national conservative Reich Minister of Justice Franz Gürtner. It consisted of lawyers who more or less sympathized with the Nazi regime, including radical Nazi lawyers such as Roland Freisler, the state secretary in the Reich Ministry of Justice, and Otto-Georg Thierack who would both later become the main proponents of legal terror in the Third Reich. The commission's aim was a new penal code that above all reflected the Nazi principles of *Volk*, race and 'healthy popular sentiment' (*gesundes Volksempfinden*). The ideological core of the new penal code, one lawyer declared, was the 'absolute protection of the people's community', relegating 'individual interests' to the background.[8] Freisler insisted that the penal code as a 'fighting law' (*Kampfrecht*) must be used as 'the self-cleansing apparatus' (*Selbstreinigungsapparat*) of the racial body by extirpating criminality and deviant behaviour.[9] The commission produced a first draft of a new penal code in 1936, and another, more radical one in 1939, in the wake of the *Anschluss*, which had necessitated the merging of the Austrian with the German penal code. The Nazis never enforced a new penal code, however, because the progressive radicalization of the regime, increasingly less concerned with legal codifications, outdated the commission's various drafts.[10] Nevertheless, the debates within the commission shed light on leading Nazi lawyers' attitudes towards suicide.

The commission originally wanted to legalize assisted suicide and involuntary euthanasia. In the end, involuntary euthanasia and assisted suicide were not legalized, not because of any concerns about the rights of the individual, but to ensure that the racial body did not lose any of its valuable members.[11] The Nazis could not realize this idea of cleansing the racial body because of the regime's regard for public religious concerns about euthanasia, which were expressed most famously by Bishop Galen in 1941.[12] Needless to say, the legal discourse on euthanasia did not matter much when thousands of physically handicapped and mentally ill people were murdered under extrajudicial provisions after the outbreak of the war. The T-4 euthanasia campaign ceased essentially because of popular protests, articulated most clearly by Galen, although euthanasia murders continued in disguise.[13]

However, in the case of valuable members of the 'people's community', suicide, the Nazis argued, was to be outlawed because the will of the *Volk* had superseded the will of the individual, according to the Nazi mantra 'the common good has priority over self-interest'.[14] This resembled official attitudes towards suicide in Stalinist Russia. There, an official had already

declared in 1926 that 'life and death cannot be decided on one's own'.[15]
The Nazis planned to make paragraph 216 of the penal code referring to
assisted suicide more severe. The duty of 'every member of the people's
community' was to contribute to its well-being, rather than to attack it
by committing suicide, as suggested by commission member Wenzel von
Gleispach, an Austrian Nazi and professor of law in Berlin.[16] Insofar as
Germans had a duty to pay taxes and to perform labour and military
service, they also had the duty to serve the national community, wrote the
Cologne lawyer Dr Weimar in 1936. He dismissed 'the obsolete idea that
everyone can freely dispose of his body or his life'.[17] For these reasons,
he demanded a new legal evaluation of suicide, which the commission for
the reform of the penal code had already been considering. In 1933 and
1934, it planned to make incitement to suicide a new statutory offence.
Those inciting enemies of the *Volk* to suicide should not be punished,
however, since the self-extermination of enemies of the *Volk* was a good
thing.[18] During the war, the proposal to criminalize incitement to suicide
was withdrawn, as the regime at that time did not really care about legal
questions.

In its deliberations on changing the method of capital punishment in
1934 and 1935, the commission also discussed suicide. Many Nazis saw
the execution of criminals and 'inferior' people as a 'general prevention
of racial degeneration' and thus as an act of extermination rather than
of retribution.[19] Following the contemporary discourse on selectionist
Social Darwinism, the Nazi writer Ludwig Binz had already written a
lengthy article in the *Völkischer Beobachter* in January 1929, stressing that the
extermination of 'inferior' people had superseded the state's need to punish
criminals. If criminals were given the opportunity to eradicate themselves,
this would be much easier for the state authorities than executing them. This
suggestion was a radical break with tradition. Prison authorities normally
tried to prevent suicides amongst those on death row, thereby asserting the
state's powers over their lives. Pointing to the blurring between suicide and
murder under the Third Reich, Binz insisted:

> It makes no sense to 'punish' those who break the law, only to dispose of
> them. The right belongs to every person condemned to death to die by
> one's own hand, to commit suicide, but of course only within a limited time
> period … Annihilation it has to be, for the sake of deterrence and safety. If
> the murderer or person who commits crimes against the nation turns down

the chance to die freely, then he is to be killed in due course by chemical means.[20]

At the commission's meeting on 1 March 1934, Freisler suggested that those condemned to death be given a chalice of poison with which they could kill themselves within five minutes if they wanted to avoid execution. Freisler, enthusiastic about this new method of execution, declared: 'Perhaps a high moral value resides therein.' The Nazis saw those put on death row to be so degenerate and racially inferior that they were not worthy of anything but self-extermination.[21] The ancient notion of capital punishment by taking an enforced draught of hemlock at a time and in circumstances of one's own choosing had allowed the condemned to retain some sense of dignity and self-determination over their life and body, as well as a degree of political heroism. The Nazi proposal fundamentally differed from this notion as it left the condemned no choice of either the time or the circumstances and robbed them of any dignity.

Others in the Nazi state welcomed Freisler's proposal. The general state prosecutor of Hesse commended the idea to give those condemned to death the opportunity to commit suicide, while he also voiced some concern over possible protests from both Catholics and Protestants. He declared in September 1934:

> Giving appellants or those already denied clemency the official or unoffical opportunity to kill themselves is at the very least desirable in many cases ... It is, however, inadvisable to codify regulations on suicide in the penal code in light of the feelings among Catholics and even some Protestants, who see suicide as a major sin. Some would accuse the new state of being pagan. The instances of suicide among those condemned to death, which are rare, are not a big deal and announcing these deaths under something like the rubric of 'judged himself' has almost the same impact on the population as the announcement of the execution.[22]

Anxious about sharp protests from the churches, however, the Nazis never introduced this new method of extermination as a substitute for execution.[23] Nazi views on suicide sometimes clearly overlapped with the Nazi agenda on exterminating criminals and 'inferior' people: suicide was to be welcomed if eugenically weak people exterminated themselves through suicide. Traditional religious concerns about suicide being a violation of God's power to decide over life and death did not play a role in Nazi discourse. But Nazi views on suicide were more complex.

# II

The problem of suicide concerned many Nazi leaders other than Hitler. Among many other things, it concerned Heinrich Himmler, Reich Leader of the SS. He saw it as a threat to the survival of the Germanic race. In a 1939 speech, Himmler declared bluntly: 'Suicide motives [are] trivial in 90 out of 100 cases', thereby denouncing suicide as an act whose 'deeper cause [is] usually cowardice...'. Suicide stood in sharp contrast to Himmler's ideal: the 'fighting spirit of the SS... to choose the difficult path'.[24] In an interesting parallel to the Christian taboo on suicide—rather ironic given his radically anti-Christian attitudes—Himmler ordered that the SS must not participate in the funeral of any SS officer who had killed himself for 'trivial' reasons such as 'fear of punishment, fear of an exam... lovesickness'. In March 1944, a drunk SS officer killed himself in Russia in remorse after he had clubbed to death a Russian woman. A furious Himmler announced that he reserved the right for himself to report cases of suicide to the suicide's relatives, and to decide whether relatives were entitled to a pension.[25]

In a decree of February 1938 circulated among the Order Police (since 1936 also part of the SS), police general Kurt Daluege declared that reports on suicide within the police 'were very serious. Not only do they reveal an increase in suicide levels, but also a deep-seated psychic misery.' Reportedly, it was especially policemen aged between 35 and 50 who committed suicide. According to Daluege, reflecting Himmler's point, these suicides had often been committed for 'trivial' reasons. Daluege demanded total commitment from the police and glorified the experience of the First World War in order to discourage his men from killing themselves. He referred to 'the experience of the front line in the Great War, during which many "lost their nerves", but regained it thanks to their comrades' encouragement and even surpassed themselves in the decisive moment'. Suicide was an act of weakness that was inappropriate for a National Socialist. Daluege insisted:

> We learn from suicide investigations that the motivating factor behind suicide in the overwhelming majority of cases is ignorance of the physical degeneration of mind and body at this age. Those affected have a totally wrong attitude towards these natural processes and lead a bad lifestyle. Time and again, we can see that the deterioration of the will to live among those affected results in totally inappropriate inferiority complexes,

which...cause 'depression'. In this state of depression, people decide to commit suicide, which is in turn often caused by a trivial reason, which the person affected totally overrates (eg marriage problems, job-related problems, being humiliated etc).[26]

In practice, however, neither Daluege's decree nor Himmler's radical views could prevent suicides within the SS, the most loyal pillar of the regime. From July until September 1942, for example, 30 suicides were recorded within the SS. A secret list was compiled for Himmler's attention. In this list, most suicides were denounced as weak or ill ('suffering from venereal disease', 'mentally ill', 'psychologically abnormal', 'hereditarily inferior'). Other SS men allegedly killed themselves because of 'fear of an expected punishment' after stealing from their comrades.[27]

Himmler did, however, make one exception to his general condemnation of suicide when he applauded it as a means of restoring one's personal honour. In January 1944, Himmler encouraged a married SS officer, who had supposedly had an affair with another woman, 'to end his failed life himself', thereby giving him the opportunity to restore his honour and at the same time purging the SS of an undesirable element.[28] Yet this appears to have been an exception. The former Saxon Minister of the Interior, SS Brigadier Fritsch, killed himself in April 1944 after cheating his wife with another woman and his degradation. Himmler personally ordered Fritsch's SS insignia to be removed from his grave and melted down.[29]

But not only leading Nazis thought that suicide was an act of weakness. In December 1940, the poet and doctor Gottfried Benn, who was at the time working in the supreme command of the Wehrmacht where he was responsible, among other things, for dealing with the suicides of soldiers, wrote in a letter that:

> There can be no doubt that most of the persons who commit suicide belong to the imperilled and labile types whose reproduction is not necessarily desirable according to the ideal of today's state biology...One could regard suicide as a process of racial elimination, and therefore, one cannot describe suicide as being immoral, neither in an individual nor a *volkhaft* sense.[30]

While Benn's role in the Third Reich remains controversial, his views here overlapped with Nazi thinking. Suicide as a means of self-extermination of the eugenically unfit and ill was to be welcomed, rather than to be condemned. The Nazi discourse on euthanasia, as the 'extermination of those unworthy to live', overlapped with suicide discourse in Benn's statement. There were of course many different views on suicide expressed by academic writers in the Third Reich and some major academic monographs on suicide were not written in explicitly political or racial language. But this is not surprising in the light of what Günther Hecht, from the Racial Political Office of the NSDAP, wrote: 'As a political movement, National Socialism rejects any equation with any scholars or researchers or with any branches of research within the life sciences... National Socialism is a political movement, not a scientific one.'[31]

The Nazis thus used those scientific ideas that fit their purposes, and the ideas of scientists had a variable impact on Nazi practices. Scientific discourses on suicide indeed somewhat differed from prevailing Nazi attitudes, and were often far more cautious. Thus in 1940, Hans-Walter Gruhle, a leading psychiatrist, denied that there were any clear links between racial factors and proneness to suicide, declaring that 'the impact of the racial factor is still unknown'.[32] Others went further. In a 1937 monograph on suicide that could only be published in Switzerland, Raphael Weichbrodt, a German-Jewish psychiatrist, dismissed the view that there was any relationship between suicide and race, savaging racial science as unscientific.[33] Gustav Donalies, a German suicide expert, condemned Weichbrodt's book in a highly critical review. Donalies subscribed to the racial view. Dismissing Weichbrodt as a biased Jew, he declared: '[the] author tends to place special emphasis on economic aspects and is more dismissive about the roles of race and heredity than one might expect from his—undeniable—bias...'.[34]

Racial thinking had long featured in suicide discourse in one way or another. The two intellectual founding fathers of involuntary euthanasia in Germany, the lawyer Karl Binding and the psychiatrist Alfred Hoche, had justified their demands for the decriminalization of involuntary euthanasia in 1920 with explicit references to suicide. Their work was frequently cited in Nazi Germany. Binding, responsible for the legal issues, deliberately conflated voluntary death with forced euthanasia and demanded its legalization. He took the impunity of voluntary suicide as a given to justify the legalization of involuntary euthanasia. Binding asked the rhetorical question: 'Shall the right to the legal extermination of life remain restricted to suicide, as it is in current law (except in emergencies), or shall it be legally extended to the killing of others, and, if so, to what extent?'[35] Binding went on to complain that 'the harsh and cold term *Selbstmord* was tendentious' in describing the act of self-killing. In likening the 'battlefields covered with thousands of dead youths' to 'our mental asylums', he exploited the massive German casualties of the First World War to demand the extermination of the costly and useless existence of the eugenically weak.[36] Binding's assertion that the race should take precedence over individuals was recurrent in Nazi writings on suicide. Of course, many Nazis, including Hitler, shared the belief that the state and the racial body were the final arbiters of life and death, rather than the individual.

This view was reflected in Wolfgang Liebeneiner's 1941 film *I Accuse!* (*Ich klage an!*), a propagandistic justification of involuntary euthanasia. In it, the killing of the 'incurably ill' is illustrated with reference to a woman suffering from multiple sclerosis who requests her husband's assistance in committing suicide. When her husband honours her request, claiming that he had 'ended her suffering', he is put on trial. A debate follows in which religious and moral concerns about euthanasia are eventually brushed aside so that he is portrayed in a positive light.[37] The blurring of the categories of 'assisted suicide' and 'involuntary euthanasia' thereby exploited the fact that suicide was legal in Germany to justify the mass-murder of those excluded from the racial body by the Nazis. A report from the SS Security Service (SD) of January 1942, summing up the public reception of the film, concluded: 'The state indeed demands from us the *duty* to die; then it must also give us the *right* to die.'[38] Needless to say, those murdered in the euthanasia programme were denied the right to decide over their own lives. The conflation of the notions of suicide as a voluntary act and euthanasia as a forced act thus centred around notions of extermination and self-extermination, which were placed on the same level.

These ideas can be traced back to the late-nineteenth century when selectionist Social Darwinism became widespread among the medical and legal professions. Rather than condemning suicide as a crime against the supreme authority of God over life and death, suicide was increasingly seen in the medical and legal professions as a biological and hereditary problem. German suicidologists generally did not pay attention to the wider socio-political background against which people committed suicide, and tended to blame the act of self-destruction on inherited psychiatric disorders.[39] Religious concerns about suicide became less relevant in the discourse on suicide as wider changes in thinking about society began to emerge around the turn of the century. Social Darwinism became a central principle underlying the wider social discourse in emphasizing the struggle for the 'survival of the fittest' and 'natural selection'. The experience of violence and destruction in the First World War reaffirmed this view. The Nazis accused Weimar welfare politicians of preserving inferior and degenerate elements through the welfare system.[40] Suicide discourse became increasingly linked to a wider discourse on crime. Building upon the criminologist Cesare Lombroso's work, it claimed that proneness to suicide was an inherited weakness, just as 'inferiority' and 'criminality' were passed on via one's ancestors. Nazi authorities shared this view, as a case from the Reich Security Head Office's files reveals. A circular from the Kiel criminal police from 1935 reflects the Nazi view that suicide was a hereditary deficiency. In 1935, a 23-year-old mechanic drowned himself in the Baltic Sea near Kiel. His grandfather had reportedly hanged himself, and his father had drowned himself in the River Elbe in 1925, having attempted at the same time to kill his two sons, one of whom now committed suicide ten years later. The article concluded: 'Thus three generations ended because of suicide.'[41]

Criminologists and psychiatrists in the Third Reich argued that most suicides were mentally ill. In a character profile of the adolescent Werner Pufert, who had attempted to kill himself in 1941 after trying to murder a 24-year-old woman with an axe, the psychiatrist Johannes Schottky carefully reconstructed the life of the would-be suicide. Schottky complained that Werner had not taken his service in the Hitler Youth seriously and that he had been a petty thief. Though of 'predominantly Nordic type', Werner was, after all, a hereditary criminal (*Anlageverbrecher*). Schottky insisted: 'Even if P has not yet committed any grave crimes, his inclination towards socially aberrant behaviour, as evidenced by his development up to now, is already unavoidable.' Pufert was sentenced to ten years in gaol 'because of his demonstrated emotional brutality and the need to protect the people's community'.[42] Not all criminologists explicitly welcomed suicides of 'eugenically weak' people. However, there were strong undertones of suicide as a means of selection in scientific discourse. As many suicides (according to one estimate, between 30 and 50 per cent) were 'inferior' people 'as a result of the hereditary biological deterioration of the race', their self-destruction was not a loss to the racial body.[43] Similarly, many racial scientists and medical doctors constructed the argument that Jews, as a particularly 'inferior' race characterized by 'excesses and degeneration', were more prone to suicide than others.[44]

The Nazis and many scientists thought that the 'eugenically fit' should not commit suicide, whereas they welcomed or even encouraged suicides amongst the 'eugenically weak'. Nazi thinking about suicide was therefore contradictory. But most commentators and Nazi politicians agreed that the Third Reich had resolved the problem of suicide, thereby denying the persistence of suicide in Nazi Germany. Nazi suicide discourse was closely attached to selectionist Social Darwinism. Nazi discourse on suicide and state intervention was not a mere return to the pre-Enlightenment notion of monarchical sovereignty over the lives and bodies of his subjects, under which suicide was penalized as a felony; the link between suicide in Nazi Germany and the Nazi extermination programmes was too close to allow such a view. The Nazi discourse on suicide was not 'barbaric' or uncivilized, inhumane as it was. Eugenicist and Social Darwinist views on suicide were by no means restricted to Germany, as Morselli's arguments have shown. But the Nazi regime, above all concerned with racial engineering and living space, purported to transform fundamentally the ways in which people experienced and represented suicide.

# III

During the Weimar Republic, as we have seen, suicide was widely reported in the press. Especially in the early 1930s, best-selling Berlin newspapers, among them the *8 Uhr-Abendblatt* and the *BZ am Mittag*, ran regular, often sensationalist, reports on suicide. Yet, after 1933 and the Nazi coordination of the press, newspapers hardly printed any stories on this topic. Economic deprivation and emotional problems had featured as a general explanation for suicide in the Weimar press. The press in the Third Reich, if it reported suicides at all, usually placed the blame on lovesickness, thereby supporting the Nazi view that unemployment and problems of a socio-economic nature had been overcome in the Third Reich. Thus for example on 25 April 1935, the *BZ am Mittag* ran a story, stripped of any political significance, on its front page on 'Tragedy of Jeaolusy: Murder and Suicide at Berlin's Gates'.[45]

Other contemporary dictatorships too tried to create the illusion that they had overcome suicide. Suicide was an inconvenient phenomenon for regimes striving to control every aspect of life and death. The Third Reich and other contemporary dictatorships were concerned about reaching unanimous popular support, so high suicide rates would have reflected badly on a dictatorial regime's image. In Italy, the Fascists had banned publication of any reports on suicide and suicide attempts with effect from September 1932. They tried to create the illusion that Fascism had overcome the suicide problem. Nevertheless, this ban did not lead to a reduction in suicide levels.[46] In the Soviet Union too suicide disappeared from the public sphere in the early 1930s. The publication of stories and studies on the subject ceased.[47] The Nazis did not ban the reporting of suicide. Nazi instructions to the press, usually dictated by Reich Press Chief Otto Dietrich, explicitly demanded a more careful, less sensationalist treatment of suicide to maintain the illusion that suicide was a problem of the past. A press instruction of 31 March 1937 reflected concerns about the Third Reich's image abroad. It demanded:

> Recently, some German newspapers have published 'compilations' of suicides, that is, proper suicide lists. Because of their impact abroad, compilations of this sort should in the future be avoided under all circumstances. It is acceptable to distribute evenly suicide reports among the various sections of a newspaper, however.[48]

The implicit warning that such reports might prompt 'disoriented people' to kill themselves was quite revealing, since it implicitly admitted that the Nazi regime had not done away with suicidal factors such as unemployment and emotional trouble. Indeed, Dietrich was aware of this and insisted, in another press instruction of 9 April 1938, that gas should not be described in press reports 'as the most convenient way to commit suicide'.[49] Here the Nazi attempt to discourage suicide amongst supposedly hereditarily sound individuals found a practical expression.

Suicide levels in the Third Reich did not in reality justify this banishing of suicide from the public sphere. Unlike in Stalinist Russia, the Nazis continued to publish suicide levels until the outbreak of the Second World War. In early 1933, after the Nazi seizure of power, Füllkrug wrote: 'Now we can wait to see Germany's suicide statistics for 1933. Has the national revolution of the last few months led to an excited feeling among many German national comrades and, therefore, has the number of cases of suicide decreased?'[50] The academic Dr Ernst March declared in an article in the trade journal of the Protestant Church's Inner Mission:

> One hears and reads increasingly less of people who have taken their lives, since unemployment, it has been established, has decreased in recent years in Germany. It is our great pleasure to report that in the newspapers, sensational reports about suicide have all but ceased. If a suicide comes to pass, it is

at most mentioned briefly. The motivation is usually specified as mental disturbance or temporary insanity, shattered familial relationships, serious illness or 'reasons unknown'. It is striking how few reports there are in the press about suicides caused by unemployment or economic misery. To this one can add that many papers, which thrived on sensationalism, have since disappeared. But has the number of suicides in Germany really decreased? Not at all. In his great speeches of 17 May and 24 October 1933, the Führer pointed out the connections between suicide and the Versailles Treaty and protracted unemployment. For these reasons, [the suicide rate] rose every year until 1932. The results of 1933, which will only be able to be established at the end of this calendar year, will certainly show us whether the National Socialist revolution and the new state were in a position to change the number of suicides significantly. We hope so, God willing![51]

Despite his doubts about the supposed decline in suicide, March was only too pleased about the Nazi coordination of the press, and the banning of 'sensationalist' newspapers. But his scepticism, though couched in cautiously pro-Nazi terms, was palpable. In 1936, Adolf Senff, a young academic, expressed a similar view:

> The National Socialist state's various welfare and social policies are, to a much greater extent than under the previous system of government, based on a deep confidence in the *Volk*. They raise strong hopes that they will help overcome the moral and social misery of our German national comrades.[52]

In fact, these hopes were not fulfilled. Suicide levels remained on a level with those of the late Weimar years until 1939, the last year for which national statistics are available. Despite the fact that the economy was recovering, suicide rates did not drop. At no time in the Third Reich did the suicide rate clearly fall below the relatively high level of the last two years of the Weimar Republic. For most of the 1920s the rate had been lower. There was no clear statistical difference across these seven years.[53] The available statistical material does contain a rough breakdown by sex. Both male and female suicide rates were roughly stable, in keeping with the generally low fluctuations of suicide levels altogether. The male suicide rate was consistent and was approximately 10 per cent higher than in 1913. Female levels fluctuated considerably and were around 40 per cent higher than in 1913. This must have reflected the fact that war widows were amongst the most impoverished sections of the community.[54]

An economic periodical claimed in 1936 that 'the creation of new job opportunities for the German worker, the unification of businessmen in their struggle for survival and not least the protection of the soil for the German peasant had strengthened energy and drive and the will to live.'[55] Correspondingly, as we have seen, there were many predictions that economically determined suicide rates would fall. But this did not happen, as evidence from Munich reveals. According to police statistics, 15 per cent of the 327 suicides registered in Munich in 1936 were still motivated by 'economic misery'.[56] In fact, unemployment remained a problem until the mid-1930s, and the living standard did not rise significantly for the overwhelming majority of the population.[57]

But suicide rates still remained high even in the later 1930s, a period of relatively low official unemployment. Some historians claim that the suicide rate reflected the extent to which Germans had to cope with existential problems and psychological stress during the Weimar and Nazi eras, and certainly the Third Reich did introduce many new kinds of stress and anxiety.[58] Another scholar argues that the suicide rate remained very high in first few years of the Third Reich due to increased stress, for instance the brutal treatment of political opponents and Jews (and other groups discriminated against because of their race and behaviour).[59] However, since there were very few Jews in Germany (less than one per cent of the population), it is unlikely that their suicides accounted for the high suicide levels; the stress was wider in its impact.

Despite propaganda claims, the continued high levels of suicide did not go unnoticed by the party leadership. On 2 September 1935, an official from the Berlin Nazi party region, appointed by the Reich Leadership (*Reichsleitung*) of the Nazi party, appeared at the Berlin criminal police headquarters at Alexanderplatz and asked for some statistical material detailing the number of suicides in Berlin.[60] Hitler himself also took an interest in suicide statistics, so Goebbels had regular statistical information on suicides presented on a special typewriter with big letters so that the myopic Hitler could read it.[61] This regular reporting of suicides had an interesting parallel in the Soviet Union, where Stalin viewed suicide as an indicator of something amiss with society and the Party.

The Soviets examined suicides within their own ranks carefully, largely focusing on political rather than private motives, as the Party's leadership believed that were no reasons to kill oneself in the Soviet system.[62] They did not, of course, release this material to the public. The Nazis also took suicides within their own ranks seriously. Gestapo reports, compiled for the attention of Prussian Minister President Göring, include suicides of low-ranking party members and state officials accused of corruption. On 24 March 1936, the District Governor (*Regierungspräsident*) of Magdeburg reported the suicide of Mayor Wagner of Schwaneberg in the Prussian province of Saxony, allegedly because he had been accused of being responsible for 'irregularities in cash management'.[63] In a similar case, on 6 January 1937, the Magdeburg *Regierungspräsident* wrote to Göring that a clerk from Calbe in the Prussian province of Saxony 'has ended his life by shooting himself. Reportedly, the reason is that the official had embezzled some state funds.'[64]

The regime did everything it could to prevent the reporting of suicides of Nazi party members. On 21 October 1938, Dr Silvio Conti, for instance, County Director (*Landrat*) of Prenzlau, near Berlin, and brother of the Reich Health Leader Dr Leonard Conti, shot himself in his office after a row with SS officials over his authority in his county. Immediately after he shot himself, his wife, afraid that her husband had not died, shot him again. He had evidently told her what he was going to do, and obtained her promise to assist—an illegal act. However, she was not prosecuted presumably because the police concluded that he was already dead when she fired the second shot.[65] According to the criminal police, Conti had a great deal of trouble with party and SS officials since taking office in 1933, a somewhat typical experience for many state officials, even if, like Conti, they were Nazis themselves. Anxious that Conti's rather obscure death might cast negative light on the Nazi regime, Dietrich expressly forbade the press to mention the case. The press decree of 23 October 1938 stipulated: 'There must not be any reports on *Landrat* Dr Conti's suicide in Prenzlau.'[66]

Nazi and state officials were worried about high suicide levels and compiled regular reports. On 18 July 1938, for instance, the senior state prosecutor (*Oberstaatsanwalt*) of Limburg, a Catholic town in what is today Hesse, wrote that the number of suicides had increased since the previous report. He was concerned that relatives were 'often ... trying to conceal' suicides, probably because in a Catholic town like Limburg, many saw suicide as a disgraceful act.[67] Absolute numbers of suicides in Bavaria confirm that a higher proportion of Protestant suicides were officially registered in the Third Reich than Catholic ones. In 1934, the Bavarian Statistical Office registered 1,178 suicides in an overwhelmingly Catholic Bavaria (according to the 1933 census, 69.9 per cent of Bavarians, including those living in the Palatinate, were Catholic, and only 28.7 per cent were Protestant).[68] 904 Catholics and 727 Protestants committed suicide in 1934 in Bavaria.[69]

Suicides' relatives often tried to conceal the reason for death. This concerned the police leadership. So Himmler, Chief of the German Police since 1936, introduced a new method of reporting suicides in February 1939. Himmler, obsessed with bureaucratic detail, decreed that suicide statistics (including attempted suicides) must be compiled more efficiently and centrally, as previous suicide statistics and death certificates had been too unreliable. Moreover, Himmler was worried about 'political aspects of suicides or attempted suicides', which from now on had to be reported to the Reich Security Head Office.[70] Previously, local policemen and registrars filled in a so-called suicide data sheet (*Selbstmordzählkarte*), which they then sent to the Reich Statistical Office, a method deemed inefficient by both Himmler and scientists. One suicide expert claimed in 1939 that the data sheets were 'useless'.[71] The Prussian State Criminal Office (*Landeskriminalamt*) revealed in 1936 that a post-mortem of every corpse had been obligatory only in Bavaria, Württemberg, Baden, Hesse, Bremen, and Hamburg. In the other German states, including Prussia, only corpses found in big cities generally received an autopsy. Pleading for the introduction of compulsory post-mortems in the Reich, the author declared: 'Each year, many capital crimes remain un-atoned, because they were not recognized as such.' An investigation of the Hanover Criminal Police Head Office (*Kripoleitstelle*) revealed that 36 suicides had gone unnoticed between January 1931 and March 1936 because of the absence of proper post-mortems.[72]

Himmler's decree aimed at a simpler and more centralized procedure. It required local policemen and registrars to certify the suicide's motive and to consult, if necessary, an official doctor (*Amtsarzt*) to investigate the case and arrange for an investigation by the state prosecutor (*Staatsanwalt*). Both the registrar and the local police then sent their files to an intermediate branch of the criminal police (*Kripostelle*), where the reports were checked against each other. For every quarter of the year, the criminal police branches were required to compile a suicide statistic, pass it on to the Criminal Police Head Offices which then forwarded the material to the Reich Security Head Office.

Information on national suicide levels for 1940 has survived in the files passed on to Hitler. These statistics, diverging from those quoted above, do, however reveal a sharp decrease in the suicide rate in 1940 that was probably

due to the outbreak of the war.[73] Suicide levels compiled according to the
new method also exist for the third quarter of 1940. In contrast to the third
quarter of 1939, before the outbreak of the war, the number of suicides
and suicide attempts in Greater Germany (including Austria) dropped from
7,362 to 6,420 in the third quarter of 1940. This decrease appears to
confirm the assumption that fewer people commit suicide during wars, as
even the most isolated people are drafted into the war effort.[74] Of course,
front-line soldiers could easily commit suicide by exposing themselves to
enemy fire, and such cases would not be recorded as suicide. The former
Commander-in-Chief of the Army, Werner von Fritsch, accused of being
homosexual in early 1938 and dismissed from his office, is said, for example,
to have deliberately exposed himself to enemy fire near Warsaw where he
died on 22 September 1939.[75] Still, the drop is a notable one.

Table 1 also gives evidence about the ways in which people died. Most
men hanged themselves, which was a readily available and efficient way to
die. Other easily available and therefore often-used methods were gassing
oneself, which was especially popular among women, whereas shooting
remained a largely male way of dying.

Unsurprisingly perhaps, suicide methods in the Third Reich were
generally the same as they had been in the Weimar Republic. As with

Table 1. Means of suicide in third quarter of 1940 (adapted
from BAB, R 58/158, Bl 43–4: Betr, Statistik über die im 3.
Vierteljahr 1940 im Reichsgebiet verübten Selbstmorde und
Selbstmordversuche, 10 March 1941)

| Means of suicide in the third quarter of 1940 | Men | Women |
|---|---|---|
| Hanging and strangulation | 1,826 (48.2%) | 530 (20.1%) |
| Gassing | 421 (11.1%) | 874 (33.2%) |
| Poisoning | 202 (5.3%) | 461 (17.5%) |
| Drowning | 318 (8.4%) | 391 (14.9%) |
| Shooting | 460 (12.2%) | 42 (1.6%) |
| Being run over by train or car | 202 (5.3%) | 74 (2.8%) |
| Jumping from height | 93 (2.5%) | 152 (5.8%) |
| Self-injury through cut or stab | 240 (6.4%) | 99 (3.8%) |
| Other means | 23 (0.6%) | 12 (0.3%) |
| Total | 3,785 (100%) | 2,635 (100%) |

murder methods, women chose indirect methods that did not involve physical violence and men chose more violent methods, reflecting gender stereotypes. Beyond gender-related differences, the choice of the means of suicide explains a great deal about the determination of a person to die. To some extent, choice was also restricted by its availability. Working-class people usually could not afford to buy a gun, though men from the generation which had served in the First World War, and, of course those fighting in the Second World War, had firearms. In the third quarter of 1940, for instance, most male suicides died by hanging or by shooting themselves.[76]

In 1940, the statistician Erich Schmahl stressed 'societal or church-related reasons as to why relatives of a suicide or a potential suicide conceal … the true motives'.[77] Nevertheless, Himmler still ordered information to be compiled on motives. The motives given in Table 2 reflect what Himmler and the German police thought to be the most common motives for suicide.

Depression or nervousness was the most common officially recognized causes for suicide in 1940, followed by incurable disease, family discords, fear of punishment, love problems, and other causes. The extremely low percentage of suicides caused by 'economic hardship' furthermore echoes Nazi propaganda about the Third Reich having overcome economic

Table 2. Official motives for suicide in third quarter of 1940 (adapted from BAB, R 58/158, Bl 43–4: Statistik über die im 3. Vierteljahr 1940 im Reichsgebiet verübten Selbstmorde und Selbstmordversuche, 10 March 1941)

| Official reasons/motives for suicide | Absolute number (percentage) |
| --- | --- |
| Economic hardship | 92 (1.4%) |
| Fear of punishment | 582 (9.1%) |
| Depression | 2,241 (34.9%) |
| Incurable disease | 1,099 (17.1%) |
| Family discords | 756 (11.8%) |
| Love problems | 496 (7.7%) |
| Other causes | 1,154 (18.0%) |
| Total | 6,420 (100%) |

difficulties. 'Depression' may, of course, have been caused by economic hardship, indeed by any one or more of a number of other factors. By listing it as a 'cause' in itself, the statistics suggested that it had no rational grounds and therefore reflected the hereditary weakness of the suicidal personality. The choice of these categories thus broadly reflected Nazi views on suicide as a problem of inherited moral weakness and physical and psychological degeneracy.

# IV

Nazi politics had a direct impact on some suicides. Thanks to the continuity of personnel within the criminal police, the investigative mechanisms discussed in the previous chapter remained largely intact, as an internal memorandum from the Berlin homicide squad reveals.[78] At the same time, however, for obvious reasons, the police became extremely reluctant to pursue the possibility that apparent suicides might have been the result of murder by Nazis. Nevertheless, there is some evidence of many political suicides in the wake of the coming of the Third Reich.

In the aftermath of Hitler's appointment as Reich Chancellor on 30 January 1933, and especially after the Reichstag fire, the Nazis arrested many socialists and communists, among others, in a wave of terror.[79] On 22 March 1933, the 41-year-old street sweeper Bernhard K, an active member of the SPD and a trade unionist, was found hanged in a goods train at Hermsdorf station, a suburb to the north of Berlin. His sister had reported him missing on 13 February 1933. Initially doubting that K had killed himself, the police interrogated his friends and relatives. His sister told the police that K had been carrying 200 Reichsmark with him, while Ludwig H, a waiter in K's favourite pub, voiced the suspicion that K had had a clash with 'political enemies'—that is, with Nazis. H, anxious that the police might tell the Nazis, did not dare identify these people. The criminal police had generally welcomed the Nazi seizure of power. They did not investigate this case further and closed the file on 27 March 1933. By then, the Nazis had unleashed a general wave of terror against the SPD and the KPD in the wake of the Reichstag Fire Decree. The police predictably concluded that K had indeed hanged himself.[80]

In Wanne-Eickel, a mining town in the Ruhr Valley, an SS officer and two storm troopers dragged Karl E, a Communist miner, out of his flat on the night of 27 April 1933, acting in conformity with Göring's appointment of SA and SS men as auxiliary policemen in Prussia.[81] Near a canal, the Nazis fired gunshots at him. Apparently traumatized by this mock execution, a common Nazi method of intimidating their opponents, E supposedly hanged himself a few days later. The Bochum state prosecutor considered pressing charges against the three Nazis, but he knew that the Prussian Ministry of Justice, led by the Nazi Hanns Kerrl, would rebuke him if he did so. Many judges and state prosecutors tried at this time to open legal proceedings against Nazis, especially on charges of murder, manslaughter and bodily harm. But in July 1933, a Central State Prosecutor's Office (*Zentralstaatsanwaltschaft*) was set up in Prussia to deal with criminal cases in which Nazis were involved. Some exceptional cases aside, Nazis were never punished during the Third Reich for their violent excesses in the wake of their seizure of power. In August 1934, this process of whitewashing Nazi violence culminated in the Reich Amnesty Law that exonerated Nazis for criminal charges in relation to their violent political activities. Political interest thus determined the outcome of suicide investigations in the E case and others.[82]

In the wake of the Nazi seizure of power, especially after the passing of the Reichstag Fire Decree, suicide thus became deeply associated with politics. For the Nazis' political opponents, suicide was often the last resort for keeping one's dignity amidst Nazi torture and arrest in the furore of the arrival of the Third Reich. While giving a Reichstag speech explaining the social democratic opposition against the Enabling Act on 23 March 1933, Otto Wels, leader of the SPD in the Reichstag, is said to have been carrying a cyanide capsule which he would have swallowed if the storm troopers had arrested and tortured him afterwards.[83]

At this time, newspapers, not yet fully coordinated, frequently reported the suicides of political opponents, usually describing them as cowards. On 25 April 1933, the 58-year-old General Intendant of the Upper Silesian Theatre in Beuthen, Arthur Illing, shot himself on the express train from Beuthen to Berlin. He had been accused of having pocketed state subsidies for his theatre for himself, a common charge levied by the Nazis in 1933 against Weimar officials. The Nazi trade union of his theatre had then turned in a vote of no confidence against him. A 'National Socialist investigating committee', set up after the seizure of power, had reported Illing to the state prosecutor, who in turn issued an arrest warrant. This allegedly prompted

Illing to kill himself. It is unlikely that he had been murdered by the Nazis.[84]

Toni Pfülf, a leading Bavarian social democrat deputy in the Reichstag, killed herself in June 1933. She was ashamed and desperate because the SPD deputies had voted for a Nazi resolution in the Reichstag on 17 May 1933, urging, in cynically propagandistic terms, German equality at international negotiations over disarmament. Pfülf refused to attend this session and instead took the train back to Munich. She poisoned herself on the train. In a farewell letter to a close friend, she wrote:

> My dear friends, I have to go the last part of the journey myself. I greet all of you and say thank you for your trust that I have always tried to gain. With all best wishes to you and those at home and to our cause I bid farewell to you.

She survived, but was determined to die, although her socialist friends had tried to discourage her from killing herself. Suicide, they thought, would be a resignation to the Nazis. In June 1933, she wrote to her friend:

> Because of the recent *malheur* on the train, my home journey was slightly delayed. I leave today. I hope I will arrive at the destination. Of course, it is a bit disloyal to all of you. Don't be angry and don't think it's an escape, which it isn't. Say hello to all good friends ... and all the best ...

She committed suicide shortly thereafter and died on 8 June 1933.[85]

It is hard to tell how many political opponents of the Nazis killed themselves in the wake of the Nazi seizure of power. The Nazis often killed or tortured political and racial opponents to death, and claimed that these people had committed suicide or had been 'shot while trying to escape' (*auf der Flucht erschossen*). 'Suiciding' opponents would become a widespread instrument of terror in the Third Reich. One early case was that of Ernst Oberfohren, parliamentary leader of the DNVP, the Nazis' coalition partner. The Nazis no longer needed the DNVP's support after the passing of the Enabling Act on 23 March 1933. He was found dead in his office on 7 May 1933. The Nazis claimed that he had spread rumours accusing them of having set fire to the Reichstag. According to the police, Oberfohren had shot himself, while an exile publication, with some justification, claimed that the Nazis had killed him.[86] Another early case in which the Nazis 'suicided' a political opponent is that of Dr Friedrich Odenkirchen, a city councillor from Düsseldorf. On 12 April 1933, the national-conservative *Nachtausgabe* reported his suicide. In retaliation, the

Nazis had taken him, like many others, into 'protective custody' on corruption charges.[87] Odenkirchen was found hanged in a room in the town hall. Did Odenkirchen kill himself or did the storm troopers torture him to death?[88] When the Nazis declared that political opponents had killed themselves in protective custody, they denied responsibility for these killings. Furthermore, they denounced these people as cowards who were not able to take the responsibility for their political actions before 1933.

Especially in the early months of the Third Reich, the Nazis often encouraged imprisoned opponents to kill themselves, even bringing them rope with which to do it. For contemporaries, hanging was a particularly disgraceful way of capital punishment, reserved for criminals.[89] Giving prisoners rope with which to hang themselves was therefore particularly humiliating. After being arrested, Friedrich Schlotterbeck, a communist, was told by Gestapo officers shortly before Christmas 1933: 'The best thing you can do is hang yourself... You'll save yourself a lot of trouble that way.'[90] A man from Düsseldorf who had been arrested and interrogated by the Gestapo in 1933 confirmed this practice. He later remembered that the officer interrogating him had threatened: 'We'll make you talk. We have very nice methods. Tomorrow your comrades can write of you that you were 'suicided by the Gestapo'.'[91]

Political opponents were also 'suicided' in the concentration camps. In the wake of the Reichstag Fire Decree of 27 February 1933 and the Enabling Act of 23 March 1933, Nazi and state institutions set up concentration camps. Up to 200,000 inmates, chiefly communists, trade unionists and social democrats, were held in the early concentration camps in 1933. The Nazis killed several hundred inmates of the concentration camps in 1933/34 and almost always denied responsibility.[92] Take the case of Erich Mühsam, an anarchist poet and playwright. Not only had he been involved with Ernst Toller and others in the 'regime of the Coffee House Anarchists' in Munich in 1919, but he was also Jewish. Initially, the Nazis took him to the notorious Sonnenburg concentration camp, where the pacifist writer Carl von Ossietzky and other political opponents of the regime were also interned. Later, he was transferred to the Oranienburg concentration camp near Berlin. After refusing to sing the *Horst Wessel* song, the Nazi party's anthem, he was badly maltreated and found hanged in a camp latrine on 10 July 1934. Despite Nazi claims that he had committed suicide, it is

unlikely that Mühsam had killed himself.[93] Camp authorities did not have
the power to kill camp inmates until the outbreak of the war. The SS
still had to report cases of unnatural deaths to the judicial authorities; they
could not get rid of prisoners, which is why they deliberately misreported
murders as suicides.[94] Camp commandants and guards declared that these
inmates had 'been shot while trying to escape' (*auf der Flucht erschossen*)
or that they had committed suicide, thereby trying to avoid judicial
investigations.[95]

Nevertheless, it is clear that concentration camp inmates committed
suicide in sheer despair over the abominably brutal treatment by the Nazis.
In Dachau, there were between six and seven suicide attempts per week
in 1937, according to reports of agents of the SPD in exile. In one such
case, the brother of a former communist Reichstag deputy, in Dachau
since 1933, had hoped to be released from Dachau shortly before Christmas
1936, following promises by the camp guards. When he was not released,
he tried to smash his skull with a hoe in despair. A camp guard stopped
him in order to maintain the total claim of the SS over the lives of inmates.
An hour later, he tried to hang himself with his braces. Once again, he was
stopped, this time by an inmate. Eventually, he slit his wrists with a piece of
metal and was found lying dead in a pool of his own blood.[96] Uncertainty
as to whether they would ever be released was a common cause of despair
and suicide among prisoners.[97]

There were also many genuine suicides within prisons. Albert Funk,
a former communist Reichstag deputy and trade-union leader from
Dortmund was arrested on 16 April 1933 by the police and taken to
prison. When his wife wanted to see him, she was told rather curtly
that her husband had poisoned himself in his cell. A contemporary exile
publication, while not denying Funk's suicide, reported that the Nazis had
tortured Funk so badly that he, in despair, jumped out of the window into
the prison yard. The Nazis allegedly encouraged other prisoners witnessing
Funk's death to follow his example. The guards reportedly shouted: 'You
Moscow swine can jump out of here, too.'[98]

In April 1934, following the fiasco of the Reich Court's acquittal of
Georgi Dimitrov, head of the Western European Bureau of the Communist
International and defendant in the Reichstag Fire Trial, Hitler set up the
People's Court for all cases of treason, including working-class resistance.
In 1936 Otto-Georg Thierack, a radical Nazi lawyer, became its president.
Sentencing became much harsher. Between 1934 and 1939, the People's

Court sentenced around 3,400 people, almost all of them communists or social democrats. Those who did not receive a death sentence were normally sentenced to an average of six years in prison. In practice, communists were often sent to concentration camps for 'protective custody' after their release from prison.[99] Some members of the working-class resistance committed suicide. Those in gaol and subject to Gestapo torture were afraid of betraying their comrades by telling their names to the Nazis. Many deaths of working-class resisters were in fact not suicides, although the Nazis classified them as such, but murders. Even where they did kill themselves, it would in many cases be more accurate to classify their cases as 'assisted suicide'. In May 1934, Erich Krause, known as 'Franz', appeared in Düsseldorf. 'Franz' and other communists printed leaflets and distributed at least 5,000 copies to workers. When the Gestapo uncovered their group, 'Franz' committed suicide in the local Gestapo gaol. 'Franz' knew about the group's links to Berlin party groups. Maltreated by the Gestapo and confronted with his assistant in the Gestapo office, he committed suicide because he did not want to betray his comrades.[100] Here was suicide as an act of solidarity. Gestapo torture led to at least nine suicides and one suicide attempt among political prisoners, probably communists and social democrats, in the first three months of 1935 in the Düsseldorf area alone, according to a confidential report by the Düsseldorf general state prosecutor to the Reich Ministry of Justice.[101] There must have been many other such cases here and elsewhere in Germany. They reflected the depth of commitment—bordering on fanaticism in the case of the communists—of many active political opponents of the Nazis in this period.

The Nazis did not only purge Germany of opposition politicians, they also tried to get rid of those artists they regarded as 'degenerate' or 'Jewish' in their pursuit for a 'pure' Germanic culture and spirit. Many artists and intellectuals left Germany in the wake of the coming of the Third Reich, since the Nazis had expelled them violently from cultural institutions and had made a living impossible for them in Germany. Previously established and successful artists suddenly had to face the financial hardship and the general uncertainties of life in exile. Among them was Paul Nikolaus, the conferencier of the Kadeko Club in Berlin, and one of the leading political comedians of the time. Unable, like many émigrés, to find work in Switzerland, where he had fled, Nikolaus killed himself in a hotel in Lucerne on 31 March 1933. In a patriotic suicide note, he emphasized his love for Germany: 'For once, no joke…I am taking my own life. Why?

I could not return to Germany without taking it there. I cannot work
there now. I do not want to work there now, and yet unfortunately I have
fallen in love with my Fatherland. I cannot live in these times.'[102] Ernst
Ludwig Kirchner, the expressionist artist, shot himself in his Swiss retreat
on 15 June 1938. He had been expelled in July 1937 from the Prussian
Academy of Arts, and some of his works were shown in the notorious
1937 Degenerate Art Exhibition. Kirchner depended on the German art
market for his livelihood. Ill and strained by his marginalization as an artist,
he shot himself in the heart. Shortly before his suicide, he wrote: 'I had
always hoped that Hitler was for all Germans, and now he has defamed so
many and really serious artists of German blood. This is very sad for those
affected, because they—the serious ones among them—all wished to, and
did, work for Germany's fame and honour.'[103]

# V

After coming to power, the Nazis increasingly were confronted with
suicides within their own ranks. In their regular reports on public opinion
in Nazi Germany, agents of the SPD in exile reported in early 1934:
'Suicide rates dramatically increase. Over the last six weeks, 18 men of
the Berlin SA alone have killed themselves. The official suicide motive is
depression and disappointment.'[104] Indeed, there were many suicides within
the Berlin SA at that time. The SA had lost its role and sense of direction.
There was a growing dissatisfaction amongst storm troopers with the new
government. Top Nazis, including Hitler and Hermann Göring, and the
Wehrmacht leadership were anxious about the competition of the SA as a
huge potential new army. They became less enthusiastic about the SA and
its demands for a continuation of the 'National Socialist Revolution'.[105]

On 25 February 1934, Botho von V, a storm trooper and administrative
worker at the headquarters of the Berlin-Brandenburg SA died in his office.
Only months later, on 28 August 1934, after the Nazis had murdered
members of the SA leadership, including the leader Ernst Röhm, and
stripped the SA of its power on 30 June 1934 in what they called the 'Night
of the Long Knives', Botho's mother, Ella von V, the owner of a bed and
breakfast, complained to the police. She did not believe that Botho had
committed suicide. An SA official had told her: Botho had died from a shot
from his boss's revolver. He had, in fact, had an argument with his boss

R about the general direction of Nazi policy. According to R, Botho had had the nerve to say that 'he had a different idea of National Socialism in practice. He could not believe that these fat cats would remain in power.' Many storm troopers, confronted with unemployment, and disillusioned with top Nazis letting down the SA, shared this view, which prompted some to take out their aggression upon Jews and others. All available evidence suggests that Botho had indeed killed himself after a drunken row with R. The official obituary, drafted by R and published in the *Angriff,* a Berlin-based Nazi newspaper edited by Goebbels, simply claimed that Botho had died in 'a tragic accident'. The regime could not admit that Botho had committed suicide, an act of weakness in the Nazi view.[106]

There were many more suicides within the SA after the Nazi seizure of power. The 24-year-old senior squad leader (*Oberscharführer*) Richard P from the Berlin working-class district of Kreuzberg shot himself on 18 April 1935. During an outing of his local unit to Blossin in Brandenburg, the storm troopers had got very drunk at a pub. At around 1 am, P's comrade storm leader (*Sturmführer*) Hans-Johannes H felt the need to relieve himself in the garden of the pub. While H was squatting, with his pants pulled down, P suddenly appeared and grabbed the revolver out of H's belt and shot himself. Although the SA had been deprived of any real political influence a year earlier,[107] ideas of class struggle still prevailed among ordinary storm troopers. Bruno L, also a storm trooper, testified to the police that P had complained to him about his inability to make a living: 'Now look, what have you got, you're making 100 Reichsmark a month and for that you have to work, even an old fighter like myself. They can all kiss my arse; the best thing to do is to shoot myself dead.'[108] In fact, P had been sacked from his job at the German Labour Front, although he managed to find another, if low-paid, position within the same organization, probably because he was an 'old fighter' within the Nazi movement. The criminal police concluded that P's suicide had been motivated by the reduction of his salary.[109] P and most of his comrades belonged to the group of storm troopers who had never known economic stability or durable employment in the Weimar years and had never managed to get permanent jobs and social recognition even under the new regime. In this situation suicide reflected the disappointment that gripped the movement after the seizure of power.

The deaths of storm troopers who had fallen into disfavour with the Nazi leadership were also subject to police investigations. Needless to say, the police had no real interest in finding out whether the Nazis had been responsible for these deaths. However, the investigation files shed light on the ways in which the police decided what constituted a suicide. In the Third Reich, unlike in the Weimar Republic, political interest often determined the outcome of a suicide investigation. On 20 January 1934, Wilhelm Brückner, one of Hitler's adjutants, wrote to Rudolf Diels, at the time still head of the Prussian Secret Police Office, the *Geheimes Staatspolizeiamt (Gestapa)* later to become the Gestapo.[110] Brückner complained that the disappearance of the staff leader (*SA-Stabsführer*) Helmuth U had not been resolved. U's father had written several letters to the *Gestapa* and Hitler, asking about the whereabouts of his son, who had disappeared on 24 June 1933. Like many storm troopers, U was unemployed, even after the Nazis came to power. After reporting his son missing to the police, U's father asked the police to start a murder investigation on 26 July 1933. Reflecting a broad Nazi understanding of the legal system, which saw above all Hitler as the final arbiter of law and justice, U's father insisted:

> It may never come to pass in the new Germany that a fighter for the swastika disappears without a trace, nor is it the Führer's will that not even the parents are told what has happened to their only son. Aside from everything else, it is illegal. I will not rest until I have learnt the whole truth about this dark incident *officially*.[111]

Prompted by the order from Hitler's staff, Diels set up a special commission on 23 January 1934 and opened an investigation. The Nazis accused U, a 27-year-old SA functionary, of having informed on the SA's internal affairs to the SPD and the Jewish-owned Ullstein publishing house. It was a typical Nazi accusation against someone who had fallen into disfavour to claim that they had had contacts with socialists and Jews. Count Helldorf, leader of the Berlin SA, and later to become police president of Berlin, had already accused U of spying for the communists and the political police as early as 1931.[112] On 28 February 1933, U had therefore been cashiered from the SA. This eviction had prompted U to issue the following request:

> I would like to speak to my supreme SA leader Adolf Hitler in person! I have full confidence that my Führer will give me an audience! I request that my honour be fully reinstated. I can no longer bear this existence as a beaten, discarded dog, and all of my hopes for this life and my once-proud goals depend on this final report.[113]

Needless to say, U did not receive a response. During an interrogation by some Nazi leaders, U, reportedly showing some remorse, had allegedly confessed that he had been spying. Nevertheless, the *Gestapa* and the SA had had to have him released, since there had not been 'any opportunities for police proceedings against U'. On 14 March 1934, Kurt Daluege, the Nazi head of the Prussian police, was interrogated by a state prosecutor about U's whereabouts. Daluege denied *Gestapa* responsibility for U's disappearance. U's corpse had not yet been found. Daluege declared that 'suicide remains a possibility, given U's emotional outburst after his interrogation'. Brushing aside any specific accusations against the *Gestapa*, Daluege speculated 'that U has been bumped off by SA or SS men'. His former comrades killed him in revenge after the Nazis had come to power. The state prosecutor as well as the *Gestapa* thought that it was best to close the file, stressing that suicide, an act of cowardice in the Nazi view, was the most likely explanation for U's fate.[114] Yet U's father was still not happy about the outcome of the investigation and accused the former standard leader (*Standartenführer*) Karl Belding of having killed his son. Belding was murdered in his turn on 30 June 1934, together with many other SA leaders, when top Nazis, led by Hitler, wiped out the SA leadership in the 'Night of the Long Knives'. The Nazis accused the SA leadership of staging a rebellion.[115] Thus the case was brought to a convenient conclusion.

# VI

The Nazis also settled old scores on 30 June 1934, and gunned down conservatives disillusioned with the regime. Among them were the former Reich Chancellor General Kurt von Schleicher and his wife, Vice-Chancellor Franz von Papen's secretary Herbert von Bose, and the right-wing intellectual Edgar Jung. Without giving any credible evidence, the Nazis claimed that these people had been conspiring with Röhm. In at least two cases, the regime concealed murders as suicides to deny responsibility. At 1 pm on 30 June, a very warm and sunny day, Kurt Gildisch, an SS officer (*Hauptsturmführer*) accompanied by two SS men, marched into the office of Erich Klausener, a senior official in the Transport Ministry and head of the Catholic Action, a popular Catholic movement. Gildisch claimed during his post-war trial that Reinhard Heydrich, chief of the SS security service, had ordered him to kill Klausener whom the regime saw as a potential threat. A few days previously, Klausener had given a speech at the Catholic Action's annual rally in Berlin-Hoppegarten, criticizing the regime's attitudes towards the Catholic Church. Also, Klausener had been in charge of the Police Department in the Prussian Ministry of the Interior in the Weimar years, investigating, among other things, the Nazi party's illegal activities. Upon entering Klausener's office, Gildisch asked him for some identification and then told him to accompany him to *Gestapa* headquarters. Klausener packed his briefcase and fetched his hat. Suddenly, Gildisch produced a 7.65 mm Mauser pistol and shot Klausener twice in the back at close range. Gildisch then immediately called Heydrich from the phone on Klausener's desk, reporting the execution. Before leaving Klausener's office, Gildisch put his pistol into Klausener's hand to cover up the murder as a suicide. Gildisch left the Transport Ministry at 1:15 pm, posting two SS guards outside Klausener's office. Nobody was allowed in. Klausener's corpse was then taken to a morgue and kept locked away. The regime claimed that Klausener had committed suicide. Heydrich had Klausener's body cremated to prevent any investigation. The Bishop of Berlin, Nikolaus Bares, did not believe this version and celebrated a memorial mass for Klausener. Canon law forbade the ecclesiastical burying of suicides or celebrating memorial masses. Celebrating a mass for Klausener was thus an open statement that the Catholic Church did not accept the Nazi claims over Klausener's alleged suicide. It was obvious that Klausener had been murdered, yet the regime stuck to its version to deny responsibility.[116] Here again was murder covered up as suicide.

The regime also declared that Gregor Strasser, the Nazi party's chief organizer until his resignation in 1932, had killed himself. In fact, he was murdered in the *Gestapa* prison at 8 Prinz Albrecht Strasse. Leading Nazis, including Hitler, Himmler, and Göring saw Strasser as a potential threat to the regime because of his good contacts with the conservatives around Schleicher. Strasser's widow, depending on her husband's two life insurance policies, wrote to the Reich Ministry of the Interior, requesting more details about the circumstances of her husband's death. The insurance companies followed their general policy on suicide and refused to pay any money to Mrs Strasser. Despite Hitler's Reichstag speech in which he openly endorsed the murders and the passing of a law, giving the purge subsequent retroactive legality on 13 July 1934, the *Gestapa* refused to give out any information to the relatives of those killed, since this would have been an implicit confession that the *Gestapa* had murdered them. At the Interior Ministry's request, the *Gestapa* wrote to Mrs Strasser in October 1934, insisting that her husband had 'passed away on 30 June 1934 at 5:20 pm by suicide'. Some senior officials from the Reich Ministry of Justice were unhappy with this outright lie. They were concerned about Mrs Strasser's livelihood. The Ministry of Justice's officials intervened with the insurance companies, telling them unofficially about the actual circumstances of Strasser's death. The insurance companies, though anxious to cultivate good relations with the Nazi party, still did not want to pay any money to Mrs Strasser. Eventually, after long negotiations between the Ministry of Justice and the life insurance companies, Mrs Strasser received the money in late 1935.[117]

After murdering parts of the SA leadership, Hitler was uncertain what to do with the SA chief of staff Ernst Röhm, one of his oldest comrades. At a garden party on 1 July, probably under pressure from Himmler and Göring, Hitler agreed to have Röhm shot. Hitler was keen to give his old friend the opportunity to kill himself. Theodor Eicke, the commandant of Dachau concentration camp, was appointed to go to the Stadelheim prison in Munich where Röhm was arrested. Eicke gave Röhm a pistol and the latest issue of the *Völkischer Beobachter* with the details of the alleged Röhm putsch. Eicke hoped that this pressure would persuade Röhm that shooting himself was the only action left to him. There was a widespread belief among the SS, as we have seen, that shooting oneself out of honour was acceptable in such a situation. When no shot was heard after ten minutes, Eicke and two SS men went into Röhm's cell and finished him off. In his published announcement, Hitler justified this cold-blooded murder with Röhm's refusal 'to draw the consequences of his treacherous behaviour'.[118]

The ruthless purge of the SA leadership saw the consolidation of Hitler's dictatorship. In August 1934, Reich President von Hindenburg died. His death graphically symbolized the completion of the Nazi capture of power. The Nazis called a referendum in which they asked Germans to endorse Hitler's unification of the office of Reich President with that of Reich Chancellor. Some historians have stressed the popularity of the regime among 'ordinary Germans' at that time, allegedly reflected in the reportedly almost unanimous yes-votes in referenda called by the Nazis.[119] In fact, the Nazis rigged the referendum and created a 'terror-atmosphere' as secret SPD agents reported. Altogether, at least 5 million Germans did not endorse the law, either by voting 'no' or by spoiling their ballot papers.[120] On 19 August 1934, the day of the referendum, the 21-year-old storm trooper Erich G, a construction worker from Godrienen near Königsberg, was found hanged in the cellar of an SA club house. G, in charge of security at a polling station, had cast his ballot paper and had voted against the Nazi proposal. Under the Nazi dictatorship, there was, of course, no secret ballot. After G had filled in his paper, the election clerk looked at the ballot paper and then shouted: 'An SA man with his honorary dagger has voted like that!' G's superior was informed, and G was arrested. It turned out that G and some of his friends, ostensibly dissatisfied with the regime after the Nazi purge of the SA, had decided to vote against the Nazi proposal.

After his arrest, G was stripped of his brown shirt and viciously beaten by two storm troopers. Three hours later, two storm troopers found him hanged in his cell. Afraid of this case's potential impact on the foreign press 'by casting doubts over the genuinely free nature of the elections', the state prosecutor called for an investigation. G, a Catholic, was given a funeral ceremony by a priest, who implied in his oration that G had been killed by the Nazis. Two hundred people attended G's funeral. The Bishop of Königsberg announced his intention of writing to Hitler and the Pope. The state prosecutor was nevertheless unimpressed by these threats and insisted that G had committed suicide. He described how the two storm troopers had mistreated G, allegedly just causing him 'some nosebleeding'. The Königsberg court acquitted them of murder, but fined them the rather modest sum of 20 Reichsmark. On 15 January 1935, the court acquitted them altogether, since the SA had already punished them by arresting them for a week. G had been killed. By claiming that G had killed himself, the regime, concerned with its allegedly unanimous popular support, denied responsibility for murdering a storm trooper dissatisfied with the Nazis.[121]

So, suicide had a very strong political dimension especially in the wake of the coming of the Third Reich. The regime began to 'suicide' some of its opponents immediately after coming to power to deny responsibility for killing them. Since the Nazis did not consolidate fully their power until Hindenburg's death, 'suiciding' was a particularly common strategy in the Third Reich's early years to prevent any judicial investigations and to cultivate good relations with the conservative, law-abiding middle classes.[122] As the regime's self-confidence grew vis-à-vis the judiciary, the practice of 'suiciding' opponents probably became less frequent, at least outside the concentration camps. On the other hand, there were also many genuine suicides among political opponents of the regime. Finally, Nazis disillusioned with aspects of the regime committed suicide. But were there also suicides among those persecuted by the Nazis because of their race or their status as social outsiders?

# VII

The Nazis targeted people for not conforming to a socially and morally acceptable lifestyle in the Third Reich. Many of these people committed suicide.[123] The available evidence is sparse. Some cases have, nevertheless, survived in the files which the Hamburg Police Authority compiled in 'cases of unnatural death'.[124] On 3 January 1938, the 63-year-old tramp Martin L was found hanged in a doss house in Hamburg. An inmate there since 1926, L had recently been reported to the police for a homosexual offence under paragraph 175 of the German penal code. The investigating policeman declared: 'It is difficult to know what reasons led to the suicide. One can assume that L felt morally compromised because of his drunkenness, which was revealed during the police officer's interrogation, whereupon his nerves gave way and he committed suicide.'[125] Probably carried out in a brutal and threatening way, the police interrogation of L had, among other factors, motivated him to take his own life.[126] There is no direct evidence that the police officers killed him during interrogation, but this must remain a possibility. In Hamburg, local civil servants in charge of the homeless had been making life more difficult for them since 1931, amidst growing pressure on the welfare system due to mass unemployment. Authorities were trying to get rid of homeless people. The radicalization of such a policy in 1933 saw the deportation of vagrants to concentration camps.[127]

The Nazis thought that homosexuals were a threat to the survival of the Germanic race by refusing to have children; they were supposedly weak and degenerate, and a danger to the state. In Imperial and Weimar Germany, male homosexuals could be prosecuted under Paragraph 175 of the German penal code. The Nazis were not slow to intensify the prosecution of male homosexuals, especially after the purge of the SA leadership led by the openly gay Ernst Röhm. In December 1934 alone, the police are said to have arrested some 2,000 men.[128] In Würzburg, a 32-year-old railway worker named Julius H hanged himself in the Würzburg prison on 17 July 1935, following his arrest for homosexual offences.[129] A few weeks before, on 28 June 1935, Nazi and state authorities had made paragraph 175, which concerned male homosexual relationships, more severe. Section 175 no longer referred to 'unnatural acts', but simply to 'indecency'. This looser definition of homosexuality widened the scope of prosecution for the authorities.[130] And from October 1936 onwards, a new Reich Head Office for the Combating of Homosexuality and Abortion coordinated the efforts of the Gestapo and the criminal police to target homosexuals. Between 1933 and 1935, only 4,000 men were convicted for homosexuality. After the amendment of paragraph 175, more than 22,000 men were sentenced between 1936 and 1938.[131]

Many of those accused of having illegal homosexual relationships committed suicide to avoid the humiliation of public shame and long prison sentences. In Berlin, a professor in custody attempted to take his life while awaiting trial in 1936. And in March 1937, the 24-year-old worker Rudolf Z, afraid that the police might force him to tell them the names of his gay friends, gassed himself in his mother's flat in Berlin. Shortly before his suicide attempt, he penned a farewell missive to his mother. In total despair, he declared, still emphasizing his loyalty to his former lover:

> I don't know what else I would have to confess … I don't see any other way out. Because of what I said today it's over. I have never been interested in anyone as much as 'Hans'. But that [relationship] has been over for a while and with it my passion for life. And now they're going to grab him by the neck. I just imagine being confronted by him. Anything but that. I'd rather die. I loved him so much …[132]

He survived his suicide attempt, and was sentenced, like his former lover, to one year and four months in prison. In its verdict, a Berlin court particularly emphasized the fact that Z, a former storm trooper, and his lover, a former block warden of the German Labour Front (*Deutsche Arbeitsfront*), must have been aware of the wickedness of their relationship 'in the knowledge of the proceedings during the Röhm affair'.[133]

Eighteen-year-old Herbert M, accused of prostitution, tried to kill himself in 1939. In a note to his parents, he wrote: 'Since I have no more strength and am too afraid of everything, I want to say good-bye to you. Don't mourn me, I'm not worth it because I know that I'm a total sissy. But always this constant anxiety and my personal state of affairs has just depressed me so much…' Here he seems to have internalized contemporary ideas about the weakness of homosexuals. The police found him and took him to the hospital of the Moabit prison. Eventually, he was sentenced to one year and two months in prison and 'subsequent security confinement' (*anschließender Schutzaufsicht*).[134] After serving their sentence, many homosexuals were immediately rearrested by the Gestapo or the SS and put into a concentration camp. Estimates suggest that between 10,000 and 15,000 homosexual men were taken to the camps between 1933 and 1945. There, they were subject to especially brutal treatment by both the guards and fellow inmates, given that they were on the lowest rung of the hierarchy of prisoners.[135]

Others, who faced forced sterilization according to the Hereditary Health Law of 14 July 1933, sometimes opted for suicide instead. On 15 January 1938, 50-year-old Fritz Wilhelm S, who came from a working-class background, killed himself in Hamburg. According to his brother, the Hereditary Health Court had recently told him to appear at the local Health Office for sterilization. After receiving this note, Fritz-Wilhelm, not willing to accept the Nazi attack on his bodily integrity and his life, had become depressed and begun to drink. He hanged himself.[136] Nazi policies thus drove people into suicide. Seeing no way out, suicide remained the last resort for keeping one's dignity. It is hard to say whether suicides amongst 'social outsiders' really led to a substantive increase in suicide levels in the Third Reich, perhaps making good the decline in economically-influenced suicides, but this must remain a possibility.

# VIII

At the same time, there were also ostensibly apolitical suicides. The collection of suicide notes quoted in the previous chapter again offers fascinating insight into the ways in which ordinary people, overwhelmingly from the working class, justified their suicides. There is little indication in these notes of a potential impact of Nazi discourses on suicide. Rather, many ordinary people still felt the need to justify their suicides, as they associated the act of self-destruction with disreputable and extraordinary action, deserving of an explanation.[137]

Next to emotional problems, many Germans justified their suicide with reference to their economic situation. A 44-year-old unemployed woman, Erna J, from the Schöneberg district of Berlin, left a suicide note on 14 April 1934 for the attention of the welfare office and the criminal police. Insisting that she wanted to die, Erna declared: 'You already know the reason for my first failed suicide attempt... Please don't take me to the hospital; let me die here in my home!'[138] Socio-economic deprivation, continuing well into the Nazi years, was not denied at this very basic level of reporting. Max S, an unemployed salesman, from the working-class Prenzlauer Berg district, cut his arms with a razor blade, yet survived. The police commented that his attempted suicide had been due to 'economic deprivation' (*wirtschaftliche Notlage*).[139]

On 14 April 1935, the widow Lina W was found drowned in a river near Bad Nauheim, a spa near Frankfurt. In her suicide note she wrote to her children: 'Thank you very much for all you have done for me. Forgive me, I am really so very sorry to leave you. Please don't blame Paula. I will really miss your kindness! Please send me the washing later. Wishing you all the best, I remain your loving mother.'[140] The police commented that she had been suffering from hallucinations. And indeed, her request to her children to send her the washing after she was dead does testify to a discernible degree of derangement.

On 4 February 1935, the 21-year-old hairdresser Irmgard K, from Berlin-Schöneberg, gassed herself. While it is not clear whether Irmgard really wanted to die, or whether her opening of the gas pipe was rather about making her friends aware of her problems as a 'cry for help', remains unclear. The fire service rescued her. The criminal police commented: 'The motive is lovesickness. Irmgard was in a relationship with a *Reichswehr* soldier who broke off the relationship ...'[141]

More complex personal motives were at work in the case of the 29-year-old Hildegard B, wife of a civil servant, who gassed herself in April 1935 in Berlin. Leaving a suicide note to her husband, she wrote:

Even doctors couldn't help me give up smoking. My only passion. Is this a crime? You won't buy me a skirt, won't go with me to the theatre, nor to the movies, nor to a concert. I'm only allowed to work. I told you five times to wear a different suit so I could mend the black one. But you don't do it and today you show me your trousers and tell me that I'm not a good housewife. I can't accept that. God knows I lived only for my husband and my household. The only vice that I could not give up were the cigarettes. Is that a crime?[142]

Accusing her husband of not respecting her, B justified her suicide with recourse to domestic problems. Was her suicide a cry for help to show to her husband that something was wrong with her and their marriage? The only background information we have is that B was drunk when she wrote her suicide note, as an annotation of a police officer from the Reinickendorf police station reveals. The reference to her inability to stop smoking hints at the Nazi anti-smoking campaigns of the late 1930s and early 1940s in which heavy smokers were denounced as enemies of the health of the racial body.[143]

Some suicides, however, did make explicit references to the political situation. On 16 August 1933, the bricklayer and SS man Hermann S, aged 42, shot himself in his flat in Berlin. He wrote to his SS superior, blaming his wife for his suicide:

> Because my wife is setting me up for great pain and emotional difficulty, I see that I must take the chance to part voluntarily from this life. It was with great joy that I remained true to our Supreme Leader and Chancellor of the People Adolf Hitler in SS *Sturm 3/III/42*. Final, heartfelt greetings to you and all of my dear comrades. I much regret that I will not be able to contribute further to the rise and completion of the Third Reich. I declare before God and all mankind that my sense of honour will not allow me to let myself be tainted by my wife's many [mis]deeds. And by God, let my wife prove a single case of adultery … [144]

Schmidt's wife had accused him of adultery, and he felt the need, if not the duty, to express to his superior that he was innocent and had not brought the SS into disrepute. Here was the kind of suicide out of honour that Himmler seems to have approved of.

Bella K, a 44-year-old middle-class woman, gassed herself on 11 July 1935, ostensibly after arguments over money with her husband. Her lucidly written, rational-sounding suicide note, addressed to her daughters and then to her husband, with no spelling or grammatical mistakes, suggests that she was serious about her admiration for the Nazis. She seems to have written the note after she had opened the gas pipe. She stressed that she had sacrificed herself for the Nazis who would, she hoped, look after her daughters.[145] She was aware that her children would be devastated to find their mother dead:

> My little girls! Forgive me, but it was just not working out. Remember me with love, as I remember you. I made sacrifices to the very end. Heil Hitler! Your Mother. Don't stay in Berlin. Be brave and strong. Your mother is fine

now. Stay with the movement and do your duty, even if it will be different for you now. My life was dedicated to my husband and children. I was [his] loyal companion with all my soul. But that is no longer possible. Thank WW for his apprenticeship. You are free now. I wanted to fight alongside Adolf Hitler, as I did in the *years of struggle*. I rose up the ranks and became young again. But now you have destroyed it for me. I love you too much to keep on living like this.

I know that I am doing you wrong, [but] today for the first time I am thinking about myself and so am departing from this world. Say hello to my sister Grete and thank her for all of her help. Tell my boy that I expect him to become a good, honourable man and fighter. If people are going to reject me, then I will leave voluntarily. If you had only granted me a proper chance to relax just once but, as it is, I no longer know myself in this muddle. The gap inside of me was unbridgeable. The responsibility is crushing me. Just 8 days in nature without having to worry about everything in household. Now you'll have to get along without me. Then maybe things will work out. My head feels heavy. Farewell! Heil Adolf Hitler!

Only a few thousand Mark and this marriage that endured so much would not have been split up. I really loved you beyond measure, but my energy is gone. Mother.[146]

She emphasized her loyalty to the regime and her expectation that the Nazi party would look after her children. Bella bitterly complained about her husband who had spent some thousand Mark, probably on alcohol, instead of giving it to her. She also lamented that she had been refused benefit. Here was suicide as an act of revenge as well as despair, since Bella knew only too well that her husband would feel guilty after her suicide.

Selma R, a war widow, aged 46, gassed herself in Berlin-Reinickendorf on 13 March 1936. She declared:

I'm not killing myself because I feel *guilty*. My strained nerves also caused my pale appearance and thus I decided to [get treatment] but now you can spare the expense. I swear to the grave that there was no *deeper* reason that I was so chatty. My thoughts certainly were not *bad*. What I said flowed freely from many others' mouths. This is a *malicious* plot and revenge of some colleagues and my last request is that this matter be looked into. Frau D will confirm that I campaigned for this cause. That I saved [money] is also not a crime, and my [financial] relationships are clear and transparent, as befits a good citizen. Isn't it so amazingly scandalous, so many colleagues [ganging up] against a single one? I have always been serious throughout my life, which was bitter and hard. If my colleagues don't try to hide something, check into it. I would have been a scoundrel if I had come out *against* our government. The only shame is that I couldn't be loyal to our SPD government, even though it did many good things for me, and that depressed me. I regretted this very much and I swore to be true to my employer and to the flag to which I swore an oath, but unfortunately I have been totally *misunderstood*. I leave you with a final Heil Hitler.[147]

Her suicide was probably motivated by bullying. Selma had commended the welfare policies of the SPD government, presumably of Prussia. This had prompted her colleagues to bully her, and Selma was probably afraid of being charged with accusations of 'malicious gossip'.

Selma penned another farewell missive, this time to her siblings. In it, she stressed her admiration for the Nazis and the legacy of her husband, who had died in the First World War:

> Dear siblings,
>
> My final farewell. Forgive me. Hope you will always be alright because you deserve it, you good souls, Selma. I don't leave guilt-ridden; otherwise I would be worthy of dying. I had the greatest sympathy for our *great* Führer, all statesmen and for the *Third Reich* and for my family. Never stopped to thank God for that great achievement. What is a woman, used to suffering like me, and a warrior's legacy compared to an army of enemies? I would have really loved to see my beloved Fatherland to get great and powerful. This I wish wholeheartedly. Sieg Heil!![148]

Selma had clearly written her suicide note under great emotional stress. Probably afraid that the Nazis might retaliate against her siblings, she was anxious about emphasizing her loyalty to the regime.

In another case, the 16-year-old school student Kurt R shot himself on 26 January 1938 in the Tiergarten. In his pocket, he had left a note, saying: 'My father is to blame for my death to a great extent.' Kurt knew that his father would be devastated to read this accusation. Kurt had had a serious row with his father. From a hard-working, lower-middle class background, his parents, owners of a small grocery shop, had sent Kurt to a fee-paying grammar school. Kurt had just received a warning letter from his school for disobeying his teacher. Kurt had been under the influence of wealthier children. This had annoyed his father who thereafter refused to speak to his son.[149] Here, too, therefore, was suicide as an expression of hatred.

On 27 May 1939, another adolescent, the 16-year-old Helmut G, an apprentice toolmaker, tried to gas himself in his parents' flat in the working-class district of Treptow. He had been playing a card game by himself. After drawing the ace of spades, he decided to kill himself, leaving a note on the reverse of the card, saying 'This card decided that I had to die. They couldn't stop it...' Helmut survived. His motive remains obscure. Sharing the wider discourse that suicide was passed on by one's ancestors, the criminal police found a neat explanation in the fact that Helmut's mother had been diagnosed with mental problems some time previously.[150]

Suicides from emotional motives also continued. On Christmas Eve 1938, the 43-year-old printer Hugo G dressed up as Father Christmas and shot the lover of his wife before killing himself; this too was an act of hatred and revenge—a calculatedly bitter Christmas present to his errant wife.[151]

# IX

Some suicides were influenced by wider political and socio-economic changes such as the Nazi seizure of power, the alleged Nazi elimination of unemployment and the supposed strengthening of the national community. Some groups of people were affected to a greater extent by these political events, as was the case with those directly targeted by the Nazi regime. For some people, Nazi policies thus created an environment in which suicides occurred easily, as Durkheim proposed when writing on anomic suicide.[152] The concept of anomic suicide, if understood as an overturning of norms and values on a *private* level, allows us better to understand some suicides in the Third Reich. For people targeted by the regime, suicide, apart from emigration, was very often the only way out of a desperate situation, and one which allowed them to keep some form of dignity vis-à-vis looming Nazi threats of torture or murder. To a degree, therefore, suicide with a political connection may have replaced suicide from economic motives.

By officially classifying the death of political opponents killed or tortured to death as suicide, the Nazis denied responsibility for them, and accused these people of being cowards unable to stand up for what they had done. Additionally, Nazi eugenic and racial policies as well as the Nazi persecution of political opponents constituted a condition of an anomie for some. In some cases, suicide took place under direct pressure from the Nazis.

The experience of ordinary people with suicide shows that it remained, to a great extent, a private act devoid of wider political meaning. In the long-term perspective on the history of death, which the French cultural historian Philippe Ariès has considered, suicide was, indeed, a private act.[153] Ordinary people, usually belonging to the working class, justified their suicides after 1933 for the same reasons as in the Weimar Republic, namely the lack of future prospects, brought on by unemployment or emotional stress. Unsurprisingly perhaps, the Nazi regime did not manage to penetrate fully the emotions and basic private resources of ordinary people—their lives and bodies—despite the Nazi claim that people's lives and bodies belonged to the *Volk*.

Suicide in the Third Reich from 1933 until 1939 was a paradox. On the one hand, the Nazis saw it as a direct indicator of the social and political stability, thereby heavily politicizing suicide discourses. On the other hand, relatively few suicides can be directly related to political factors. The fact that the Nazis, particularly immediately after Hitler came to power, 'suicided' many of their opponents in order to deny responsibility for killing them is, however, striking. All in all, there was a lack of any pattern to suicide in the Third Reich's pre-war years. Nazi racial policies, however, had a clear impact on some suicides, apart from those already studied here. These are the suicides of German Jews in the Third Reich, which will be considered in the next chapter.

# 3
## Suicides of German Jews, 1933–1945

### I

In the Third Reich, suicide became a routine phenomenon among German Jews. This chapter concentrates on Nazi Germany, but also goes beyond the confines of the Third Reich: to exile, to Auschwitz, and to later times. It focuses on German-Jewish suicides during the Third Reich and analyses the links between Nazi racial policy and German-Jewish suicides. There is a rich literature on the suicides of prominent Holocaust survivors, such as Jean Améry, Paul Celan, Primo Levi, and Bruno Bettelheim, who killed themselves decades after the final solution. The existing literature suggests that these suicides can be broadly seen as the result of long-term traumatization during the Holocaust. This literature is not very helpful, however, as it brushes over the fact that not all post-war Jewish suicides were carried out as a reaction to the circumstances of the Third Reich. Some, of course, had other causes.[1]

But how politically significant were the suicides of German Jews in the Third Reich? This question guided the research of two historians, Konrad Kwiet and Helmut Eschwege, who treated the suicides of Jews in their 1984 monograph on 'Jewish self-assertion and opposition'. They mainly focused on statistics and argued that suicides of German Jews were not necessarily acts of resistance, but nevertheless disrupted the deportations and therefore have to be seen as acts of opposition.[2] Kwiet and Eschwege studied suicides of German Jews in a wider context of other Jewish responses to Nazi racism, such as open resistance, going into exile, or hiding.

To begin with, suicide rates among German Jews had been higher than corresponding Catholic and Protestant rates since before the First World

War. Regardless of this fact, German-Jewish suicides were a particular response to Nazi racial policy. Marion Kaplan introduced the concept of 'social death' to describe how German Jews were gradually excluded from German society.[3] But the present chapter goes beyond her useful survey of survivors' memoirs written after the Holocaust that document suicides at second-hand in the context of the camps. This chapter primarily concerns the social and political context of German-Jewish suicides and their individual motives, going beyond Kwiet and Eschwege's largely statistical analysis. It introduces hitherto neglected archival sources, including suicide notes of German Jews. These sources allow us to assess the impact of Nazi racial policies on individual suicides. This chapter also asks how far, if at all, Jewish suicide was a form of resistance towards Nazism, or how far, on the other hand, it was an act of despair and hopelessness.

# II

In the months after the Nazis came to power on 30 January 1933, storm troopers frequently and arbitrarily attacked Jews. Many Jews committed suicide under the impact of this violence. A few examples must suffice to illustrate the circumstances. The factory owner Hans Sachs from Chemnitz shot himself on 18 March 1933 after storm troopers had tried to arrest him.[4] The boycott of Jewish businesses on 1 April 1933 led to hundreds of suicides among German Jews.[5] Max Reiner, a journalist who had been working for Ullstein, the great Jewish publishing and newspaper business, forced to retire in 1933, noted in his diary on 24 April 1933 that he had recently been to a Jewish cemetery in Berlin. There he had seen many new double graves. A friend told him that these were the graves of couples who had committed suicide together.[6]

The severe measures and laws directed against Jewish professionals such as the Law for the Renewal of the Professional Civil Service of 7 April 1933 and the creeping Aryanization of Jewish business not only caused severe financial problems, but also resulted in the humiliation of many Jews who had perceived themselves as Germans. On 3 April 1933, Dr Hans Bettmann, a Jewish lawyer, shot himself in a Heidelberg cemetery, after being dismissed from court; and Professor Jacobsohn of Marburg University, upon being sacked, committed suicide on 28 April 1933. Many Jewish doctors, whom the Nazis gradually forced out of their jobs, killed themselves. These doctors thought of themselves as Germans and not as Jews, especially if, like Victor Klemperer, they were registered members of a Christian church.[7]

Fritz Rosenfelder, a Jewish businessman from Stuttgart and a passionate member of a local gymnastics association, shot himself in the summer of 1933. His club, like most sports associations at that time, was about to kick him out, along with its other Jewish members. His suicide note, reprinted in a contemporary anti-Nazi exile pamphlet, conveys his feeling of stigmatization:

> My dear friends!
>
> Herewith my final farewell! A German Jew could not stand living with the feeling that the movement with which the German nation wants to be saved regarded him as a traitor. I depart without hatred and resentment. An inner desire inspires me—may reason return in due course!…What a Jew feels—you may understand from my action. How much I would have preferred to sacrifice my life to my Fatherland! Don't mourn—but try to enlighten and to help the truth become victorious.[8]

The extreme anti-Semitic Nazi paper *Stürmer*, edited by Julius Streicher, *Gauleiter* of Franconia, quoted from Rosenfelder's suicide note and commended his suicide as a positive contribution to the solution of the Jewish question in Germany:

> If the Jew Fritz Rosenfelder wanted to contribute to a change of the attitude of Germans towards the Jews, he died in vain. We think of him, now that he is dead, without any feelings of 'hatred and resentment'. On the contrary, we feel happy for him and would not mind if his racial comrades sent their regards in the same way. Then, 'reason will have returned to Germany', with the Jewish question solved in a simple and peaceful manner…

To underline the point, the paper printed the story on its front page.[9]

Kwiet and Eschwege claim that the Jewish suicide rate dropped after the boycott of April 1933, even after the promulgation of the Nuremberg laws in 1935, since Jews initially felt less threatened by Nazi thugs and thought that their legal position had been clarified.[10] It is not possible to verify this claim statistically since national suicide statistics from this time did not specifically refer to Jews. However, what is clear is that the criminalization of sexual relationships between those branded as racial Jews and non-Jews in the Nuremberg laws did lead to some suicides that might not have happened otherwise.[11] The Nazis were aware of rising Jewish suicide levels since 1933 and especially in the wake of the Nuremberg laws. A Saxon Gestapo report from October 1935 dismissed the claim that 'Jews had committed suicide in high numbers because of their bad treatment'. The report was quite revealing, implying that many people were aware of increased suicide rates among German Jews because of the regime's racial policies. In a similar vein, the Leipzig police president commissioned a survey of Jewish suicides in Leipzig. The survey predictably concluded that most Jewish suicides had had to do with 'illness', thereby denying any potential Nazi responsibility.[12]

Hertha Nathorff, a Berlin Jewish doctor, observed many suicides in the wake of the Nuremberg laws. In September 1935, she noted in her diary: 'A victim of the Nuremberg laws! Poor girl. She did not have anything but her relationship with the Aryan man... and now this relationship must be broken off. Therefore, she took Veronal. And such cases happen every day.' Mostly, it was the Jewish partners of such relationships who committed suicide. Courts treated Jewish suspects much more harshly than their non-Jewish partners.[13]

On 22 March 1936, a storm trooper spotted a Jewish man, the 61-year-old Isidor S, together with the non-Jewish 28-year-old Auguste B in a hotel near Würzburg. Assuming that the two were having an illegal sexual relationship, he reported them to the Gestapo. Isidor S was immediately taken into custody. Auguste B was allowed to go home, since she had to look after her five-month-old baby. Interrogated by the Gestapo the same day, Auguste confessed that she had known 'the Jew S' since 1929 and that they had last had sex some four weeks previously and not at the time of being caught by the storm trooper at the hotel. Probably put under pressure by the Gestapo interrogation officer, she called herself a 'complete, stupid bitch [gutes, dummes Luder]', and confessed that 'she had heavily sinned'. She asked the Gestapo for leniency, not least because of her child. Isidor S reminded the interrogation officer of his war service, and claimed, although being aware of the Nuremberg laws, that he had not been thinking of them while courting Auguste B. He also claimed that he had not penetrated Auguste. On the night of 25–26 March 1936, seeing the hopelessness of the situation, especially after Auguste B had confessed under pressure, he hanged himself in his cell.[14] It is a moot point whether Isidor S really committed suicide or whether he was tortured to death by the Gestapo. But his situation would not have occurred without the Nuremberg laws. Moreover, in addition to this, Jews had to cope with a string of local anti-Jewish measures and violence throughout this period, with only a brief and partial let-up in the first half of 1936, as the Berlin Olympic Games loomed and the regime, as a consequence, did not want to offend international opinion.[15]

In 1937, the Berlin Jewish Community was so worried about the growing number of suicides that it commissioned a study of it. Unlike the Leipzig police's survey, the aim of the Berlin Jewish community's study was to blame Nazi persecution for increasing suicide levels. The results were reported in a Dutch press circular in November 1937. Whereas in 1924–6, there had been around 50.4 suicides per 100,000 Jews living in Berlin, these levels had increased in 1932–4 when there were 70.2 suicides per 100,000. This increase was partly due to the changing age structure of the German-Jewish population. Generally, young Jews left Nazi Germany, whereas older people remained. Elderly people are more likely to kill themselves than young people.[16] In addition, some of the increase was also probably the result of the Great Depression. According to the Dutch press circular, the Gestapo banned publication of this somewhat inconclusive study, since it showed a link between Nazi racial policies and suicides among the Jews.[17]

The direct effects of the Nazi regime on Jewish suicides were clearer to see after the *Anschluss* of Austria in March 1938. Here, anti-Semitic violence outdid anything seen in Germany up to that point. All the different stages of Nazi anti-Jewish policy and actions came together in a tremendous outburst of violence meted out to Austrian Jews in the process. Austrian Nazis humiliated Jews in public, forcing them to kneel down on the streets and clean the pavements. Anna Freud asked her father, the Viennese psychoanalyst Sigmund Freud, immediately after the *Anschluss*, whether it would not be a good idea to commit suicide. Freud, who shortly thereafter emigrated to England, is said to have responded: 'Why? Because they would like us to?'[18] Hundreds of Austrian Jews committed suicide amidst the open Nazi violence against Jews and suicide became an everyday phenomenon.[19] In the ten days from 12 to 22 March, at least 96 Viennese Jews committed suicide, including the cultural historian Egon Friedell who jumped to his death out of a window on 16 March when storm troopers tried to arrest someone else in his house. Even the Nazis acknowledged that some suicides had to do with what they euphemistically called the 'change in the political situation in Austria'. Pleased about the many Jewish suicides, Goebbels noted in his diary on 23 March 1938: 'Many Jewish suicides in

Vienna. Previously, Germans committed suicide. Now it is the other way round.'[20] Nevertheless, concerned about the reaction of the foreign press, Goebbels cynically downplayed the very high number of Jewish suicides at a mass rally in Vienna on 29 March 1938. He declared: 'In Vienna, there are at present fewer suicides than before, with the main difference being that some time ago only Germans shot themselves and now there are also Jews [who commit suicide] ...'[21]

The British *News Chronicle* reported in March 1938 'More Suicides as Austrian Purge Goes On', detailing that 'doctors and chemists are pestered by people asking for poisons or drugs to end their existence, which seems to have lost all purpose.'[22] Nazi officials forced Viennese Jews to sign a declaration committing themselves to their imminent emigration and then told them that the 'way to the Danube [was] always open', thereby encouraging them to kill themselves. After a Jewish shopkeeper had committed suicide together with his family in Vienna, storm troopers plastered his shop windows with placards saying 'Please imitate'.[23] There were so many suicides in March 1938 that Vienna's death rate reached a record high, a British newspaper claimed.[24] *The Anschluss*, with its accompanying anti-Semitic excesses, gave a tremendous boost to anti-Semitism across the whole of Germany and was a significant step towards the long-term Nazi aim: to purge Germany of the Jews.[25]

On the night of 9 November 1938, the Nazis unleashed the next anti-Semitic excess in what came to be known as *Reichskristallnacht*. The Nazis set synagogues on fire across Germany and destroyed Jewish shops. They murdered at least 91 Jews, according to official Nazi accounts—the actual numbers were undoubtedly far higher. There were also hundreds of suicides.[26] Altogether, hundreds of Jews died in the wake of *Kristallnacht*, if not one or two thousand.[27] The pogrom clearly revealed that Jews had no place in Nazi Germany.

On 11 November 1938, the Hamburg police investigated the suicide attempt of Dr Emil H, a 73-year-old Jewish doctor, who had overdosed on morphine. His sister told the police that he 'had been depressed over the last few days', not least because he had been forced, like all Jewish doctors across Germany, to close down his surgery for non-Jewish patients by the end of September 1938.[28] On 18 November, Dr H, having survived his suicide attempt, appeared at the police station and declared: 'As a result of my tragic and personal circumstances, I have recently been so desperate that I did not want to live any longer and attempted to take my life...'

He did not dare mention the pogrom explicitly because he was afraid that the Nazis might retaliate against his family. The shock of the violence and the Nazi invasion of people's homes meant a real loss of any security to Jews. Many Jews who survived the pogrom were never the same again. Dr H was determined to die, and finally succeeded in killing himself on 28 November. His wife went to the police station and handed in a death certificate and two suicide notes, which the police typed up and put into Dr H's file. His first suicide note dates from 11 November 1938:

> My dear Else!
>
> It will be incredibly difficult to depart from you. I have loved you so much. I thank you for all your love and faithfulness! Keep on loving the children and grandchildren! Please apologize and think of me with love. Your unhappy H. Say hello to Henny and thank her for all her love. I do not want to be given a post-mortem, only if my insurance demands it. If that's alright for you, give my fur to E and my watch to my little godchild.

Jewish suicides in the Third Reich were generally not expressions of hatred towards those left behind or against the own unloved self. Relatives usually did not condemn suicides for violating the Judaic taboo on suicide.[29] In the upsetting environment of the Third Reich, suicide became an acceptable way out of despair. In his second, more desperate suicide note, which he had written before his second and finally successful suicide attempt, he underlined his wish to die: 'My dear Else! I cannot live any longer and I do not want to live anymore. Let me sleep quietly, do not call a doctor and don't let them take me to hospital! Thanks for all your love. Your H.'[30] The atmosphere of fear and terror created by the pogrom prompted many more German Jews to commit suicide.

In the direct aftermath of the pogrom, the Gestapo arrested at least 30,000 Jewish men across Germany and took them to concentration camps.[31] Number 381 on the arrest list of the Hamburg Gestapo was an elderly doctor, Salomon K. When the Gestapo agents showed up at his flat, they did not arrest him, allegedly because he was very nervous after the pogrom. Instead, the Gestapo agents searched the flat, and found one of the bedrooms locked. Their suspicions aroused, they told the person inside the locked bedroom to open the door immediately otherwise they would break it down. The man inside turned out to be Martin C, a 46-year-old Jewish musician, as the landlady told the Gestapo. Terrified of being killed, he refused to open the door. Finally his landlady broke a glass panel in the door so as to unlock it from inside. When the Gestapo agents entered the room, C had already jumped out of the window, probably since he did not see any other way out to escape what he thought to be his imminent death.[32] Such actions were sometimes explicitly welcomed. In Hofgeismar, a small town in Hesse, the local representative of the SS intelligence service, the SD, reported on 17 November 1938: 'Unfortunately, there have been no suicides or cases of death at this time.'[33]

Weeks after the pogrom, 76-year-old Hedwig Jastrow, a former teacher and feminist, wrote in her suicide note on 29 November 1938:

> Nobody must undertake any attempts to save the life of someone who does not want to live! It is not an accident, nor an attack of depression. Someone leaves her life whose family has had German citizenship for 100 years, following an oath and has always kept this oath. For 43 years, I have taught German children and have helped them in all misery and for much longer, I have done welfare work for the German *Volk* during war and peace. I don't want to live without a Fatherland, without *Heimat*, without a flat, without citizenship, being outlawed and defamed. And I want to be buried with the name my parents once gave me and inherited to me, which is impeccable. I do not want to wait until it gets defamed. Every convict, every murderer keeps his name. It cries to heaven.[34]

As Jastrow was aware, Jews would be forced to carry the name 'Sara' or 'Israel' from 1 January 1939.[35] Emphasizing her Germanness and her service to the German nation during the First World War, Jastrow refused to accept her removal from German society. The notion of honour also plays an important role in Jastrow's suicide note as she saw herself 'outlawed'. She thought it better to die than break the law, which she found dishonourable. The Nuremberg laws had reduced German Jews to the status of subjects rather than full citizens, but it was the pogrom of 1938, and, on a more practical level, the eviction from her flat, that destroyed Jastrow's hopes for the future. Rather than cope with more discrimination and humiliation, she preferred to decide for herself when it was time for her to die. Her suicide was indeed an act of self-assertion of her right to keep control over her life and body.

The competition among various authorities to remove Jews from public life as soon as possible particularly increased after *Kristallnacht*. Their financial situation became even more precarious as a result of the billion Reichsmarks the Nazis cynically forced the Jews to pay. In Berlin, the police president ordered a ban on Jews (*Judenbann*) as early as December 1938. Jews were not allowed to visit places of public entertainment and culture in Berlin or in any other part of Germany.[36]

In 1933, there had been 525,000 Germans of Jewish faith. For the Nazis, there were, of course, many more Jews in Nazi Germany than that because they classified Jews by race and not by religion. Many Jews who committed suicide in the Third Reich were highly acculturated. The Nazis persecuted them simply because of their Jewish ancestry. By May 1939, only around 210,000 were left in Germany, excluding Austria. The violence of the pogrom clearly showed that Jews were in physical danger in the Third Reich, even if it had not been clear enough before. In Berlin, more than half of the Jewish population emigrated between June 1933 and May 1939. As noted earlier, those who had stayed were generally old.[37]

Even some German Jews preparing to emigrate killed themselves. On 19 July 1939, 29-year-old Luise S shot herself on the banks of the Griebnitzsee, a lake to the south of Berlin. The criminal police initially assumed that she had been murdered, and therefore carried out an investigation. After they identified the corpse, the police interrogated Luise's sister, Ilse F, who had already emigrated to London, but was at that time in Berlin to help her family move. Both Ilse and Luise were from a wealthy Jewish family whom the Nazis had pressured to sell their country estate after the pogrom of November 1938. Luise and her parents wanted to emigrate to England and had already obtained the necessary visas. Jews often found it difficult to find someone in Britain, or indeed in other countries, who would vouch for them and get their case high enough on the list of those who were allowed to enter the country. Also, leaving Nazi Germany was very difficult, with many bureaucratic and financial obstacles. The Nazis forced Jews preparing their emigration to go through humiliating bureaucratic procedures and generally took away their money and possessions before eventually allowing them to leave.[38] Luise and her non-Jewish husband just could not stand life in Germany any longer 'as a result of the anti-Jewish laws', as her sister told the police. Luise's husband had already left for East Africa, where he had tried to shoot himself, but survived, though he lost an eye. Luise had been very nervous and had also been addicted to sleeping pills and morphine. The criminal police were embarrassed, since they could not directly blame official anti-Semitic policies for her suicide. In the conclusion of the highly detailed investigation report, the criminal police blamed her nervous state of mind instead: 'Ill, separated from husband and children, facing an uncertain future, she most likely killed herself. The result of the investigations so far is suicide.'[39]

Some German-speaking Jews committed suicide in exile, such as Walter Benjamin or Stefan Zweig. After the German invasion of France in 1940, Benjamin left Paris and tried to escape to the USA via Spain. Held at the Spanish border at Port Bou by Spanish officials, Benjamin was afraid of being sent back to Nazi-controlled France. He overdosed on morphine on 26 September 1940. Stefan Zweig, a highly successful Austrian novelist who had already emigrated to London in 1934, took an overdose of sleeping pills together with his wife in his Brazilian exile on 22 February 1942. Isolated from European culture and despondent about the rise of fascism in Europe, Zweig and his wife saw no other way out than suicide.[40]

# III

When the Nazis launched the Second World War in September 1939, the situation for the Jews remaining in Germany became even more distressing. In Stuttgart, the wife of Julius G, a 57-year-old textile merchant, proposed to her husband that they should commit suicide together. They had just been forced to sell their house in Stuttgart and were now living in a gloomy two-bedroom flat. Imprisoned from November until December 1939 for alleged currency smuggling, G was preparing to emigrate, when a supposed friend fraudulently absconded with a substantial sum. G's wife, Lini, killed herself on 9 December 1939. In a suicide note addressed to her imprisoned husband, she wrote:

> Dear Julius!
>
> It is incredibly difficult, so difficult that I cannot express it with words that I have to leave you behind in your despair. You are a man, you are strong, but I am too weak to take this long ordeal ... My thoughts are with you in your cell, at day and at night, all the time, you are my husband. My last request to you is to forgive and to condone what I had to do to you and think of me with love nevertheless. I greet you for the last time and say farewell to you for ever. Your Lini.[41]

Here was suicide, presented as an act of resignation and despair vis-à-vis the unbearable political situation that had impacted on Jewish private lives. Rather than express anger or hatred, Lini G stressed her love for her husband and her weakness as a woman, a reflection of the gender stereotypes she had obviously internalized. This emphasis on love towards those left behind was common in Jewish suicide notes. Julius G decided to try to survive, which he managed after emigrating to the United States via Portugal in 1940. He wrote in his memoirs after the war and his return to Europe: 'I decided to live ... I did not see another way out for myself, either, but the thought [remained with me] that a happy accident might occur, that there might be political change. Or was it cowardice, which initially prevented me from departing voluntarily from life?'[42] Unlike his wife, therefore, he could regard suicide as an act of strength rather than weakness.

As the war continued, Nazi discrimination increased. Jews were not permitted to leave their flats after 8 pm. In October 1940 Jews from Baden and the Rhineland-Palatinate were deported to Southern France, an event triggering many suicides.[43] Already impoverished because of Nazi expropriation, German Jews received lower food rations, and many Jews were drafted into forced labour. The introduction of the yellow star in September 1941 further stigmatized the Jews and was also directed at their removal from the public sphere. This 'social death' was certainly an important factor creating an environment in which suicides could easily occur.[44]

In October 1941, first systematic deportations of Jews from across Germany began. By this time, only about 160,000 Jews were left in Germany. In July 1941, according to an estimate based upon the files of the Confederation of Jews (*Reichsvereinigung der Juden*), compiled on the orders of the Gestapo, 36.4 per cent of German Jews were over 60.[45] The long-term aim of the Nazis—to evict all Jews from Germany—now materialized and finally led to mass murder in extermination camps from 1942 onwards (mass shootings of non-German Jews had already taken place in Poland since 1939 and the Soviet Union since mid-1941).

Suicide was a common reaction to the deportations. According to a list of funerals at the Jewish cemetery in Weissensee, 811 suicides were buried there in 1942, compared to only 254 in 1941. On 23 March 1943, Martha Liebermann, widow of the famous painter Max Liebermann, aged 85, was also interred in this cemetery. She had committed suicide after receiving her deportation order.[46] By then, there was a special ward in the Berlin Jewish hospital dedicated to failed suicides, which, more clearly than any quantitative data, suggests that suicide had become an everyday phenomenon within the Jewish community. Doctors at the Berlin Jewish hospital were debating whether or not to treat people who had attempted to take their lives, since they knew that once recovered they would be deported and killed anyway.[47]

After the beginning of the deportations, Nazi and state attitudes towards Jewish suicides underwent a fundamental transformation. No longer did the Nazis encourage Jews to commit suicide. At the beginning of the deportations in 1941, the Berlin Gestapo issued deportation orders a week before the actual deportation. But later, according to an eyewitness account, the Nazis changed this policy and did not tell Jews in advance of their deportation, because many Jews had used the interim to kill themselves.[48] In Würzburg, if a Jew who had been on one of the deportation lists committed suicide, the local Gestapo rounded up another Jew to fill the place that had become vacant.[49] The determination of the police and the Gestapo not to be 'cheated' and to round up all Jews is confirmed by the fact that, once the deportations had begun, policemen often inspected the pharmacy of the Berlin Jewish hospital to ensure that no poison had been issued to Jews. Herta Pineas, who had been working at the Levetzowstraße collection point for the deportees in 1942, later remembered what had happened to those who had attempted suicide, but who survived: 'If not successful, suicide was a criminal offence!' Typically of the Third Reich, this practice did not have a legal basis. The Gestapo denied survivors any food and put them onto the next available transport to the East.[50]

# IV

The wave of deportations of German Jews from 1941 until 1943 prompted about 3,000 to 4,000 suicides.[51] Nazi attempts to prevent Jews from committing suicide were not effective. A study compiled for Goebbels during the war, and presented to Hitler, calculated that the number of Jewish suicides increased from 94 in the third quarter of 1940 to 160 the third quarter of 1941, a rise of 70.2 per cent. Jewish suicide levels rose even further in the fourth quarter of 1941, when there were 850 Jewish suicides in the *Altreich*, an increase by a staggering 516 per cent compared to the fourth quarter of 1940.[52] The Nazi leadership was thus clearly aware of the wave of German-Jewish suicides as a response to the deportations. Bruno Blau, the long-time statistician of the Jewish Statistical Office who survived the Third Reich in the Berlin Jewish Hospital, believed that around one in four deaths of Berlin Jews in 1942 and 1943 had been a suicide. By this time, the majority of German Jews lived in Berlin.[53]

The Berlin criminal police compiled suicide statistics from 1941 until 1944, including Jewish suicides.[54] Like all suicide statistics, these numbers are probably underestimates. More and more policemen were drafted into front-line duty, so the police probably had even fewer resources to register suicides. Not all Berlin Jews committed suicide within the Berlin police district. On the other hand, the figures include Jews domiciled outside Berlin, who committed suicide in the city. Nevertheless, the statistics give a graphic indication of the problem. In 1941, the Berlin criminal police registered 1,818 suicides of whom 332 or 18.2 per cent were Jewish. When the deportations began in the last quarter of 1941,[55] 40 per cent of the suicides were Jewish. After the deportations commenced, Jewish suicides made up roughly half of all suicides in Berlin and, at times, considerably more than that.

Suicide levels clearly correlated with waves of deportations. The Nazis forcibly evicted Jews from their flats and took them to the Levetzowstraße transit-camp. According to Hildegard Henschel, the wife of the last chairman of the Berlin Jewish Community, many deportees took barbiturates already at this stage to kill themselves to avoid the humiliation and terror of deportation.[56] Altogether, 13,374 Berlin Jews were deported to Poland and to Riga, and 14,795 to Theresienstadt. Initial transports were bound for Lodz, Riga, and Warsaw. From the autumn of 1942, transports were bound for Auschwitz. The vast majority of Berlin Jews were deported in the autumn of 1941 and in the first quarter of 1943. In March 1943 alone, some 7,000 Berlin Jews were deported to Auschwitz.[57] At these times, suicide levels were particularly high. Many Jews knew that the deportations probably meant death.[58] This helps to explain the steep rise in suicide levels in the third quarter of 1942. Most strikingly, more Jewish women killed themselves than Jewish men. This trend remained until 1944. According to most of the literature on gender and suicide since Durkheim as well as the statistics presented earlier in this book, this was unusual. However, more Jewish women than men remained in Berlin, and those Jewish women who had stayed in Berlin were usually older than sixty years and often widowed. Widows were unwilling to leave their familiar environment and were socially isolated. This fact and the continuing everyday persecution of German Jews were among the causes of their suicides.

Younger Jews could leave Germany until the October 1941 ban on Jewish emigration, although emigration was very difficult. During the deportations, younger Jews could go into hiding. These options were not really available to elderly German Jews who were seldom able to show self-assertion in this desperate situation, except by committing suicide. They preferred suicide over Nazi humiliation. German Jews were aware that suicide levels had reached a new maximum. On 22 May 1942, Victor Klemperer noted in his diary that there had recently been 2,000 Jewish suicides in Berlin.[59] In 1942, Jews committed 39.6 per cent of suicides in Berlin. 886 Jews out of a total of 2,236 Berliners committed suicide amidst new deportations to Theresienstadt in the summer of that year. The Berlin Jewish suicide rate reached its climax in the third quarter of 1942 amidst a wave of deportations when 481 out of a total of 669 suicides were Jewish, which means that 75 per cent of suicides were Jewish. The Berlin suicide statistics also contain the numbers of suicide attempts reported to the police. The determination to die was much higher among Jews. Of those 1,138 people who survived their suicide attempt in 1941, only 64 were Jewish. Considering the numbers of 'successful' suicides in 1941, this shows that only 19 per cent of Jewish men survived their suicide attempt compared to 62.5 per cent of non-Jews. Jewish women were even more determined to die, as only 14.5 per cent of them survived their suicide attempt, which once again suggests a gender-reversal of traditional findings on suicide.[60]

Most German Jews committed suicide by poisoning. Poison, especially barbiturates such as Veronal, was, at least initially, easily available and ensured a relatively painless and quiet death. Carrying potassium cyanide and barbiturates was a matter of everyday routine for many Jews by this time. Carrying poison gave Jews a strong sense of control over their fate, and made them feel prepared for the eventuality. This culture of being prepared to die by one's own hand was an important stage on the road to suicide. But obtaining such drugs became increasingly difficult because they were extremely expensive and not easily available, as a doctor at the Berlin Jewish hospital later remembered.[61] Like many Jews, Ilse Rewald was drafted into forced labour in an armaments factory in 1941. She later recalled how one of her friends had sold a Persian carpet for 1,000 Reichsmarks to buy some Veronal. Her friend poisoned herself the following day. But this was by no means unusual by that time, and Rewald remembered that 'the suicides almost [did] not shock us anymore, we [envied] everyone who [took] the courage and who [did] not have to cope with the tortures'.[62] Suicide had become an everyday phenomenon among German Jews.

Foreign observers and ordinary people also knew of the suicides. In 1942, the American journalist Howard K Smith, a correspondent in Berlin until Nazi Germany declared war on the United States, published his account of the October 1941 deportations:

> The greatest number of suicides … occurred among Jews still in Berlin when the transportations first began. The pitiful little Jewish weekly newspaper which the Nazis allowed the Jews in Germany to publish became filled with death notices each week after the raids began. It was death one way or another, and the sensible ones chose it the sooner and easier, rather than the later and harder.[63]

Smith was right when he wrote that most Jewish suicides knew at this stage that they would die 'one way or another'. On 29 December 1942, in the course of its campaign in December 1942 to broadcast news of the persecution of the Jews, the BBC German-language service took up the theme of Jewish suicides in its comedy show *Kurt und Willi*, in which Kurt Krüger, a teacher, and Willi Schimanski, a civil servant in Goebbels's Ministry of Propaganda, discuss political issues. Kurt reports that their neighbour, an elderly Jewish woman, had just gassed herself after receiving her deportation order. Willi replies: 'No, my dear friend, a quick death from gas is much better than starving to death in a cattle wagon or being gassed as a guinea pig.'[64]

## V

How did Nazi racial policies impact upon individual suicides? The following investigation of suicide notes and police reports gives a voice to those who committed suicide. The many suicides must have overwhelmed the criminal police. The investigation reports are very short, giving almost no background information on the individual suicides. We do not know much about their lives, hopes, and expectations but it is striking that many Jewish suicides explicitly referred to their personal histories in their farewell missives. Take the case of the pensioner Dora G from Prenzlauer Berg, a working-class district in the centre of Berlin. She gassed herself in her kitchen on 4 March 1943. She was due for deportation and announced her suicide to her non-Jewish husband and her neighbours. She left a suicide note, written under great stress and almost unreadable, on the kitchen table. In it, she declared:

> For forty long years I have been married to Aryans, in my first marriage in America ... For 34 years married to an Aryan, had no contact to Jews, brought up the children in an Aryan way and took them to holy Communion, exercised no Jewish influence on them ... did not marry according to Jewish faith, 1905 in America, married according to Protestant rituals ... never did any harm to anyone, always worked (as a girl and as a woman) ... I am only sorry for my dear ill husband, I like to die, there I am safe.[65]

Dora G's suicide note reads like a public complaint against the Nazis. She emphasizes her Aryan and Protestant identity. She did not feel Jewish and refused to accept being deported like the other Berlin Jews by the Nazis.

In a similar case, Margarete L, a 58-year-old widow from the middle-class Wilmersdorf district of Berlin, took cyanide on 4 March 1943. L had been married to a lieutenant-colonel and had received her deportation order for that day. She had told her friends that she would under no circumstances accept her deportation. In her very brief suicide note, she too underscored her German identity as an officer's widow: 'I depart from life voluntarily! Margarete Sara L, b Levy, *widow of a lieutenant-colonel* ...'[66] Most Jews who committed suicide in the Third Reich were highly acculturated, like Margarete L and Dora G. Both referred to their 'Germanness'. This was common in German-Jewish suicide notes. Some Jewish men who committed suicide even wore their medals from the First World War when they killed themselves, emphasizing their German identity. The Judaic taboo on suicide did not apply to them.[67]

While most Jews committed suicide in private, people sometimes wrote suicide notes to make their desperate situation public.[68] They rightly assumed that the police and other Nazi institutions would read their suicide notes. Contrary to their intentions, Jewish suicides did not shock Nazi authorities, so Jewish suicides were not political weapons. During the deportations, suicide was above all an action to keep control of the self and to evade the deportations and what came after.

In most cases, those Jews who had attempted to kill themselves in Berlin but failed were taken to the Jewish hospital, where they usually perished. Take the case of 64-year-old Harry S from the middle-class Halensee district. He overdosed on sleeping pills at his home on 13 March 1943. The police commented on his death at the Jewish hospital rather laconically: 'Reason...: fear of evacuation. Relatives already evacuated...'[69] The police did not send a telegram to the state prosecutor, which would have been the usual procedure with non-Jewish suicides. In some cases, the police, understaffed due to the war, did not even bother to contact doctors to establish the cause of death. When neighbours found Frieda B, a 60-year-old widow, dead in her flat in Potsdamer Straße in Berlin, the police did not call a doctor, since 'as has already been mentioned, she has been dead for a few days...'.[70] This circumvention of standard procedure suggests that the police did not care how Jews died.

In Rathenow, a small town near Berlin, the local police found Martha W, a 60-year-old housewife, gassed to death. She had been driven to suicide not only by the threat of the deportations but also by Nazi intimidation and terror following her having called Hitler a 'crook, gangster etc' in anonymous letters. Probably following Martha W's denunciation by the letters' recipients, the police had ordered her to appear at the police station for investigation on 11 January 1943. But Frau W refused to show up. She told her non-Jewish husband that she had indeed written these letters and she would 'not go the way her relatives had gone', since she was well aware that this would mean death. The police concluded: 'It can, therefore, be assumed that Frau W was aware of being investigated for libelling the Führer and that she knew about her arrest and probable deportation. Thus she opted for suicide.'[71]

People facing their immediate deportation sometimes chose very violent means of suicide, which reflected their sheer despair. On 23 August 1943, two Gestapo officers rang the doorbell of 48-year-old Sophie Z in Berlin-Wilmersdorf to arrest her for deportation. The first officer remained downstairs to secure the entrance, while the other one ran upstairs to the second floor to break down Frau Z's door. Then, suddenly, she opened the lavatory window and leapt into the backyard. She died on the way to the Jewish hospital.[72]

The deportations in early 1943 were accomplished in a particularly cruel and humiliating way in Berlin. Following the widespread bombings of German towns, the Nazis became more radical in fulfilling their plan to get the Jews out of Germany.[73] On 6 March 1943, Helene M, Ella H and Bruno H, all in their early sixties, were found dead in the Levetzowstraße transit camp. They had managed to smuggle in sleeping pills and, in a last attempt to keep their dignity, took them together and died. The criminal police laconically commented: 'Reason of the deed is fear of evacuation.'[74] 'Evacuation' was a Nazi euphemism, as Jews well knew.

After 1943, when most German Jews had either emigrated prior to 1941 or had already been deported, the large-scale deportations from Berlin and other German towns stopped and the suicide rate sank drastically.[75] Jews still in Germany were facing increasing terror and persecution. Some 10,000 Jews hid during the deportations.[76] When Jews in hiding were discovered, some committed suicide.

On 12 February 1943, Hanna S, from the expensive Frohnau neighbourhood in North Berlin, reported to the police that a couple called Lohmüller had been staying in her neighbour's house for four months without registering with the police. Frau S had become suspicious. She did not like her neighbours, who were very rich, and so she decided to denounce them to the police. The police duly arrived and interviewed the suspect, Herr Lohmüller, who had lots of suitcases and food stamps with him, since he had allegedly been preparing to travel to Cologne. The police checked his identity papers, which turned out to be genuine, and then left. On the same day, the police saw his wife (who had also been staying at the rich people's house) and immediately took her to the police station. She asked for a glass of water, when suddenly 'a cyanide-like scent was smelled in the room', as one of the policemen noted in the protocol. She died immediately. A few weeks later, on 3 March 1943, the Berlin Gestapo Head Office noted that the Lohmüllers had actually been the Jewish couple, B, who had gone underground. They only learnt this after finding Herr Lohmüller, ie Herr B, hanged in the Grunewald on 27 February 1943.[77]

Having non-Jewish spouses initially protected some Jews from deportation, following Hitler and Göring's decree defining 'privileged' and 'non-privileged' mixed marriages in the winter of 1938. Once their non-Jewish partner had died, they too fell prey to the Nazis.[78] The actor Joachim Gottschalk, one of the most popular German film stars of the time, had been banned by Goebbels from appearing in any film unless he divorced his Jewish wife (this pressure on mixed marriage couples was common, with the Gestapo coercing partners, especially non-Jewish women, to divorce their Jewish spouses). He refused. When his wife and daughter received their deportation orders, they all committed suicide together on 6 November 1941.[79]

The 46-year-old Hertha D from Stettin was found gassed in her non-Jewish brother-in-law's flat in the working-class district of Kreuzberg on

30 October 1944. Her non-Jewish husband had been killed on the Eastern
front five months previously. She had lost her 'privileged' status and had to
wear the yellow star. Refusing to accept that the Nazis branded her a Jew,
she repeatedly failed to collect her yellow star from the Stettin Gestapo
office. She travelled to Berlin instead to visit her brother-in-law whom she
told that she would 'under no circumstances return to Stettin, but rather
take her life'. Since she had failed to comply with Nazi regulations, she
faced immediate deportation. She preferred to die by her own hand.[80]

The repressive mechanisms of the Nazi regime were still enforced,
perhaps more radically than before, right up until the German surrender.
Victor Klemperer records, for example, that all remaining Jews in Dresden
were being rounded up for deportation and killing as late as the first
two months of 1945.[81] Some Berlin Jews killed themselves in 1945, since
they were unable to endure the racist policies of the Nazi regime any
further. But only very few Jews were left in Berlin, once the single
biggest Jewish community in Germany. Many had married non-Jews
and had managed, with many difficulties, to evade deportation only to
find themselves summoned by the Gestapo at the start of 1945. On
15 January 1945, the Reich Security Head Office ordered the deportation
to Theresienstadt of all Jews living in mixed marriages.[82] On 6 January
1945, the criminal police in Hermsdorf, a quiet Berlin suburb, reported
the suicide of the Judge Heinrich P and his partner Charlotte A who
was, according to the Nuremberg laws, half-Jewish. A initially survived,
but later died in hospital. The suicide note, which they had written
together and left for the attention of the police, reveals their refusal to
accept the anti-Semitic policies of the regime: 'To police investigators!
Since we were prevented from living together, we have decided to die
together. Please do *not* give any trouble to our housekeeper, FL, who was
loyal to us for many years. She has had *nothing* to do with our deaths.'[83]
In Hamburg, 43-year-old Erna M, who was married to a non-Jewish
husband, took an overdose of sleeping pills on 14 February 1945. Her
husband, Hans, had found his wife unconscious at home. He told the
police very coolly that his wife had been 'very sad' about her imminent
deportation.[84]

The 69-year-old widow Natalie G, who was also Jewish according to
the Nuremberg laws, overdosed on sleeping pills on 11 March 1945. Her

non-Jewish husband had died a few days previously and thus she now faced deportation. She left a suicide note:

> My last will and testament. I...have decided that because my beloved husband is gone, I, too, will leave this life voluntarily. It is my wish that we be buried together...and that this wish be granted. I am so weary of life and have been through so much that I cannot dissuade myself from this course. I am now the third victim in my family. Kind regards to all of my neighbours.[85]

Natalie G explicitly mentioned the known deaths of her relatives, a reference to the fact that they had killed themselves for the same reason.

# VI

Most of the Jews who were deported to the concentration or death camps either died on the way or were murdered in the camps themselves.[86] Needless to say, many of those who allegedly committed suicide in the camps had, in fact, been murdered or tortured to death by the SS. SS attitudes towards suicide of camp inmates underwent a fundamental transformation once killing on a mass scale had begun. No longer did guards encourage prisoners to commit suicide. The SS severely punished suicide attempts, since suicide was an expression of self-determination. Suicide ran counter to the Nazi total claim over the lives and bodies of the inmates.[87]

Scholars suggest that there were relatively few suicide attempts in the concentration and death camps during the Holocaust. Under extreme life-threatening conditions 'there is a tremendous increase in the self-preservation instinct', one scholar notes, based on memoirs of survivors of concentration camps. The inmates' depersonalization allegedly did not allow them to reflect on suicide. This was particularly common among the so-called *Muselmänner*, inmates who had lost their individuality and desire for self-preservation, but were also so apathetic that they lacked even the will to kill themselves.[88]

Some did, however. Evidence from the Mauthausen concentration camp, set up by the Nazis near Linz after the *Anschluss*, confirms this view. On 8 September 1942, the Hamburg lawyer Otto B, a Jew, committed suicide by running into the electrified fence there. The SS wrote to his wife that her husband had been cremated and that she could apply for a death certificate by sending in 72 pfennigs.[89] In a PhD thesis written in 1943, the Austrian Jew Paul Neurath, an inmate of Dachau and Buchenwald after the *Anschluss*, before he emigrated to the USA, draws an intriguing picture of SS attitudes towards suicide, which, at least at this stage, were entirely arbitrary: 'If a guard wants to drive someone into suicide, he subjects him to chicanery until he [the inmate] cannot stand it any longer; if he wants to kill him immediately, he does; but if he wants to prevent the suicide, the man who has undertaken the failed attempt receives 25 lashes.'[90]

The author Jean Améry, a survivor of Auschwitz who committed suicide himself in 1978, remembered later that 'only relatively few had decided to run into the barbed wire ...', since inmates were so afraid of being severely punished by the SS for attempting suicide that they did not dare try in case they failed. If the SS or Kapos (prisoner functionaries) caught people during their suicide attempt, they would usually kill them in a particularly cruel way.[91] In contrast to this, the psychoanalyst Bruno Bettelheim, himself a former inmate of Dachau and Buchenwald, claimed: 'Psychologically, most prisoners in the extermination camps committed suicide by submitting to death without resistance.'[92] But in these circumstances, resistance would have been suicide too. Hermann Langbein, an Austrian survivor of Auschwitz, confirmed this. Suicide, Langbein claimed, was always a widely discussed idea at Auschwitz, due to the constant and unbearable torture and humiliation inmates had to endure. But there were relatively few suicides there, since the individuality of the inmates had been totally destroyed.[93] However, this depersonalization does not seem to have been the only, or even the principal reason for the relative lack of inmate suicide in Auschwitz. Comparison with other death camps puts the situation into a different perspective. Auschwitz was divided into an extermination and a labour camp: for those who were not taken to the gas chambers immediately on arrival, there was always some hope of survival. In a camp purely dedicated to extermination, such as Treblinka, the situation seems to have been different, and suicide out of sheer despair was so widespread that the SS forced Jewish inmates to go on night-watch to prevent other inmates from killing themselves. Nevertheless, many Jews committed suicide, either by taking poison they had found in the luggage of those who had already been gassed, or by hanging—a slow and painful way of dying.[94] German Jews usually had the means to commit suicide with sleeping pills without suffering much pain, while poorer Eastern European Jews often chose more violent methods such as jumping out of windows, hanging or exposing themselves to shootings by camp guards.[95]


# VII


Nazi racial policies, the removal of Jews from the public sphere and the deportations amounted to an overturning of normal life and its norms and values that increased the likelihood of suicide, prompted by the collapse of hope in the possibility of a future. Jewish institutions—synagogues, community centres, schools, clubs, and societies—had been destroyed in the wake of 1938, and Jewish society in Germany had been atomized as well as ostracized.[96] German Jews who committed suicide during the Third Reich were not simply alienated from existing society. Rather, they were convinced that the society in which they could exist had been destroyed. To be sure, many German Jews, if they did not emigrate, initially tried to adapt to life in Nazi Germany, at least until the pogrom of 1938. Suicide levels mounted each time the Nazis launched direct actions (the April 1933 boycott of Jewish shops, the *Anschluss*, and the pogrom of 1938), but also subsided temporarily afterwards.

Jewish suicides in the Third Reich were not simply acts of despair. Suicides very often tended to be carefully planned by the time the deportations had started. Maintaining some form of dignity was probably a more important motive than pure despair. In the overwhelming majority of cases, those German Jews who committed suicide were highly acculturated and did not feel Jewish. They did not accept being branded by the Nazis as 'racial' Jews. Most suicides discussed above did not feel bound by Jewish religious taboos on suicide. In her 1943 essay 'We Refugees', Hannah Arendt discussed the problem of Jewish refugees' suicides. She remarked: 'We are the first non-religious Jews persecuted—and we are the first ones who ... answer with suicide.'[97]

Comparatively few Jews committed suicide in the concentration or death camps during the Holocaust. For all the arbitrary decisions that governed life and death in the camps, the highly-regimented rule-bound environment gave inmates a structure to their lives. The common means of committing suicide with dignity, such as poison, were not readily available. Killing oneself by running into the wire was not a dignified or honourable end, but a kind of surrender to the superior forces of the camp's brutal environment. The terrible punishments meted out to failed suicides were a deterrent. In a single-purpose extermination camp like Treblinka, suicides were most probably acts of despair. The Nazi regime radically changed the ways in which German Jews experienced suicide. Suicide could no longer be an expression of hatred and anger towards those left behind. Despite Jewish religious proscriptions against suicide, it became a routine phenomenon as the last resort for keeping one's dignity vis-à-vis Nazi racial policies that eventually left no freedom for Jews—other than suicide. In the end, this is what mattered, far more than the question whether suicides of German Jews in the Third Reich were intentional acts of defiance or of political opposition against the Nazis' murderous policies.[98] In the totally exceptional situation of German Jews in the Third Reich, suicide had a clear pattern. The history of the suicides of German Jews reminds us of the fact that few Jews left in Germany after November 1938 were young. They could not be expected to start a new life elsewhere or go into hiding.

# 4

# Wartime suicides, 1939–1944

## I

On 1 September 1939, Germany invaded Poland, triggering the Second World War. In a bloody campaign, Germany quickly subjugated Poland. The suicide rate closely mirrored Germany's fortunes in the war. The Nazis, concerned with the use of statistical data by the enemy, stopped publishing statistics in 1941/42. Thus the statistics published in 1941/42 only go up to 1939.[1] However, the unpublished files compiled by the Reich Propaganda Chief for Hitler still contain some useful information for 1940 and 1941. Whatever their reliability, these are the only statistics available for this period. According to these files, suicide levels dropped quite significantly in 1940. In the *Altreich* (German pre-1938 territories) there had been 6,326 suicides in the third quarter of 1940, and in the same quarter of 1941, only 5,986, a drop of 5.4 per cent.[2]

There is no evidence of what the Nazis thought about this decrease, but one can speculate that they associated the drop in suicide levels with the war, and the alleged strengthening of the national community. Popular support for Hitler was at its highest when Germany overran Denmark, Norway, the Netherlands, and France — Germany's most powerful opponent in the First World War — in stunningly successful military operations in 1940.[3] In Berlin, too, suicide levels declined in 1939, a trend that lasted until 1942. Indeed, at times of German victories, fewer people killed themselves. Germany's military successes came to halt in late 1941 after the attack on the Soviet Union in June 1941.[4] The Berlin suicide rate rose in 1942. (Given that there were very few Jews left in Germany and Berlin at this time, the upsurge in Jewish suicide rates probably did not significantly affect overall rates.) When Germany's military fortunes turned in 1942, and Germans were increasingly subject to Allied bombings, more people committed suicide. The increasing difficulty of everyday life in this situation clearly played a role. In a sense, economic factors were coming back into play. People were bombed out, their family and friends killed, their menfolk dead, missing, or captured in increasing numbers. Rations became tighter and food more difficult to obtain. But this was not all. The policies of the Nazi regime also played a role. This chapter tells the familiar story of the Third Reich at war from a different, individual perspective. This chapter's material goes beyond Nazi reports on public opinion which many historians cite in support of the now fashionable hypothesis that the behaviour of 'ordinary Germans' during the Second World War is best understood in terms of consent and collaboration with the regime. Powerful, individual cases of suicide cast into doubt this argument and emphasize the significant role of Nazi terror in keeping the German population at bay.[5]

# II

The war led to an immediate escalation of legal terror by the Nazi regime. Draconian new laws were brought in, and even relatively trivial offences now met with very severe punishments. As in the opening phase of the Third Reich, this led to a number of suicides of people hunted down by the Gestapo and mortally afraid of the consequences. The following case illustrates this atmosphere of terror.

On 2 September 1940, following the German military successes in France, Johann R, a 44-year-old servant from Marktbreit near Würzburg, shot himself. He had been in serious trouble with the Gestapo ever since an SS man had denounced him. The SS man allegedly overheard R, who was apparently drunk, say in February 1940: 'If the war is not over by July 1940, we'll lose it.' In March 1933, an emergency decree had been passed on the prevention of malicious attacks against the government. From December 1934 onwards, the regime and the judiciary enforced a new law against 'malicious attacks' on the state and the Nazi party. The Nazis and the courts deliberately defined very broadly what constituted an offence under this law to intimidate and possibly suppress open criticism of the Nazi state.[6] These laws were applied with particular severity during the war. In the same conversation, R had reportedly confessed that he was still a communist. The Gestapo, without checking whether the SS man's allegations were true, arrested R on 20 February 1940 and accused him of undermining the war effort. Courts, especially towards the end of war, often meted out death sentences on those charged with this offence. The officer in charge of R's interrogation noted: 'R's statements are likely to cripple or destroy the German *Volk*'s will to defensive self-assertion, particularly because R made these statements to members of the armed forces...' The Gestapo also searched his flat, but found neither compromising material nor any proofs of his membership in the Communist party. The local police of Marktbreit wrote to the Gestapo that R had allegedly been involved in the 1930 murder of Horst Wessel, a Nazi martyr. This claim was not true at all. The local Nazis, including the Mayor and the local Nazi leader, hated him and described him 'as a Communist and archenemy of the National Socialist Reich'. R, threatened by brutal Gestapo officers, stated during his interrogation on 21 February 1940 that he had not wanted to undermine the war effort. Almost certainly forced by the Gestapo to confess in order to save his life, R signed the following declaration:

> What I once told Gretl R about my participating in the murder of Horst Wessel didn't correspond to the facts...But in this case, too, I was just boasting. Based on the explanation of charges against me, I can see that I deserve to be punished. I accept it. When I am again free, I will behave such that I will no longer come into conflict with the law.

The Gestapo also forced him (like others) to sign a declaration that he had been 'given a severe warning' and that he would have to reckon with 'indefinite confinement in a concentration camp'. R was terrified of being taken to a concentration camp. He thought this would have meant his death. R died after his suicide attempt on 5 September 1940, a few days before his trial was due to begin.[7]

Others, too, killed themselves after the Gestapo had opened proceedings against them, as the case of Julius S, a 63-year-old retired businessman, shows. On 3 October 1940, he jumped out of the window of the Gestapo office at Aschaffenburg, a small town on the River Main. He died immediately. His neighbour, Maria M, a postman's wife, had denounced him to the Gestapo on the previous day for listening to the BBC, which was not only illegal but punishable by death.[8] Maria M, it turned out, was one of Julius S's tenants. He had recently complained about her children making too much noise; and she had warned him that he should not make too much fuss, given that he was listening to foreign radio stations. As in most denunciations, Maria M's motivation was not primarily political, but personal.[9] When the Gestapo called on Julius S the following day, they found him listening to the BBC, whereupon they arrested him. Frightened, Julius S jumped out of the window and died.[10]

The war against the Soviet Union, planned from the outset as a war of extermination,[11] also witnessed a new dynamic of radical Nazi policies against those considered politically or racially undesirable. Four personal fates illustrate the escalation of Nazi terror. The first case is that of Matthäus M, a 71-year-old locksmith from Lower Franconia. He hanged himself in prison on 17 October 1941, four months after Germany invaded the Soviet Union. A vagrant, Matthäus M, who had been prosecuted and arrested some 50 times already, was now arrested for 'vagrancy and violation of the Malicious Gossip Law'. Reportedly, M had claimed that the German soldiers fighting the British in North Africa were unaccustomed to the desert climates and thus they would not return home. Furthermore, M had allegedly said that Germany would not win the war in 1941. He claimed that he had been a member of the SA, and that he had even shaken hands with Hitler at a Nazi party rally in Frankfurt am Main in 1930. But this did not help him. He was sent to prison. Probably aware that he would never be released from penal institutions or the concentration camps, Matthäus M hanged himself.[12]

The second case is that of 23-year-old Margarethe von R from the Osthavelland on the outskirts of Berlin. Local policemen reported her suicide on 23 February 1942. Margarete von R had swallowed an overdose of 20 sleeping pills. The police commented: 'Reason for the suicide: fear of punishment as a consequence of her immoral conduct (continuous refusal to work, loitering, venereal disease).'[13] Margarethe von R's allegedly immoral way of life, and her refusal to work, reduced her to the status of an asocial in the view of Nazi authorities in spite of her noble descent. She probably feared police authorities would send her to a concentration camp or to a Labour Education Camp (*Arbeitserziehungslager*), camps run by the Gestapo. During the war, the police were granted new powers to detain anyone the Nazis deemed racially or morally deviant, and policies against such undesirables became more radical.[14]

The third case is that of 44-year-old Heinrich K. On 4 September 1943, he hanged himself with a gauze bandage in a Nauen police prison cell. He had escaped from the Neuengamme concentration camp near Hamburg, but the police recaptured him. He knew that he faced execution.[15] The fourth case is that of 44-year-old postal worker Otto P.

On 19 December 1943, members of the 30th police precinct in Hamburg found him dead in the police station's arrest cell. P had been jailed for stealing parcels sent to front-line soldiers, a capital offence under the Racial Pest Decree (*Volksschädlingsverordnung*) of 5 September 1939. Theft of goods was common because of rationing. Afraid of being executed, P hanged himself. The criminal police laconically commented: 'In this case, one can say with certainty that this crime was not caused by another person; there is no need for further investigation, and this is clearly a suicide of a thief of soldiers' mail…'[16] As Germany's fortunes in the war turned, the regime intensified its pressure on the civilian population, increasingly terrorizing those who fell out of line.

After the outbreak of the war, courts also massively extended the death penalty.[17] As popular support for the regime began to decline after Germany's failure to defeat the Soviet Union by winter 1941, the Nazis considered even more draconian measures to suppress any potential unrest. They feared that criminals, asocials, and political enemies would undermine the war effort.[18] At a lunchtime meeting on 20 August 1942, Hitler complained that German courts meted out sentences that were far too lenient at a time when soldiers, in Hitler's view 'positive elements', were being killed in the war. Reflecting notions of Social Darwinism, Hitler insisted that 'negative elements', including criminals, must be killed in much larger numbers to make up for this loss of 'eugenically valuable' men. Hitler and other Nazis thought that if the judiciary continued to mete out 'lenient' sentences, a new 1918 might be possible. Back then, political criminals, with the help of degenerates, had staged a disgraceful revolution and had thereby destroyed Germany, Hitler thought, conflating notions of political opposition, criminal behaviour, and racial degeneracy. Hitler ordered the judiciary to disregard existing laws and act according to Nazi ideas of 'healthy popular feeling'.[19] In October 1942, Minister of Justice Thierack insisted: 'It goes without saying that the looter who assaults the belongings of our national comrades after our enemies' terror attacks deserves only death.' By that time, Thierack was sending out regular directives to German judges, thereby effectively undermining the long-established German tradition of judicial independence.[20] In the autumn of 1942, Thierack ordered 'asocials' singled out from prisons for 'extermination through labour' and the killing of those held in 'security confinement'. In a speech at Breslau on 5 January 1943, Thierack insisted: 'It is not right that the idealist dies outside and the inferior scum is preserved inside.' A summary of this speech in the *Völkischer Beobachter* reiterated Thierack's call for the 'ruthless extermination and extirpation of incorrigible criminals'.[21] The radicalization of the criminal justice system terrified people and led repeat-offenders to commit suicide. Two cases show how these radical policies impacted on individual suicides.

The first case is that of Johannes R, a 39-year-old metal worker from Darmstadt, a town heavily attacked by the Allies in September 1944. Accused of being a racial pest (*Volksschädling*), R hanged himself with his tie in his cell of the Darmstadt gaol on 9 August 1944. Arrested a few days before, he confessed that he had sold the contents of seven pieces of express luggage which he had obtained on the black market, increasingly a place where Germans bought and exchanged rationed goods. Afraid of the death penalty, R killed himself. In a letter to his wife, he justified his suicide: 'Dear wife! When you receive this letter, I will be dead already. It is better that way. Farewell and don't forget your Hans! I am very sorry that I am hurting mother and you so much, but in the end this is my only refuge. Again my best wishes to all my loved ones at home. Farewell...'[22]

The second case shows how Nazi terror was specifically directed against an individual. On 3 March 1943, the deputy *Gauleiter* of Mainfranken wrote a letter to the Gestapo to complain about the factory owner Georg H from Wertheim near Würzburg. The local Nazi party had denounced him. The deputy *Gauleiter* branded Georg H a war profiteer:

> I have been told in confidence that Georg H...has made irresponsible remarks about the Führer and the war. Aside from that, he is a profiteer. H apparently spends a lot of time in Würzburg and spends lots of money, great sums of which he has earned because of the war, lives the high life, and says more or less that in Stalingrad 400,000 German soldiers had to die because Hitler didn't follow his generals' advice and that the Führer is unsparingly sacrificing German lives... If this man is such a conspicuous profiteer and a criminal agitator, we must get hold of him. Perhaps we can arrange for the SD to investigate him...

The Nuremberg branch of the SD could not prove that Georg H had made such allegations. Nevertheless, probably in retaliation, the deputy *Gauleiter* ensured that Georg H was drafted into the Wehrmacht as an ordinary soldier. H shot himself on 10 September 1943 near Karlsruhe, according to the local Gestapo which had kept observing him, 'after a major drinking bout'. The Gestapo's threats to confine him to a concentration camp seem to have been a major motive for his suicide.[23]

After Hitler's attack on the legal system in 1942 and his appointment of Thierack to the office of the Reich Minister of Justice in the same year, the legal system increasingly served as a means of terrorizing and exterminating deviants. Although popular knowledge of the full extent of the concentration camp system is notoriously difficult to ascertain, people were terrified. The cases discussed above furthermore suggest that many people, like Margarethe von R, were terrified by imprisonment in other penal institutions, too, as the conditions in prisons dramatically deteriorated amidst the escalation of legal terror in the war.[24]

Suicides from such motives continued till the end of war, as Nazi terror increased. On 15 February 1945, Minister of Justice Thierack set up drumhead courts martial (*Standgerichte*) in regions near the front line. These consisted of a judge, a Nazi party officer, and a Wehrmacht officer, who were to sentence everyone to death who in their opinion undermined the war effort by trying to give up fighting or making 'defeatist remarks'. Often, those sentenced to death by the *Standgerichte* were hanged in public.[25] In the administrative chaos that accompanied defeat, Himmler decreed on 3 April 1945 that everyone trying to surrender was to be shot without trial. Most civilians were at that time generally concerned with ensuring their survival, rather than with showing ideological commitment to the Nazis.[26] Take the case of 25-year-old Annemarie E; she was found gassed in her mother's kitchen in Karlshorst, an eastern suburb of Berlin, on 18 February 1945. She had just been sacked from her job as a typist in the county office of Niederbarnim near Berlin for making a defeatist remark. Since the Gestapo had started an investigation, which would probably mean her death at this time, she preferred to die by her own hand.[27]

Men who had sex with other men who became known to the authorities were also subject to increasing Nazi terror during the war. Obsessed with male homosexuality, the Gestapo claimed in 1941 that there were four million homosexuals in Nazi Germany. The police often obtained confessions from 'homosexuals' by coercion and torture. The only way to combat homosexuality, the Gestapo thought, was to castrate homosexuals. Other institutions, including Wehrmacht doctors, wanted to 'cure' homosexuals by giving them the opportunity to prove themselves in battle. There were also medical experiments on homosexuals, using hormone treatment.[28] While legal conviction rates for homosexual men fell after the beginning of war, other agencies, such as the Gestapo, intensified their extra-legal persecution of men who had sex with other men. During the war, the Reich Ministry of Justice took up the Gestapo's view and included the forcible castration of homosexuals in the draft law against community aliens, illustrating the radicalization of anti-homosexual attitudes within the Nazi state.[29] Homosexual men were normally treated very badly in prisons and concentration camps, reflecting contemporary anti-homosexual stereotypes.

Four cases illustrate the radicalization of the Nazi persecution of male homosexuals. The first case is that of Franz B, an inmate of the Sachsenhausen concentration camp. Accused of having had sex with other men while in the camp and put on trial in Berlin in May 1940, B testified that an SS officer had suspended him from a wooden post, a normal punishment in the concentration camps and a particularly cruel way to torture inmates. Franz B had probably been rearrested on release from prison on the Gestapo's order. In despair, he hanged himself with his jacket. He survived because the jacket tore.[30]

The second case is that of Walter Z, aged only 15 years. On 24 February 1942, Walter was run over by a train near Falkensee. The police wondered whether Walter had committed suicide, especially after his mother had accused an anonymous man of murdering him. Walter, it turned out, had been suffering from syphilis, which he had caught while having sex with men. His friends and his boss, probably trying to ingratiate themselves with the police, accused him of having been lazy and effeminate. These accusations included the claim that Walter had avoided his service in the Hitler Youth. His colleague at work, the 15-year-old Kurt R, told the police that Walter had told him that his partner, a Luftwaffe soldier, looked like Hermann Göring. 'He did not say whether he is as fat as Hermann Göring', he added.[31] Although the police did everything they could to find the unknown man, they never found him. Walter's mother even accused the lawyer of one of Hitler's favourite actors (whose name cannot be given for legal reasons) of having been Walter's partner. The police duly interrogated the actor on 13 May 1942. He denied any accusations against his lawyer.[32] Walter likely committed suicide because he knew he would face a serious sentence, and also by this time indefinite confinement in a concentration camp, if the police caught him.[33]

Fear of indefinite confinement in a concentration camp also prompted other homosexual men to kill themselves, as the third case reveals. On 21 June 1944, the stationmaster of the Berlin-Wannsee station found the 33-year-old librarian Walter S unconscious in a train compartment. S had overdosed on sleeping pills. He died the following day in hospital.

He had been working at the National Socialist Welfare Organization (*Nationalsozialistische Volkswohlfahrt*), but had just been sentenced to nine months in prison for 'unnatural intercourse'. Awaiting his prison sentence, he was despondent about these accusations and planned his suicide very carefully. On 15 June 1944, he called on a doctor, who prescribed him 25 Veronal pills. He also penned a suicide note, addressed to an aristocratic female friend in Bonn. Walter S declared: 'My dear and honourable Countess! A life such as the one I have before me is no life at all. And so I strip myself of it. Please take a nice souvenir for yourself. Take my watch as a token of my gratitude. My last thoughts will be with you. Walter S.'[34] Afraid of his confinement in a concentration camp, Walter S preferred to die by his own hand.

The fourth and final case brings home the fear and desperation of a man the regime targeted as a paedophile. A Berlin court charged 17-year-old Harry S with having homosexual relationships in January 1945.[35] A month earlier, on the morning of 13 December 1944, the criminal police tried to arrest a man who had allegedly seduced Harry at his fashionable West Berlin flat. To arrest the 'homosexual seducer of the young', the police pretended that they wanted to speak to a female opera singer who also lived in this flat, but nobody let them in. This refusal annoyed them, and they were about to call a locksmith to unlock the door, when they again rang the doorbell. As they did this, the police heard a gunshot, and this time the opera singer did open the front door. A grisly scene was revealed. Dr Paul K, a 41-year-old first lieutenant in the Luftwaffe had shot himself, but was sitting in an armchair, apparently still alive. He died on his way to hospital. Desperate about his likely confinement to a concentration camp, and already cited for 'unnatural intercourse with men', Dr K committed suicide.[36]

The Luftwaffe, as well as the Wehrmacht leadership, had been concerned with homosexuality for a long time. Army psychiatrists advised the Wehrmacht leadership to take a tough stance on soldiers who had homosexual sex. In the spring of 1943, Field Marshal Keitel, one of the Wehrmacht's leaders, insisted that 'true' homosexuals, those with a genetic disposition, were to be handed over to the civilian authorities for punishment. Those soldiers only caught in a single homosexual incident were to be put under surveillance in special punishment units. How to detect 'true' homosexuals remained an unresolved question for the army leadership until the end of the war.[37]

In many cases, those accused of homosexuality were handed over to the criminal police and the Gestapo and confined to concentration camps. This would have probably also been Dr K's fate. The Law for the Prevention of Hereditarily Ill Offspring of 14 July 1933 enabled courts to order the sterilization of the 'congenitally ill'. Sex offenders, like Dr K, were to be castrated, according to the Law Against Dangerous Habitual Criminal and Sex Offenders of 24 November 1933. The 1935 revision of paragraph 175 broadened the scope of what constituted homosexual offences. Prison doctors could arrange for the castration of suspects even before the case had gone to the court. The Nazis thought that castration would eliminate not only the homosexual sex drive, but the criminal drive, too.[38] Facing castration and confinement to a concentration camp, Dr K committed suicide.

These suicides had their origin in the Nazi legal and extra-legal terror, which increased as the war went on. Nazi terror dramatically affected the lives of people accused of deviant behaviour. The Nazi racial utopia did not leave any space for these people and systematically terrorized them. In this context, suicide was an act of desperation, but also a last resort of showing some self-assertion. Many people persecuted by the Nazis preferred to die by their own hand, rather than face confinement to a concentration camp, castration, or, indeed, the death penalty.

# III

Ordinary, conforming German citizens came under extra pressure during the war, too. Unlike in 1914, most ordinary people did not welcome the outbreak of war in September 1939, afraid of its implications for their everyday lives, which, for those old enough, had been so badly affected by the First World War. Take the case of 52-year-old housewife Olga K, from the working-class district of Hamburg-Altona. On 7 December 1939, the Hamburg police investigated her death. She had jumped out of a window. Her husband, a tramway conductor, told the police: 'Since the war [began], my wife has been very nervous. She does not find her way around... She's always complaining about ration cards, which she could not get used to... In a word, she did not move with the times.'[39] Olga K had experienced the First World War, of which she probably had very bad memories, especially of malnutrition.[40] Like many Germans, she was unenthusiastic and anxious about the new war. She felt unable to cope with her new situation. When her husband complained about her failure to adjust to the new everyday challenges, he implied that Olga's suicide expressed her refusal to follow Nazi exhortations to mobilize everything and everyone for the war effort and simultaneously distanced himself from her deviant conduct by implying thereby that he did not refuse 'to move with the times'. One cannot ultimately know whether the war's outbreak alone caused Olga to jump out of the window, but it is telling that her husband emphasized this possible suicide motive in his interrogation by the police.

Despite the lack of enthusiasm in September 1939, popular support of the regime was massive in the early stages of war, reaching its peak in June 1940 after Hitler's successful conquest of France, for many Germans, the arch-enemy. This and other *Blitzkrieg* victories raised hopes among the population that the war would soon be over.[41] Gradually, especially after the first Allied bombings of German towns in 1941/2, there was anxiety about the air raids and concern about the everyday hardships caused by the war. As the war went on, Germans on the home front increasingly felt its impact. Of course, the war had been affecting people's lives since its beginning. Many men had to join the armed services. Food and other consumer goods were rationed. This directly affected the lives of people, especially of women, who were usually responsible for running the household. There were constant air-raid precautions, including blackouts at night, and many people, especially women, were drafted into the war effort.[42]

Full-scale Allied bombings of German towns began in 1942. Life became more difficult for ordinary people, as goods and foodstuffs became scarcer and black-marketing increased. The Allied bombings became more severe in 1942/3.[43] From 1943, the British and the Americans bombed German towns following a round-the-clock-bombing strategy. Estimates suggest that about one third of the German population suffered directly from the bombings. More than 25 per cent of German houses were destroyed. Almost five million people had to evacuate their homes because of the bombings. Around 300,000 people were killed.[44] In Hamburg suicide numbers increased from 553 in 1942 to 585 in 1943, an increase of 6 per cent, likely related to the bombings in 1943.[45] And in Frankfurt am Main, the criminal police recorded a substantial rise in suicide levels in the wake of the heavy bombings of March 1944. Eleven cases in Frankfurt resulted supposedly from 'depression, during which the act is committed because they fear bombings or because they lost everything because of them'.[46] Whatever the truth of this claim, relating suicides to the Allied bombings was convenient for the Nazi regime, since this allowed the Nazis to stress German victimhood due to what they called Allied 'terror raids'.

The Allied bombings of Hamburg, also known as *Operation Gomorrha*, in July and August 1943 were some of the heaviest bombing raids of the war and left at least 34,000 people in Hamburg dead and 125,000 injured. The raids left 900,000 Hamburgers homeless. Half of the flats were destroyed.[47] SD agents reported on 29 July 1943 a 'feeling of insecurity and hopelessness' among people as a direct reaction to the raids on Hamburg.[48] On 2 August, the SD reported that 'various Anglo-American terror attacks on Hamburg have triggered a pronounced shock-effect among the population in all parts of the Reich'. The same report continued to lament 'rumours about alleged unrest in Hamburg'. Alarmingly, it went on to allude to the revolutionary situation of 1918: 'These totally unfounded rumours have created a situation throughout the Reich whereby people speak of a "November mood", since the German people cannot stand these attacks and protests against them.'[49] Yet people were so shocked by the extent of the destruction and so busy with securing their livelihoods that they did not turn against the regime.[50] The Nazis, concerned with popular support, yet at the same time rigidly persecuting any dissent, managed to contain this potential of popular dissatisfaction until 1944 by mounting a propaganda campaign that promised German retaliation for the Allied bombings. SD reports from early 1943 referred to high hopes among civilians for retaliation. When the Allies invaded Normandy on 6 June 1944, it was clear to many Germans that the Nazis' propaganda campaign had failed and that the war was lost.[51]

Suicide was an extreme response to the bombings. Files on suicides in the wake of the bombings are sparse. The police did not have many resources for documenting suicides in the chaotic milieu of the bombed-out cities. Some individual files have survived in Berlin and Hamburg. They shed light on individual reactions towards the bombings. Friedrich S, a roofer, aged 68, from Berlin-Schöneberg lost his house in an Allied bombing. He committed suicide on 23 March 1943 in an allotment in Falkensee on Berlin's outskirts. Allegedly, he was so despondent about losing his house that he shot himself. The criminal police blamed his suicide on 'nervous breakdown after losing his home in an air raid'.[52] The raids had destroyed

Friedrich S's livelihood and he did not see any other way out other than suicide in the chaotic environment of the bombed-out city.

In Hamburg, many suicides related to the bombings took place some months after the *Gomorrha* raids when people had realized the full extent of the destructions. On 17 December 1943, 35-year-old Peter T died in the University Hospital at Eppendorf. He had tried to kill himself on 24 September 1943. The police ascribed his suicide to 'depression'. His wife explained to the police that they had lost their house, together with all of their belongings and savings, in a bombing. She declared:

> My husband could not get over this loss and day by day became more and more pensive ... He could no longer stand to see the rubble in the city and could no longer sleep. My husband was constantly afraid of new terror attacks and repeatedly announced his suicidal intentions. He often said that he would hang himself when the alarm sounded the next time.[53]

But not only men concerned with their livelihoods committed suicide in the wake of the bombings. On 8 January 1944, 62-year-old Paula W, a butcher's wife, hanged herself from an apple tree in Rahlstedt, on the outskirts of Hamburg, where she and her husband had been evacuated after the bombings. Returning to Hamburg was hard, especially because Allied bombings continued until April 1945, killing at least another 5,000 people and leaving about 6,000 injured.[54] Like many, Paula W and her husband had lost all of their property in the bombings and found it hard to re-establish themselves. Her husband told the police that Paula 'had lost her zest for life. Although she had never expressed suicidal thoughts, we always suspected suicide was a possibility with my wife.'[55]

Richard J, a 59-year-old dock-worker, hanged himself on 7 January 1944. His wife told the police that their family had been split up, with their son missing since the bombings and their daughter evacuated to Warnemünde on the Baltic Coast near Rostock. Following the bombings, Richard and his wife, like many other Hamburgers, had been relocated to Nordhausen in the Harz mountains. They decided to return to Hamburg because they did not want to settle in an unfamiliar environment. His wife later told the police that Richard worried about future bombings:

> My husband always worried that we would move back here and be in danger again. I reassured him repeatedly and told him that if anything were to happen, then we would be in the same situation as other people and that we

would overcome it. But my husband wouldn't settle down and he couldn't get over our deeply missed son.[56]

In Berlin, people also directly related suicides to Allied air raids. On 18 January 1944, a female corpse was found near the Plötzensee penitentiary after a bombing. It turned out to be the 51-year-old widow Frau K. Her daughter told the police, after she identified her mother, that the deceased 'suffered greatly from the bombings and the general difficulties caused by the war'. Erich K, Frau K's husband, also found a suicide note. Frau K, ostensibly suffering from a nervous depression, declared: 'Farewell, forgive me for doing this. Dear Erich, you had to suffer a lot because of me.'[57] Many more people must have committed suicide in the wake of Allied bombings. The regime was increasingly unable to cope with the impact of the bombings, more and more suppressing any dissent among the population and increasing terror against German civilians.

# IV

The increasing Nazi terror affected not only Germans. Ever since the war began, large numbers of foreigners had been working in Germany. In the summer of 1941, there were almost three million foreign workers. In 1942, Fritz Sauckel, the Plenipotentiary for Labour Mobilization (*Arbeitseinsatz*), systematically brought in more foreigners, especially from the Soviet Union. By the summer of 1944, some 7.6 million foreign workers were in Germany. The largest contingent, 2.8 million, were from the Soviet Union, followed by some 1.7 million Poles.[58] The Nazis were concerned that the foreigners were a serious threat to the 'preservation of the German *Volk's* purity of blood'.[59] The SS Security Service warned in 1942: 'The conscription of many millions of German men into military service, the lack of a general prohibition against sexual relations for foreigners, and the incorporation of additional foreign workers, have all increased the threat of infiltration of the blood of the German *Volk*.'[60] Yet, sexual contact between Germans and foreigners had in fact been outlawed. From 1939 onwards, the Nazis banned such contact with prisoners of war, including sexual relationships. The Nazis claimed that this rule was necessary because of concerns over racial purity, alongside sabotage, espionage and the undermining of morale. The Gestapo and the Wehrmacht raided foreign workers' camps to prevent such contact, though without much success. Courts often meted out stiff prison sentences and humiliating public punishments on German women who had been cheating on their husbands with foreign workers. These punishments included the public shaving of women's heads. In October 1941, Hitler personally banned such public punishments.[61] But the general enforcement of the ban of these relationships continued. The March 1940 Polish decrees, which the Nazis later applied to Soviets too, reflected Nazi racist notions. Many German women who had been caught having a relationship with Polish or Soviet men were sent to concentration camps. Polish or Soviet men were often sentenced to death by special courts. From 1942 onwards, following an agreement between Thierack and Himmler, 'racially inferior' foreigners, such as Poles and Soviets were no longer dealt with by the German judiciary but by the SS and the police. This agreement led to an upsurge in executions of Poles and Soviets, since the police and not the courts now decided which foreigners were to be executed.[62] The Security Service wanted to ban all sexual contacts between Germans and foreigners to reassure German soldiers that 'the wives they had left behind would come to no harm'.[63] The following cases reveal the impact of these policies on women who were afraid of being investigated by the Gestapo.

On 5 January 1942, the Hamburg police reported the suicide of 25-year-old Elfriede S. Her husband had been drafted into the Wehrmacht. She had turned on the gas. Although the fire service rescued her, she later died in hospital. The police commented: 'One can see that the motive for the act was fear of confrontation with her husband in that he is currently in Norway and will soon come home on leave. During her husband's absence, she let herself get involved with Dutch men and through her careless lifestyle ran up debts.'[64] The threat of soldiers' wives being unfaithful to their husbands was constantly present during the war. This notion reflected sexual double standards, since soldiers were usually allowed to go to brothels while at the front. As one historian has argued, based upon an extensive study of Düsseldorf Gestapo files, both the regime and ordinary people suspected many soldiers' wives of having illicit sexual relationships with foreign men. It seems likely that Elfriede's mother had denounced her to the Gestapo. Although her mother claimed that she liked Elfriede's Dutch lover, Elfriede had been owing her rent for two months. Feeling unable to settle her personal problems with Elfriede, Elfriede's mother, like many denouncers, turned to the Gestapo.[65] Elfriede killed herself, afraid of being persecuted by the Gestapo which had begun to investigate her.

Twenty-seven-year-old waitress Hildegard S, from a working-class neighbourhood in the centre of Berlin, gassed herself in her kitchen in January 1942. Her husband, a soldier on the Eastern Front, could not believe that his wife had killed herself and therefore asked the criminal police to investigate her death. Like most other soldiers whose wives were cheating on them with other men, Hildegard's husband had not reported his wife to the police authorities before, since this would have undermined his own position as a man. If he had denounced her, he would have seemed a weak husband. Hildegard worked at a pub near the Silesian Railway Station in East Berlin, an area traditionally dominated by prostitution, gambling, and crime. With her husband being away at the front, she had become more independent and enjoyed her new freedom. She had got to know many soldiers on leave and slept with them. The police confirmed that she had killed herself, and complained that 'the deceased had been involved with men and drank a lot. She allowed men to take her home, if she had not to be taken home due to her drunkenness.'[66]

In Lower Franconia at least two young soldiers' wives killed themselves in August 1942. Such suicides seem to have been quite common, since the SD made special mention of it in an official report on public opinion. The SD was worried that German women dating foreign workers would hurt public morale. Other women in the same region of Lower Franconia tended to blame the Nazis for women dating foreign men, and implicitly for such suicides, because the Nazis had let foreigners into Germany in the first place.[67] Nevertheless, the Reich Ministry of Justice insisted on 14 January 1943: 'German women who engage in sexual relations with prisoners of war have betrayed the home front, done gross injury to their nation's honour, and damaged the reputation of German womanhood abroad.'[68]

Thirty-four-year-old worker Hildegard R gassed herself in her flat in Potsdam on 14 April 1943. The criminal police related her suicide to the fact that she had cheated on her husband with several prisoners of war. Unlike most other men in this situation, her husband had filed for divorce since he probably found it disgraceful that his wife had affairs with foreign men while he served at the front.[69]

Despite such liaisons, the Nazis and many ordinary German workers treated foreign workers, particularly those from the East, quite badly. Racism became a matter of everyday routine for many Germans.[70] Living conditions for foreign labourers from the East were catastrophic. They were subject to starvation, beatings, and the death penalty for petty offences. The situation for many foreign workers from the East, away from home in an unfamiliar environment, was hopeless and desperate.

On 1 September 1941, the Halle senior state prosecutor (*Oberstaatsanwalt*) accused the 25-year-old Polish foreign worker Georg N of a violation against the Malicious Gossip Law. Allegedly, Georg N, drafted into forced labour at a Merseburg ammonium factory, had declared in a local pub in mid-May 1941: 'If he had a machine gun, he'd go back to the military and shoot. Everthing was much nicer in Poland before the Germans came. They did not bring good fortune to Poland. *The Germans are shit for him.*' Georg's open criticism of the brutal German suppression of the Poles and his intention to resist the German occupation were unacceptable for the Nazis. He faced a death sentence by the Halle Special Court. Georg hanged himself in a Halle prison cell on 1 September 1941, exactly two years after the German attack on Poland.[71]

Michał S, a 17-year-old Polish worker at a paper factory in Wittenberge near Berlin, committed suicide in a particularly cruel way on 3 June 1942; he lay down on a railway line so that the incoming train decapitated him. Although the terrible living conditions he and other foreign workers faced most likely motivated his suicide, the criminal police laconically commented: 'Reason for the suicide: S had expressed suicidal thoughts to his co-worker. The suspected motive for the act is homesickness.'[72] Fear of Nazi terror prompted 39-year-old Czech Franziska W, a Czech foreign worker at one of the armaments factories in Hennigsdorf, near Berlin, to overdose on sleeping pills on 3 January 1943. She died a few days later in hospital. According to the police, W had made defeatist remarks and the Gestapo had started proceedings against her, which would have normally meant her death.[73] Fear of the death penalty led to many more suicides among foreign workers, especially towards the war's end when the regime became increasingly radical in its policy to exterminate 'community aliens'. In February 1945, the police of Eberswalde, near Berlin, found the Russian foreign worker Nikolai K, aged 29, hanged. Probably struggling with hunger, like the overwhelming majority of foreign workers from the East, K had stolen some foodstuffs to survive. The police commented 'fear of punishment because he has … perpetrated a number of serious thefts', implying that K would have been executed for his thefts, as was the rule at that time.[74] Twenty-five-year-old Soviet citizen Maria T, a forced labourer, drowned herself in a lake near Berlin in March 1945. The criminal police stated tersely that she had escaped from a foreign workers' camp. She feared punishment, which those days almost certainly would have meant death.[75] Such acts must have been common among foreign workers.

## V

It was not only the bombings that affected people at the home front. Fear and anxiety about the impact of an ever more likely German defeat became widespread after the Sixth Army's defeat at Stalingrad in early 1943, 'the greatest single blow of the war [to German morale]'.[76] Many people saw Stalingrad as a turning-point. Nazi propaganda had promised an imminent German victory over the Soviets there.[77] On 3 February 1943, a man from Hamburg noted in his diary: 'Stalingrad has been reconquered by the Russians... how was that possible? Why doesn't Hitler control the situation? Why does he let an enemy that is already defeated force him into such actions?'[78] And an SD report of 4 February noted: 'The report of the battle of Stalingrad's end has led to a great shock among the entire people.'[79] After the German defeat at Stalingrad and the Allied declaration at Casablanca to fight Nazi Germany until unconditional surrender, Nazi leaders demanded the total mobilization of Germany's economy and society, lest the war would be lost and Germany overrun by Bolshevik terror. The Nazis increasingly referred to their struggle to power during the Weimar Republic. Nazi leaders tried with some success to mobilize the various party organizations for propaganda purposes. Civilian defence was put under party control with the appointment of the party regional leaders as Reich Defence Commissioners. Goebbels and other Nazi leaders disseminated the view that winning the war was a possibility, if not a historical necessity, given that the Nazis had survived their bitter defeat on 9 November 1923 and had risen to power again by means of violent struggle.[80]

At that time, men began to kill themselves out of despair at Germany's run of defeats and fear of what would come after the fall of the Third Reich. On 10 February 1943, a few days after the battle of Stalingrad ended, 53-year-old senior civil servant and Regional Labour Leader Dr Kurt Leopold von F, a captain in the First World War, blew out his brains in his flat in Potsdam. F, probably afraid of being labelled a coward, justified his action in a suicide note, addressed to his father, a former general. The police perused his farewell missive and complained 'that he no longer believed in a German victory. He would have to kill his father, his wife and his daughter, he writes, when Bolshevism overwhelms us, ie the German *Volk*. There is no longer any doubt that this will happen, according to his note.'[81] In F's opinion, there was no doubt that the Bolsheviks would flood into Germany and rape his wife and daughter, in which case it would be his duty to shoot the women. Because of the defeatist impact that news of F's suicide might have on the German public, the criminal police kept its investigation secret and denounced F as mad, even as it forwarded the report to the Reich Security Head Office. Stalingrad prompted F's belief that he and his family lacked a future, and that he as a German officer would be required to maintain some sense of honour regarding his and his family's lives and bodies amidst the threat of a Soviet invasion. This case confirms, at least to some extent, the anti-Russian and anti-Bolshevik stereotypes keenly advocated by the Nazis, which built on a long tradition of German anti-Russian propaganda that went back to the First World War.[82] F's suicide was not an isolated response to the German defeat at Stalingrad. On 9 March 1943, Walter von D, a 60-year old retired major general, shot himself near Berlin. His wife told the criminal police that her husband had 'portrayed Germany's future in the blackest of colours and completely lost belief in a German victory'. The report went on, 'the person concerned no longer agreed with the state's leadership and he has always been an outsider, as is well known here'.[83]

Suicides reflecting despair at Germany's imminent defeat continued. Karl S, a 56-year-old teacher from Weissensee, a Northern district of Berlin, killed himself on 21 August 1943 after a failed suicide attempt, for which he feared being held accountable. Karl S was concerned about not being sent with his pupils to a child evacuation (*Kinderlandverschickung*) camp, a scheme designed to send children from 'areas threatened by air attack' to the countryside for six-month spells.[84] In his unusually long suicide note, addressed to his wife, he referred to his despondency about Germany's future and his fear of a Bolshevik victory:

Dear Mama!

The stupidity of tossing myself from the window because I wasn't going to be sent away with the children is something I only realized today because of its inevitable consequences. I stigmatized myself as a criminal, as my colleagues' behaviour after the fact proved. It happened in a moment of panic; I lost my nerves because until that moment, I firmly believed that I would be sent away with the children. Since this attempt will surely be reported and aside from being sacked I can also expect additional punishment, I can find no peace. Paranoia has overtaken me because I will probably be arrested by the police when the train with the children departs. I can no longer bear this kind of life. A happy life with you, dearest Inge, and with our most beloved daughter is also unthinkable because any possibility to make a decent living in the future no longer exists on account of the war, which appears to me a lost cause because of Bolshevism's invincibility and because America has entered on our enemies' side. The first and last reason for my despondency is that victory is a lost cause. Many, including you, don't think that the end will be so bad, and I envy you and from the bottom of my heart I wish that everything will go well for you and our little Elke without me. I thank you for all of the good things that you have done for me over the years. My unnatural death will cause you lots of sorrow and pain, but you'll overcome it and in a short while it will be all over. And besides, unnatural death seems to me hereditary, since too many of my relatives have chosen this path. Well, I bid you both farewell and for the last time, a heartfelt greeting from your unhappy daddy.[85]

Like many, Karl S was convinced that the Soviets and the Americans would defeat Germany. Karl S had clearly internalized Nazi ideas about the hereditary nature of suicide. The Nazi leadership condemned such politically motivated suicides, which they thought subversive and cowardly.

Soldiers afraid of fighting in a war that could not be won also committed suicide. Erich S, a 43-year-old Wehrmacht recruit, gassed himself in his flat in Brandenburg, a small town near Berlin on 26 April 1944. According to the police, who condemned his death as cowardly, he had committed suicide: 'Probably because he was afraid to be sent to the frontline.'[86] Similar cases were reported in the nearby town of Eberswalde, following the drafting of all men, aged between 16 and 60, into the *Volkssturm*, which had been established on 18 October 1944, the anniversary of the 1813 'Battle of Nations' in Leipzig against Napoleon.[87] On 1 February 1945, amidst the threat of the Soviet invasion of the area around Berlin, 47-year-old forest worker Erich D drowned himself after having cut his throat. The police investigation concluded that his suicide was due to his 'fear of being drafted into the *Volkssturm*'.[88] Nazi terror and fear thereof prompted many to commit suicide, especially after 1943. Nazi terror also affected ordinary people, as we have seen, and not only social outsiders and foreign workers. Many Germans worried at this time about surviving the war, rather than about ideological issues.[89] Public morale did not remain good until the war's end.[90] These powerful individual case studies suggest that the now fashionable argument of 'ordinary' Germans' collaboration and consent with the regime during wartime is deeply flawed. Ordinary people did not, unlike in liberal democracies, have a free choice between supporting or resisting the regime and the war. It is time for historians to overcome this 'voluntarist turn' and emphasize the crucial role of Nazi terror in keeping the German population at bay.[91]

# VI

Resistance towards Nazism revived during the war. In February 1942, the Gestapo exposed one of the largest communist resistance groups, the Uhrig group, and arrested its leaders Robert Uhrig and Josef Römer. Altogether, the Nazis arrested some 200 members across Germany. The police murdered sixteen of them before trial and at least 36 received death sentences. At around the same time, members of a communist group in Mannheim, the Lechleiter group, were also arrested. Nineteen members were sentenced to death. Two committed suicide.[92] There were also suicides within the Berlin communist resistance group the 'Red Orchestra'. Its members, among them Harro Schulze-Boysen, a first lieutenant in the Luftwaffe, Arvid Harnack, an official in the Reich Ministry of Economics, and their wives, Mildred Harnack-Fish and Libertas Schulze-Boysen, had been supplying the Soviets with military secrets. In late August 1942, the police began to arrest members of the 'Red Orchestra'. Altogether 139 men and women had been arrested by March 1943. The courts meted out death sentences on the overwhelming majority of them. Some of those arrested by the Nazis committed suicide because they did not want to betray their friends to the Gestapo under torture. At least three members of the 'Red Orchestra' attempted suicide in prison. During a Gestapo interrogation Walter Husemann jumped out of a window on the top floor. Hans Kummerow, another member, smashed his spectacles and swallowed the glass. He survived, and slit his wrists. Mildred Harnack-Fish, executed on 15 February 1943, is said to have attempted suicide by swallowing drawing pins.[93]

A wider but looser coalition of conservative groups and individuals tried to assassinate Hitler on 20 July 1944. Most of those involved in the assassination plot wanted to restore a pre-democratic Germany that would include recent German territorial acquisitions.[94] The military members of the resistance were very often characterized by a strong sense of honour and duty. On the night of 20 July 1944, Wehrmacht and SS troops loyal to Hitler put down the military insurrection in Berlin. General Ludwig Beck, one of the leaders of the putsch, asked General Fromm who had arrested him for permission to commit suicide instead of being shot. Fromm granted Beck his last wish, reflecting an old military tradition. Beck shot himself twice but survived, until Fromm ordered a soldier to finish him off.[95] Henning von Tresckow, chief of staff of the Second Army at the Eastern Front and one of the leaders of the plotters, killed himself on 21 July 1944 with a grenade, before the Nazis could arrest him.[96] Major von Oertzen, also complicit in the plot, committed suicide on the same day in a Wehrmacht barracks in Berlin. After flushing some compromising material down a lavatory, Oertzen managed to obtain two hand grenades, which were lying about on a corridor. He then asked for permission to go to the lavatory again. There, Oertzen exploded the first grenade. His guards thought him dead. A wounded Oertzen suddenly exploded the second grenade in his mouth. He died instantly.[97] On 28 July, Lieutenant-Colonel Werner Schrader committed suicide in his barracks in Zossen, near Berlin. His suicide note captures the feeling of many of those complicit in the plot: 'I won't go to gaol; I won't allow them to torture me.'[98]

Many more officers complicit in the plot committed suicide in the wake of 20 July 1944. In a powerful reminiscence of his service in the First World War, General Otto von Stülpnagel, Military Commander of France, also part of the plot, shot himself near the battlefield of Verdun. Generals loyal to Hitler had ordered him to report in Berlin. He survived, though blinded. The People's Court later sentenced him to death. He was hanged like most of the other survivors of the plot.[99] The Nazis accused Field Marshal Erwin Rommel of being disobedient to Hitler's orders and of being involved with the assassination attempt of 20 July 1944. They gave him the opportunity to kill himself by taking poison in late 1944 rather than being court-martialled. Rommel took the poison and received a state funeral. A court martial would have shed negative light on the Nazi regime, not least because Rommel was very popular.[100]

The Nazis persecuted members of the plot until the end of the war, as the following case reveals. On 10 March 1945, Baron Kurt von Plettenberg, a lawyer and estate manager of the Hohenzollern family, killed himself by jumping down the staircase of the Reich Security Head Office in Berlin.

The Gestapo had arrested him two days before, but they did not tell Plettenberg's friends and relatives how he died. The Nazis would have executed Plettenberg, so it is highly unlikely that they 'suicided' him. In the death register of the Kreuzberg district of Berlin, Plettenberg's death was officially classified as 'suicide by jumping from the 2nd floor of Prinz-Albrecht-Str 8.' Plettenberg, like Tresckow and others, did not want to betray his friends by telling the Nazis their names under torture.[101] Nazi terror therefore gave a new impetus to the military tradition of suicide out of honour in the aftermath of the failed 20 July plot.

## VII

As the war intensified and a German victory became increasingly unlikely, suicide levels rose within the armed forces.[102] Between 1 April 1939 and 30 September 1941, the army's Health Inspectorate (*Heeres-Sanitätsinspektion*) registered a total of 1,196 suicides. Between April and September 1943, there were at least 6,898 suicides within the army.[103] After the Allied invasion of France in the early summer of 1944, suicide levels rose within Luftwaffe units stationed there, according to a Luftwaffe circular of 1 August 1944 captured by the Allies. It complained, without giving any numbers: 'Since the beginning of the invasion, the number of suicides and attempted suicides has increased considerably.' The circular identified 'psychological burdens brought on by fighting, terror raids on the homeland and temporary cancellations of [soldiers'] vacations etc' as the likely motives.[104] Many soldiers were unable to cope with the stress of the war.

In May 1944, after several defeats of the German army on the Eastern and Southern Fronts, Martin Bormann, head of the party chancellery, sent a lengthy telegram to Heinrich Himmler's adjutant in which he complained that there were too many suicides within the Wehrmacht. In his telegram, Bormann demanded commitment from soldiers in a typically Nazi manner and asserted sovereignty over the bodies of every German. Bormann reiterated the views of Freisler and other Nazis on suicide and insisted: 'The life of the individual belongs to the *Volk*. Therefore, he may not voluntarily bring his life to an end. If he does it nevertheless, he forgets his duty vis-à-vis his *Volk*. This is particularly the case during the war.'[105] The Nazis thought that suicides of soldiers, and by implication, of civilians on the home front, were cowardly. According to the Nazis, suicides must be treated as acts of desertion, since people tended to justify them by cowardly motives such as 'fear of punishment' and 'nervous breakdowns'. The telegram continued to lament that 'investigations revealed that suicide was chosen even in circumstances in which brave fighting and tireless work for the *Volk* were still possible, more courageous and more honourable'. Those who had failed their suicide attempt were to be shot, according to Bormann, as they had violated their duty to the people's community (*Gemeinschaftspflicht*). While there is no evidence that this decree was implemented, its message was clear: soldiers and civilians must keep fighting until the last bullet. Deciding the fate of one's own life and body was only permissible under grave circumstances, such as when a soldier faced captivity. Reflecting Social-Darwinist notions of the survival of the fittest, the Nazis did not condemn the suicide of incurably ill or wounded soldiers. Nevertheless, anyone facing punishment had to show that 'he could atone for this deed only by bravely sacrificing his life for the entire *Volk* (*Volksganze*)', as they would relieve the body of the *Volk* of useless elements when they exterminated themselves. Bormann wrote a final draft of his anti-suicide decree on 17 July 1944.[106] By this time, the Allies had landed in France. He also endorsed the suicide of Germans facing 'Soviet captivity', whose survival might be a threat to the *Volk*. He implied that such suicides would be honourable and almost a duty. Bormann's decree neatly summarizes the major Nazis' views on suicide; Himmler 'fully agreed with it'.[107]

Bormann may have been thinking of General Friedrich Paulus's refusal to die what the Nazis considered a 'heroic' death in Stalingrad in February 1943. Hitler had appointed Paulus, the supreme commander of the Sixth Army in Stalingrad, a field marshal even though the battle of Stalingrad had already been lost in January 1943. Hitler had expected Paulus to kill himself by dying a heroic soldierly death in order to 'have freed himself from all sorrow and ascended into eternity and national immortality'.[108] Paulus did not kill himself, but surrendered to the Soviets. Hitler neither referred to *Selbstmord* or *Freitod* in this situation because he considered heroic suicide fundamentally different from the suicides of ordinary people, which he and the Nazis condemned. The minutes of Hitler's briefing with his generals on 1 February 1943 reveal Hitler's anger about Paulus's failure to die a 'heroic' death by shooting himself. Hitler thought that such a death would set a fine example for other soldiers facing similar situations in the war. The Nazis had long promoted the idea of heroic death, glorifying German casualties in the First World War as blood sacrifice, essential to Germany's rebirth.[109] Drawing upon the Roman model of Stoic suicide, Hitler shouted: 'The pistol—that's an easy one. How cowardly to shrink back in fear of such a thing! Hah! Better to let oneself be buried alive! And in such a situation where he knew completely that his death was the precondition for holding out in the next redoubt...'[110]

Dismissing Paulus and his staff as cowards, Hitler was worried about the effect of Paulus's capture by the Soviets on the morale of ordinary soldiers: 'I am really hurt by this because the heroism of so many soldiers is wiped out by a single, characterless weakling...' Furthermore, Hitler found it unacceptable and disgraceful that a German officer surrendered his life and body to the Bolshevik sub-humans who would put him into a 'rat cage', where he would be forced under torture to tell secrets.[111]

Other top Nazis agreed with Hitler's views on heroic death. On 1 February 1943, Goebbels, still uncertain about Paulus's fate, noted in his diary: 'In light of the situation, his [Paulus's] only option is an honourable soldier's death.' On 2 February, Goebbels voiced his worries about Paulus's failure to kill himself. Concerned with the impact on German morale of Paulus being captured by the Soviets, he opined: 'Based on Colonel Martin, I can tell how this news affects army officers. He is deeply depressed and declares that it is almost time to take off his uniform.'[112] Hitler and Goebbels were also concerned over Paulus being put on trial by the Soviets. In fact, what happened was possibly even worse for Hitler and Goebbels. Paulus went with 90,000 German survivors of Stalingrad into Soviet captivity, where he became active in the National Committee Free Germany (*Nationalkomitee Freies Deutschland*), a communist union of German soldiers that aimed for an unconditional German surrender and prepared anti-Nazi propaganda. Only released in 1953, Paulus settled in East Germany, where he died in 1957.[113]

The Nazis encouraged 'heroic' death and fighting until the bitter end, but resented suicide as an act of resignation or surrender. Nazi concerns over suicide as a cowardly act found expression in an article in *Das Schwarze Korps*, the SS journal, on 30 November 1944. While we do not know whether suicide rates were rising at this time, this article's publication at a time when the Nazis had almost certainly lost the war was significant. The article insisted: 'We don't believe that the individual human being controls his own fate; his *Volk* does. He does not have the right to withdraw from the *Volk* as long as he is able to benefit the *Volk* and harm the enemy.' The article furthermore dismissed suicide as typical of bourgeois values which the Nazis wanted to eliminate: 'In the bourgeois world, suicide played the strange moral role as a kind of overarching indulgence.' It warned: 'The *Volk* that will experience the future is not the one that has the most suicides on its honour rolls, but rather the *Volk* whose unyielding men bridge the abyss with their sense of duty, responsibility, loyalty and honour.'[114] In 1945, top Nazis would not follow this exhortation, however, as we shall see.

Nazi discourse emphasized that the individual did not have the right to suicide. A Wehrmacht guideline on the burying of dead soldiers from 1937 reflected this idea. The order insisted: 'Members of the armed services who have committed suicide must not be buried in the fields of honour. They are to be interred elsewhere in the cemetery ...'[115] And the names of soldiers who had died by their own hand must not be given to the Nazi party because their names were not to be read aloud in 'party ceremonies honouring heroes'.[116]

If soldiers committed suicide for reasons which Wehrmacht psychiatrists deemed unjustified, such as 'cowardice' or their inability to adapt to front-line duty, Wehrmacht authorities usually refused paying a pension to suicides' relatives under the regulations on War Service Damage (*Wehrdienstbeschädigung*). Wehrmacht authorities awarded pensions only to 40 per cent of all suicides whose cases were examined by the psychiatrists of the German army.[117] Leading army psychiatrists agreed that soldiers did not have the right to commit suicide. Like Gottfried Benn, they also saw suicides as acts of cowardice or inherited weakness. In-house psychiatrists examined the cases, using character references written by the superiors of the suicidal soldiers.

Towards the war's end, there were tendencies within the Nazi leadership to ban suicide, an endeavour that had failed in the mid-1930s, although the Wehrmacht leadership had already been denouncing suicides as cowards. In 1942, the supreme command of the Wehrmacht decreed: 'Suicide during the war is desertion. During war, the life of the soldier belongs to the fatherland alone, which needs it for its protection. No soldier has the right to dispose freely of his life.' Reflecting Nazi discourses on suicide, the circular dismissed soldiers' suicide motives as 'cowardice or weak will'.[118]

Some of the cases examined by Wehrmacht psychiatrists, usually professors of psychiatry who had been drafted into the army, have survived in the archives. In Berlin, Max de Crinis, a Nazi involved in the euthanasia murders and holder of the chair in psychiatry at the Charité hospital, was in charge of examining psychiatric disorders and suicides of soldiers within the Third Military District Command (*Wehrkreiskommando III*).[119] Here, superiors of suicidal soldiers had openly blamed the increasingly terrible circumstances on the Eastern Front. The murders of partisans, Jews, and Soviet civilians, not to mention increasing German casualties, caused so much unbearable stress for some soldiers that they could not see any other way out than to shoot themselves. De Crinis usually dismissed such motives and rejected any pension claims, since he thought such suicides cowards, unable to face the reality of total war. One case from de Crinis's files is particularly striking. When the 44-year-old second lieutenant Max B shot himself on 30 May 1942, de Crinis, rather surprisingly, recognized his widow's pension claim. The medical certificate read:

> His superiors speculated that B probably took to heart the many shootings of partisans and gypsies that he had to lead; [and] that he ended his life in a state of mental derangement. Since there is nothing negative from the point of view of heredity, one can safely assume that B fell into a reactive depression as a consequence of the particular effect of the military situation in which he ended his life.

As in many other cases, the report of B's superior presumably influenced de Crinis's judgement.[120] Recent research on the 'crimes of the Wehrmacht' has shown that no German soldier was shot for refusing to participate in the crimes of the Wehrmacht at the Eastern Front. However, some people like B, who obediently carried out mass executions, were so upset by doing so that they went on to shoot themselves.[121]

In Hamburg, the psychiatrist Hans Bürger-Prinz, like de Crinis also notorious for his involvement in euthanasia murders, was in charge of issuing psychiatric certificates for soldiers of the Tenth Military District Command (*Wehrkreiskommando X*). Reflecting wider psychiatric and medical discourses on suicide, Bürger-Prinz thought that suicides of soldiers, even if they were not acts of cowardice, resulted above all from inherited psychiatric disorders, not from wider social circumstances. He too rejected most claims for pensions; in fact, most of the suicides he examined had supposedly been prompted by 'fear of punishment', when soldiers were afraid of the draconian punishments meted out by Wehrmacht courts for indiscipline, disobedience, and even for minor offences such as returning late from leave.[122] In a medical certificate on behalf of Friedrich F, a reserve captain who had committed suicide, Bürger-Prinz wrote on 11 January 1943:

> According to the files, there have not been any mental problems in F's family ... he was a member of the 6th Army. F eagerly dedicated himself to his duty; he was conscientious, calm, modest ... He was very depressed by his experiences of Stalingrad and fixated on them so strongly that he was no longer interested in art, the hobby he otherwise loved passionately. The presumed motives for F's depressive turn: the experiences of Stalingrad can only be regarded as a secondary motive for his depressed mental situation ... In this particular situation, military events cannot be presumed to be the cause. However, a special case can be made here because of his good character, his earlier participation in the First World War and the extended duration of his deployment ... [123]

As a Nazi, who did not want to blame F's death on Hitler's eventually suicidal strategy at Stalingrad, Bürger-Prinz would not recognize F's front-line experiences as a primary suicide motive. Effectively, F had been suffering from a psychiatric disorder, but the positive references to his war service in the First World War ensured that Bürger-Prinz would make a special case for F's relatives receiving a pension.[124]

As the German armies lost one battle after another, Hitler and the Nazi leadership realized that a German victory would be impossible. Hitler and the Nazis constantly radicalized the war as a result up to the point of self-destruction. Contrary to a widespread interpretation, Hitler and the Nazis did not merely lose their sense of reality. For the Nazis, victory became a secondary matter. They were more concerned with 'bloodshed, racism and death'.[125] If the war could not be won, then the Nazis wanted at least to destroy totally their racial and political enemies. Even in total defeat, they believed, heroic self-sacrifice could set a precedent for future generations to keep fighting the Jews and the Bolsheviks.[126]

Goebbels considered the use of suicide missions as heroic precedent for Germans to keep fighting. The concept of suicide missions of the German Luftwaffe originated with Albert Speer in late 1943, one year before the Japanese began to use *kamikaze* airplanes.[127] Unlike in Japan, where suicide was generally an acceptable and honourable way to die, suicide was, of course, a Christian taboo in Germany. Nazi demands for suicide missions reflected not only Nazi notions of total mobilization, but also Nazi disregard for Christian ethics. Speer suggested that manned airplanes should bomb a dam near Moscow, which was out of the range of German planes unless the pilots went on a one-way mission. In May 1944, Speer suggested such missions (*Totaleinsatz*) to Hitler. Goebbels's diaries confirm Speer's suggestion and reveal his enthusiasm for this radical strategy.[128] According to Goebbels, Speer suggested on 29 August 1944 to man the *V 1*, a flying bomb used since summer 1944 for attacking Belgium and south-eastern England. Goebbels noted in his dairy: 'The *V 1* weapon is to be manned by a special squadron that will fly to its death into the English fleet at Scapa Flow. One might thereby achieve great successes. The members of the death squadrons, who apparently signed up voluntarily and in great numbers, are already being trained.'[129]

The SS also shared this idea of total mobilization. In November 1944, the SS paper *Das Schwarze Korps* propagated the idea of heroic self-sacrifice. It printed the unsolicited letter of Bernhard B, a young Wehrmacht sergeant, who volunteered for deployment on a manned torpedo. His unit rejected his application, allegedly because too many soldiers had already volunteered for suicide missions, as the SS journal was only too pleased to note. Asking *Das Schwarze Korps* for help to get into a suicide unit, B declared: 'Please don't think that you are dealing with someone who was tired of life or that sorrow or despair drove me to take this step... My brother fell on the Eastern front in 1941. If you ask me for the reason for my behaviour, I can only reply: "Because I am German." Heil Hitler!' Predictably, *Das Schwarze Korps* welcomed B's implication that it was every German's duty to sacrifice himself for the fatherland. To underline the point, it reprinted B's concluding sentence twice on the same page.[130]

Goebbels's enthusiasm for suicide missions continued, as a German victory became more and more unlikely. On 30 December 1944, Goebbels wrote in his diary: 'Self-sacrifice should now be applied on a large scale in the German Wehrmacht's struggle. There is a vast amount of young men in the German *Volk* who are prepared to die for the Fatherland a certain death, a symbol of the German youth's high and unshakeable fighting spirit.'[131] In March 1945, when German defeat was certain, Hitler agreed with Goebbels's plan to send 300 fighter planes on suicide missions against Allied bomber planes. Eventually, Goebbels himself was disappointed with the failure of this mission.[132] There is some evidence that the Luftwaffe flew self-sacrifice missions against Soviet bridges across the River Oder in April 1945. Thirty-five pilots of the *Leonidas* squadron, based in Jüterbog, near Berlin, allegedly died after destroying two bridges. Before their mission, pilots reportedly signed a declaration, saying 'I am above all clear that the mission will end in my death.'[133] Indeed, many of these pilots were Nazi fanatics who had volunteered for the self-sacrifice mission.[134] The concept of self-sacrifice (*Selbstaufopferung*) fundamentally differed from *Selbstmord*, which the Nazis condemned as a cowardly action, as noted earlier. Dying a soldier's death was more dignified than negotiating for peace, the Nazis thought.[135] The notion of self-sacrifice would feature very prominently in 1945, as we will see in the next chapter.

# 5

# Downfall

I

In the spring of 1945 the Third Reich met its end in a massive wave of suicides. We know little about this unprecedented suicide epidemic and its origins. Suicide was an extreme reaction to the decline and fall of the Nazi regime and to Allied occupation. The war's final period from July 1944 until May 1945 was by far the most lethal and violent one for Germans. More German soldiers and civilians died than in all the previous years of war put together.[1] Nevertheless, suicide, violence of individual Germans directed against themselves, does not feature in debates on the public memory of the Second World War. Instead, debates on public memory focus on other acts of violence that Germans experienced towards the end of war, such as rape, mass Allied bombings, and expulsion from the East, not to mention the massively destructive and aggressive policies of the Nazis. This silence is perhaps because suicide is a topic that does not easily allow for simplistic and moralizing views of Germans as victims and others, including the Allies, as perpetrators, or the other way round.[2]

The suicides which occurred in Germany before the Nazi regime's downfall had in common a general feeling of insecurity and the lack of a future perspective. Contemporary observers such as Thomas Mann shared the view that the Nazi suicides were acts of raw cowardice. On 23 April 1945 Mann wrote in his diary at his home in Pacific Palisades what the American media had reported about events in Germany that were geographically distant, but emotionally close to him. He was quite happy about 'the many suicides among the Nazi bigwigs, finally...'.[3] When he learned of Hitler's death by suicide in the bunker of the Reich Chancellery on 30 April 1945, the American journalist William L Shirer, who had lived as a correspondent in Berlin until 1941, declared: 'In fact, I have always been certain myself that that was what he would do in the end', thereby seeing the Third Reich as an ultimately suicidal regime.[4] Another contemporary observer, the Norwegian correspondent Theo Findahl, who witnessed the decline and fall of the Third Reich in Berlin, suggested that the end of the Nazi regime directly confirmed what Hermann Rauschning, one of the early analysts of the Third Reich, had written in 1938, namely that Nazism was a directionless revolution of nihilism, that would end in 1945 in self-destruction and total chaos. This basic diagnosis was correct, even if it lacked precision.[5]

Hitler, for one, was not unfamiliar with suicide. It affected him personally several times. In September 1931, Hitler's niece Geli Raubal died in his Munich flat. Accounts of Raubal's death differ. One author claims, based upon an eyewitness account, that Geli's death was an accident, not least because there was no suicide note.[6] Since only relatively few suicides leave farewell missives, as we have seen, this assessment is not altogether convincing. The police investigation of Geli's death revealed that Geli shot herself. Saddened by her death, Hitler soon considered leaving politics, and reportedly contemplated killing himself as well. Eva Braun, his new lover, shot herself in November 1932. She survived. As with many deliberate non-lethal suicide attempts, Braun's act was probably a 'cry for help' to force Hitler to care for her. Her second 'suicide' attempt in 1935, when she allegedly overdosed on sleeping pills, did not happen; it appears in Braun's 'diary' which is a forgery.[7] In December 1932, when Gregor Strasser, pleading for a Nazi toleration of the conservative von Schleicher cabinet, challenged Hitler's supreme authority as leader of the Nazi party, Hitler, ostensibly nervous and furious, is said to have threatened: 'If the Party falls to pieces, I shall end it all in three minutes with the pistol.'[8]

According to Sebastian Haffner, writing in 1940, Hitler was 'the potential suicide *par excellence*', able to risk everything, including his life 'to preserve or magnify his power'.[9] Suicide was always an option for Hitler, who was trying to follow the Roman example in which failed leaders fell on their swords. Indeed, in his Reichstag speech on 1 September 1939, the day Germany attacked Poland, Hitler prophesied that in the event of defeat, he was ready to make any sacrifice, including suicide. After demanding total sacrifice from the German people, he declared: 'I now wish to be nothing other than the first soldier of the German Reich. Therefore I have put on that tunic which has always been the most holy and dear to me.

I shall not take it off again until after victory is ours, or—I shall not live to see the day!'[10] Suicide in the event of defeat was already on his mind. Hitler's personal suicidal tendencies probably reflected a wider problem of the Nazi dictatorship, namely the inability of a form of government based largely upon Hitler's 'charismatic authority' to reproduce itself or to attain 'normality' or routine. The longer the Third Reich lasted, the more it destroyed all routine patterns of government and the more expansionist and destructive it became, culminating in self-destruction in 1945. As Ian Kershaw has shown, Hitler's 'charismatic authority' linked 'the social motivations which forged the bonds with Hitler, the peculiar expression of personalised power that was a chief characteristic of the form of political domination in the Third Reich, and the destructive dynamic of Nazism'. Unlike the Soviet Union which did not break down after Stalin's death, the Third Reich was, therefore, doomed to collapse with Hitler's death.[11]

In 1943, the psychoanalyst Walter C Langer analysed Hitler's mind in a study commissioned by the American Office of Strategic Services. Langer too suggested that Hitler would commit suicide. He prophesied:

> Not only has he frequently threatened to commit suicide, but from what we know of his psychology it is the most likely possibility ... In all probability, however, it would not be a simple suicide. He has much too much of the dramatic for that, and since immortality is one of the dominant motives we can imagine that he would stage the most dramatic and effective death scene he could possibly think of. He knows how to bind the people to him, and if he cannot have the bond in life he will certainly do his utmost to achieve it in death ...[12]

His basic prediction was correct, even if the psychological trimmings were not. When a German victory became increasingly unlikely, Hitler characterized suicide as a straightforward option at a military briefing on 30 August 1944: 'It's only (the fraction) of a second. Then one is redeemed of everything and finds tranquillity and eternal peace.'[13] On 30 April 1945, when the military situation had become totally hopeless and Soviet troops were progressing towards the Reich Chancellery, Hitler killed himself together with Eva Braun, whom he had married a few hours earlier in his bunker.[14] Other top Nazis were hardly surprised when they heard about Hitler's suicide. Göring declared during an interrogation in October 1945: 'We always knew that the Fuehrer would kill himself if things were coming to an end. We always knew that. There is not the least doubt about it.'[15]

Many Nazis committed suicide in 1945. Along with Hitler, top Nazis like Joseph Goebbels and Heinrich Himmler all committed suicide. Bernhard Rust, Reich Minister of Education, killed himself on 8 May 1945. Himmler committed suicide in Allied captivity. He bit into a capsule of potassium cyanide which he had carried in his mouth at an interrogation centre near Lüneburg on 23 May 1945 after the British had identified him and had ordered him to strip naked. A British eyewitness complained about Himmler's easy death, given the crimes he committed.[16] Reich Minister of Justice Thierack, responsible for the radicalization of the German legal system described in the previous chapter, killed himself in a British internment camp in October 1946.[17] Field Marshal Walter Model, a Nazi who had declared his loyalty to Hitler after the failed assassination attempt of 20 July 1944, shot himself in a forest near Düsseldorf in late April 1945. He did so to avoid surrender.[18]

When hearing the news of Hitler's death, some Nazis reportedly committed suicide immediately, thereby following their leader into death. Goebbels, Hitler's official successor as Reich Chancellor, had his children poisoned before requesting a SS guard to shoot his wife and himself. In a letter on 28 April 1945 to his stepson Harald Quandt, Goebbels claimed that his death would set a heroic precedent for a new Germany which would 'survive this war, but only if it has precedents at hand on which it can lean itself'.[19] Suicide figures among the party and SS top echelons were staggering. Eight out of 41 party regional leaders who held office between 1926 and 1945 and 7 out of 47 higher SS and police leaders committed suicide, followed by an unknown number of lower Nazi officials. For these Nazis, life was impossible after the Third Reich's downfall. Fear of Allied retribution and the notion of self-sacrifice may well have motivated these suicides. In the Army's top echelons, suicide was also widespread, perhaps because of the Army's complicity with Nazi crimes. According to a 1950 statistic, 53 out of 554 army generals, 14 out of 98 Luftwaffe generals and 11 out of 53 admirals killed themselves.[20]

Upon learning of Hitler's death *Gauleiter* Jakob Sprenger of Hesse-Nassau and his wife committed suicide on 8 May 1945 in the Tyrol, a region where many leading Nazis had fled.[21] On the same day, Nazi Germany unconditionally surrendered to the Allies. Some top Nazis immediately committed suicide. Josef Terboven, *Gauleiter* of Essen and Reich Commissioner in occupied Norway, committed suicide in a spectacular way on 8 May 1945, detonating 50 kilograms of dynamite in his bunker.

Wilhelm Rediess, higher SS and police leader in Norway, shot himself in Oslo on the same day. Odilo Globocnik, responsible for the mass murder of Jews in occupied Eastern Europe, bit on a cyanide capsule on 31 May 1945 in Austria after the British had captured him. Rudolf Höss, formerly commandant of Auschwitz, claimed in his autobiography, written whilst he was awaiting trial in Cracow in 1946, that upon hearing of Hitler's death he immediately thought of committing suicide together with his wife and children in northern Germany. Höss emphasized his loyalty to Hitler as well as his fear of being prosecuted by the Allies for the unparalleled crimes he had committed. He declared:

> On our escape we heard on a farm that the Führer was dead. Upon hearing this, my wife and I simultaneously thought: Now we have to go, too! With the Führer being dead, our world had also fallen. Did it make any sense to live? We would be persecuted and searched for everywhere. We wanted to take poison...

He went on to claim in a rather unconvincing manner that he and his wife decided 'for our children's sake' not to do it.[22] In Berchtesgaden, home to Hitler's alpine residence, some Nazis listening to the radio broadcast of Hitler's death in a pub supposedly went outside and shot themselves.[23]

Some Nazi suicides interpreted their deaths as fighting Judaeo-Bolshevism until the last bullet. At his last meeting with the *Gauleiter*, on 24 February 1945, Hitler insisted:

> What this Jewish pest does to our women, children and men in these areas is the cruellest fate that a human brain is capable of concocting. There is only one way of opposing this Jewish-Bolshevik extermination of mankind (*Völkervernichtung*) and its west European and American pimps: the deployment with utmost zeal and dogged steadfastness of all the strength a merciful God allows man to find in the most difficult times in the defence of his life. Whatever becomes weak must fade away.[24]

Hitler decided that the German people were not worthy to survive. Speer claimed that Hitler told him on the night of 18 March 1945:

> If the war is lost, then the *Volk* will also be lost. This fate is unavoidable ... After all, the *Volk* would then have proved the weaker nation, and the future would exclusively belong to the strongest nation of the east. What would remain after this fight would in any event be inferior subjects, since all the good ones would have fallen.[25]

On 19 March 1945, Hitler decreed that the German infrastructure must be destroyed so as not to hand it over to the Allies. The Nazi regime and the civil administration slowly disintegrated. Now that total victory was impossible, 'at least defeat could be total', as one historian perceptively noted.[26] Dying a soldier's death was more dignified than negotiating for peace. The significance of dying a violent death dated back to the initial period of the party's struggle for power (*Kampfzeit*) and the experience of 1918, which had led to an idealization of the soldier's death in Nazi discourse, such as in the Nazi cult of Horst Wessel. This corresponded with Nazi notions of a distinctly masculine way of dying. In this way, the suicides of Nazi leaders in 1945 were not understood as suicides as such, but as heroic self-sacrifices undertaken for the future of the Nazi creed.[27]

The author Wilhelm Pleyer penned a lengthy propaganda article, entitled 'Risk of One's Life', along these lines on 28 March 1945 in the *Völkischer Beobachter*. He claimed that 'to risk one's life does not merely mean to die, but also to really stand up for a cause...and the desire to sacrifice one's personal existence'.[28] Pleyer wanted to encourage people not to give up resisting the Allied enemies. 'Self-sacrifice' rather than cowardly surrendering was the way to maintain one's 'honour', the same newspaper claimed on 16 April 1945.[29] Likewise, in the most expensive German colour film hitherto made, *Kolberg* (1945), for which Goebbels had written most of the dialogue himself, the people of Kolberg, a town in Pomerania which had allegedly not surrendered to Napoleon in 1806/07, served as a heroic precedent for Germans facing an ever more hopeless military situation. Only a stoic attitude and a readiness to sacrifice oneself could thus lead to the final victory.[30]

In a way that strongly characterized the Nazi regime's final months, the self-historicization of the Nazi leaders drew upon references to famous heroic deaths in history. Goebbels is said to have read out passages from Carlyle's history of Frederick the Great to Hitler in the bunker. In these passages, Frederick the Great contemplated suicide by poisoning himself when the military situation had seemed hopeless to the Prussians in 1757 during the Seven Years War.[31] In a radio speech, Goebbels claimed on 28 February 1945 that Frederick the Great had only known 'victory or death'. In the same broadcast, circulated in most German newspapers on 1 March 1945, Goebbels alluded to the Stoic heroism of Roman leaders who had preferred to die rather than surrender their lives and bodies to the ruler's mercy.

Anticipating his wife's and his own suicide and the murder of his children, Goebbels declared that he 'would not find it worthwhile to live...neither for his children nor for all those whom I loved', but would prefer, if Germany were defeated, 'cheerfully to throw away his life'.[32] Thus, Roman political suicide and not the highly-ritualized voluntary suicides of the Japanese Allies served as a seeming precedent for Nazi leaders. According to rumours circulating among diplomats of those few states still represented in Berlin, Goebbels had glorified suicide at a press conference on 3 March. A conservative German diplomat allegedly commented upon Goebbels's speech dryly: 'The Nazi leadership could long ago have set a good precedent by doing away with themselves. That would have been a blessing for Germany and the world.'[33]

Nazi leaders thought that suicide or rather 'heroic self-sacrifice' allowed them to retain a sense of honour, separating them from the bulk of a German population increasingly unwilling to continue fighting. It placed them in control of the decision of when and how to die. Hitler and other Nazi leaders did not see their suicides as acts of despair.[34] Hitler thought of his decision to stay in the bunker and die by his own hand as honourable in contrast to 'cowardly escape or even surrender' and as a heroic precedent for German troops to keep fighting. In his political testament of 30 April 1945, he blamed the Jews for unleashing the Second World War and portrayed his imminent suicide as an act of heroic self-sacrifice.[35] He insisted:

> May it become, at some future time, part of the code of honour of the German officer, as it is already in our Navy, that the surrender of a district or of a town is impossible, and that the leaders here, above all, must march ahead as shining examples, faithfully fulfilling their duty unto death.[36]

A radio broadcast on 1 May 1945 claimed that Hitler had died in action, 'fighting for Germany until the last gasp'.[37]

But not all Nazi suicides staged their deaths as acts of heroic self-sacrifice. Robert Ley, the Labour Front leader, killed himself in the Nuremberg gaol on 24 October 1945. He had been indicted on all four counts put forward by the International Military Tribunal trial. Rather than trying to die a heroic death, Ley was desperate, as the way in which he died reveals. He strangled himself with a towel that he had attached to the cistern of his lavatory. He regarded himself as a 'German and a National Socialist', as he wrote in a letter to his lawyer on the day of his suicide, 'but not a criminal'.[38] Unlike Ley, Göring, the other Nazi leader who committed suicide in

Nuremberg, did not try to shirk his responsibility for Nazi crimes. He was completely unrepentant. As the Allied interrogation protocols show, Göring did not believe in the legitimacy of the Tribunal, and thought that the Allies were trying to take revenge on the Nazi leadership. When the Tribunal condemned him to death by hanging instead of death by firing squad, as he had demanded, Göring committed suicide on the night before his execution on 15 October 1946 by taking cyanide (there is no certainty over whether he had hidden the poison in his cell or whether a guard had supplied him with it). Death by hanging was a method of execution traditionally associated with dishonour and disgrace.[39] Allegedly, he told his wife at their farewell meeting 'you may be sure of one thing...they won't hang me...no, they won't hang me'.[40] Less grandiose motives for suicide should not be underestimated. Hitler and some other Nazis were aware of the unheroic death of Mussolini and his mistress, who had been shot by partisans and were then hung upside-down in public in Milan on 29 April 1945.[41] Hannah Arendt's essay on 'Organized Guilt' written in November 1944 prophesied that those responsible for war crimes and mass killings 'would not go the way of rebellion, but of suicide—just as many have gone already in Germany, where there is apparently one suicide wave after another...'.[42] There was, of course, a notable lack of guilt among the top Nazi leaders, but fear of retribution may well have prompted their suicides.

## II

In the weeks preceding the German surrender, suicide became almost a routine phenomenon in Germany, as a report written by the SS security service (SD) in March 1945 suggests: 'Many are coming round to the idea of doing away with themselves' and 'suicide in sheer despair at the certainty of approaching catastrophe is the order of the day'.[43] Suddenly, suicide lost its status as an extraordinary act, and was even discussed at a service in the Berlin Kaiser Wilhelm Memorial Church in early March 1945. Here, Gerhard Jacobi, the local pastor, spoke out against suicide as an immoral act, for which in his view only the Nazis were to blame. He told Jacob Kronika, a Danish correspondent:

> The danger of a suicide epidemic exists. Again and again I am sought out by members of my parish, who confide in me that they have secured cyanide.

They see no way out. The person chiefly responsible for the increase in suicidal tendencies is Dr Goebbels. He drummed it into the people that the Russians will bring hell in their wake. These horror stories have certainly had their impact. All Berliners know that the Russians will soon be in Berlin, and they see no alternative—other than cyanide.[44]

Jacobi's vivid illustration of the danger of a suicide epidemic nevertheless foretold the way in which members of the Soviet army would indeed behave in Germany. Many suicides did indeed occur in the immediate context of the approaching front, preceding the mass suicides of the Nazi elite. Nazi propaganda had exhorted Germans to hold out and keep fighting the 'Bolshevik-Mongol hordes'. On 26 April, the *Panzerbär*, a Nazi propaganda news-sheet for German soldiers, sketched a horrific scenario that Germans would have to face in case they lost the war. One captured Soviet major had allegedly said: 'We'll work the German scum until they croak.'[45] (Nazi propaganda did not mention, of course, that the Germans had done the same, and worse, to the Soviets.) The Nazi demonization of the Red Army, including for example eyewitness accounts of Bolshevik atrocities in Nemmersdorf, a village in East Prussia, in October 1944, helped to create a suicidal atmosphere.[46] In a leaflet distributed in February 1945 in Bohemia, Nazi propaganda claimed that if the 'Bolshevik murderer-pack' were victorious, 'incredible hatred, looting, hunger, shots in the back of the neck, deportation and extermination' would follow immediately. In an appeal to the prowess of German men, the leaflet demanded from German men *'to save German women and girls from defilement and slaughter by the Bolshevik bloodhounds.'*[47]

Red Army soldiers did indeed commit crimes such as the rape of German women, beginning in East Prussia in early 1945, and continuing towards the west as the Red Army advanced.[48] Margret Boveri, a journalist who documented the impact of the war's end on German women in a diary, described on 3 May 1945 the failed suicides of German girls who had been raped by Red Army soldiers. Her very sober style suggests that rape, like suicide, had become a normal phenomenon by this time: 'Afterward they were totally shattered, would happily have poisoned themselves, but had no poison; they found razor blades and wanted to slit their wrists, but for whatever reason, put it off.'[49]

Many women committed suicide in anticipation of being raped by Red Army soldiers or afterwards. Numbers vary considerably and are unreliable because many women did not report these sexual attacks and many women were raped repeatedly. Some historians suggest that Soviet soldiers raped up to 1.9 million German women at the end of the war. In Berlin alone, Red Army soldiers raped between 20,000 and 100,000 German women. Probably more than 10,000 Berlin women died in the aftermath of being raped, often by suicide.[50] The 17-year-old Lieselotte G from Friedrichshagen, an eastern suburb of Berlin, committed to her diary on 29 April 1945, a few days after the Soviet occupation of her suburb:

> On the first day, about one hundred suicides in Friedrichshagen are said to have occurred. It's a blessing that there is no gas supply, otherwise some more people would have killed themselves. We might perhaps also be dead. I was so desperate!...My German Fatherland had to come to this, now that we have been handed over, without any rights, to the powers of foreigners.[51]

Like Lieselotte G, many Germans in the eastern parts could not cope with Soviet occupation. After all, Nazi propaganda had claimed that the Soviets were subhuman beings. Carrying cyanide capsules was common in the months around the end of war; in Berlin, for example, the local health authority allegedly distributed capsules of postassium cyanide and women carried razor blades in their handbags. In some cases, people were anxious to store cyanide in the right way to ensure that it would not lose its lethal effect, as Boveri noted later with some surprise. Since Boveri's own dose of cyanide had not been recently renewed, she would not have died, as she later admitted.[52] Hitler allegedly gave cyanide pills to his secretaries as a farewell gift; and members of the Hitler Youth are said to have distributed poison to the audience of the last concert of the Berlin Philharmonic on 12 April 1945.[53] Though these reports may be exaggerated they nevertheless capture the subjective feeling among many Germans that everything was coming to an end.

In the Tempelhof district of Berlin, the wife of an old professor committed suicide by taking sleeping pills immediately after the Soviets arrived in late April 1945, as their landlady later remembered.[54] On 5 May 1945, the journalist Ruth Andreas-Friedrich wrote in her diary about the shock of Germans about the Red Army's arrival: 'I shudder. For four years Goebbels told us that the Russians would rape us. That they would rape and plunder, murder and pillage...'[55] Many other women committed suicide because they were afraid of being raped. Take the case of Hanna von B. She poisoned her eight-year-old daughter and then swallowed an overdose of sleeping pills in February 1945 in the upper-middle-class Lichterfelde suburb. Her husband, a captain in the Wehrmacht, testified: 'The news that the Russians had reached the Oder depressed my wife greatly. She feared that she and her child would fall into Russian hands. She told me often that she would end her life before that happened.'[56]

Any suicide raises the question of the relationship between a suicide and those left behind. One historian argues that suicide in 1945 was 'not only a consequence of fear and despair, but... also of anger and hatred', and that these two emotions reflected the psychological breakdown of German society.[57] But this point is hard to verify, as the case of Hanna von B suggests. In her suicide note, she expressed her love towards her husband; she did not express any feelings of anger or hatred towards him: 'My dear good one, dad... We won't change plans any more, daddy, and my only wish is to put this plan into practice very calmly for Peterl's [her daughter's] sake. We love you very much...'[58] Hanna probably felt that her husband was unable to protect their daughter and herself from the invading Russians.[59] Many Berliners vividly recorded the suicidal atmosphere of the early months of 1945. Hertha von Gebhardt, from the middle-class Wilmersdorf suburb, noted in her diary on 26 April 1945, as the battle for Berlin still raged, that 'Frau K [is] totally fragile, and wants to take her own life. We keep trying to make sure that she does not run outside.'[60]

Allied bombings continued to affect the everyday lives of ordinary people until the surrender. Many Berliners killed themselves after losing their property during some of the very heavy air raids on Berlin in 1945. In the chaotic context of 1945, the Allied bombings had an even more profound impact on German morale than before. On 31 March 1945, for example, the 39-year-old Erna M jumped to her death off the landing on the fourth floor of a staircase. Her husband had gone missing in action on the Eastern Front and she had lost her flat in Pankow, in north-eastern Berlin, in a bombing raid. Blaming the Allies for Erna's suicide, the criminal police noted: 'The deceased became melancholic over recent events... then her flat was totally destroyed in one of the last terror raids. She lost everything.'[61] In Hamburg, heavily bombed in 1943, as we have seen, the 67-year-old pensioner Hermann P shot himself on 15 February 1945. The police investigation revealed that he had told his wife: 'I just wanted to see whether the pistol is working... If the house caught fire during a bombing, and I did not have the opportunity to get out of the flat, I would not want to burn alive, as you will understand.'[62]

Suicide levels reached a clear maximum in Berlin in April 1945. At the climax of the battle of Berlin, no fewer than 3,881 people killed themselves. The suicide rate was at an approximate 242.7 per 100,000 population: that is, approximately five times higher than in the previous years.[63] Altogether, 7,057 suicides were reported in Berlin in 1945, an underestimate, given the administrative chaos that accompanied German defeat. There is no reliable or more precise statistical breakdown of these numbers concerning the age and sex of the suicides. According to one source, however, 3,996 women and 3,091 men committed suicide, turning upside down the traditional pattern of more men than women committing suicide.[64] Mass rape is the obvious explanation for this, along with the fact that a high proportion of men were either dead, at the front, or in captivity. Drawing wider conclusions merely from statistics about motivations for suicide is difficult, if not impossible.

# III

In order to understand the suicide epidemic, we must turn our attention to individual cases. Individual cases have survived in the files of the Berlin general state prosecutor and the criminal police. These institutions were hardly politically neutral and probably receptive of the Nazi idea of heroic 'self-sacrifice'. Ordinary people too committed suicide because they lacked any future perspective for the time after the imminent defeat. In a sense, they thought they would not survive the end of the Third Reich.

One of the most immediate problems Germans faced was the uncertainty concerning their families' whereabouts. Suicide was common especially among those who had fled the eastern territories of Germany from the Red Army or those who had had to leave their families behind. Leading civil servants and party members, such as Dr Rudolf S, a head of department in the Reich Ministry of Propaganda, committed suicide for this reason. The criminal police noted after they found him shot dead in his office in Goebbels's Ministry on 22 April 1945: 'All circumstances suggest that S did the deed himself... The present, general conditions and fear for his family have to be assumed to have been the factors motivating him. S did not know what happened to his family, but it is likely that they fell into enemy hands.'[65]

The SS officer Alwin V committed suicide with his wife on 4 February 1945 in the expensive Zehlendorf district, reportedly because of hopelessness regarding the fate of his family. According to his sister, he had been depressed: 'My brother-in-law told me of the refugee trains and how miserable it was for him. I assume that he was also thinking of his parents in East Prussia, and that the same things would happen to them.'[66] Alwin felt unable to help his parents, and this feeling of powerlessness prompted him to die together with his wife. He was probably also afraid that the Allies would take revenge on him and his family. In Potsdam, the 73-year-old widow Ida K gassed herself in her kitchen on 8 February 1945. The police commented: 'Reason ...: Fear of the Russian invasion.'[67] And on 25 March the double suicide of the 37-year-old carpenter Erich A and his 35-year-old wife Margarete was reported in Potsdam. According to the police, Erich A had written in a suicide note 'life did not have a point. Reason....: the current situation.'[68] The reports of local police stations in the countryside around Berlin and Potsdam yield similar cases. For instance, the 53-year-old dressmaker Frieda B was found dead from poisoning herself on 1 April 1945 in Wittenberg. The police stated tersely that her suicide had been prompted by 'melancholia, due to the current situation'.[69] What is striking about these police reports is that they all mention topoi like 'the Russians', 'the current situation' or 'the war'. The police and the authors of the suicide notes felt no need to explain them further. That the authors did not clarify the reasons for their suicides suggests that they believed that their relatives would know what they were talking about. Even if Nazi propaganda was not to blame for all suicides, then, it had created a common language and set of identifications for the masses of Germans who were living this war experience.

In the areas that were occupied by the Soviets in early 1945, suicide took place on a mass scale. Plenty of eyewitness accounts are available in the edition of 'Documents on the Expulsion of Germans from the East' that a team of historians around Theodor Schieder edited under the aegis of the Federal Ministry for the Expelled in the early 1950s.[70] A female clerk of the city council of Schönlanke in Pomerania, for example, claimed that during the approach of the Red Army in February 1945, the following events occurred: 'Out of fear of these animals from the east, many Schönlankers ended their lives (around 500 of them!) Whole families were wiped out in this way ... '[71] And a Protestant pastor from Schivelbein, a village in Pomerania, reported the following about the arrival of the

Red Army in March 1945 (note the shock with which he registers the disregarding of the religious ban on suicide by his congregation): 'After a short time we heard what sorts of tragedies played out in just a few short nights. Whole, good, churchgoing families took their lives—drowned themselves, hanged themselves, slit their wrists, or allowed themselves to be burned up along with their homes.'[72] And in Demmin, a town in Lower Pomerania, some 700 to 1,000 people are said to have committed suicide directly after the arrival of the Red Army.[73] In Teterow, a small town in Mecklenburg, the burial register counted some 120 suicides in May 1945 alone.[74]

In Darmstadt, in western Germany, the local court was heavily occupied in issuing death certificates for those who committed suicide while fleeing the Red Army in the winter of 1944/45.[75] At this stage, often facing financial problems and unable to remarry while their partners were officially still alive, many refugees applied to the courts for help. They wanted to know conclusively if their relatives were dead because this knowledge made it easier for them to come to terms with their own past.[76] In one case, the owner of a drugstore, Kurt P, originally from Hammer in Pomerania, a place in an area with a very high suicide rate towards the end of war, received the information he had sought. On 21 October 1954 a Darmstadt court certified the death of his wife who had 'died during the Russian invasion, probably through suicide'.[77] In a similar case, the 37-year-old farmer Franz Karl H, from Zorndorf near Königsberg, applied in July 1946 to the local court in the nearby district town of Dieburg for a death certificate for his daughter and his two grandchildren. In his testimony, he declared how the 'Russians' had invaded their village on 12 February 1945: 'As a result of the events taking place then, our daughter E became so mentally exhausted that she killed her two daughters, aged one and a half and five years, and then drowned herself.'[78]

Killing one's children and then oneself was quite common at the end of the war. In Berlin, the 45-year-old Corporal Max K shot his two sons, aged 8 and 15, before killing himself on 2 April 1945. According to the criminal police, his wife had tried in vain to stop him. The police commented that the 'reason for the deed is … the fear of the approaching enemy'.[79] As noted above, Goebbels and his wife murdered their six children with poison before killing themselves. In her final letter to her adult son by her first marriage, which she wrote to him from Hitler's bunker on

28 April 1945, Magda Goebbels announced her suicide and the murder of her children:

> The world that will come after the Führer and National Socialism will not be worth living in, and therefore I have taken my children away. They are too dear to endure what is coming next, and a merciful God will understand my intentions in delivering them from it. We have now only one aim: loyalty unto death to the Führer. That we can end our lives with him is a mercy of fate that we never dared to hope for.[80]

Suicide, in combination with killing one's family, implies a very high degree of hopelessness and identification with Nazi propaganda concerning the cruelty of 'the Russians'. Fathers and, in some cases, as we have seen, mothers, killed their children before they took their own lives because they did not see a future for themselves. The fact that it was mothers who killed their children, before taking their own lives, reflected in a sense the changed role of German men since the beginning of the war: men had failed.[81]

Suicide rates rose, though not dramatically, in some western parts of Germany, too. There were 42 suicides in Upper Bavaria during April and May 1945. In previous years, there had only been between three and five suicides during these months. Many Nazis and people from Protestant regions of Germany, now occupied by the Red Army, had fled to Upper Bavaria at the end of the war, which may help explain why there were more suicides than previously.[82] In Hamburg, too, some killed themselves. Numbers were significantly lower than in Berlin and there was no sharp increase at the end of the war. In April 1945, only 56 people committed suicide in Hamburg, according to a report by the British Control Commission in Germany.[83] On 5 February 1945, the 71-year-old pensioner Otto V was found gassed to death in his flat in the Fuhlsbüttel suburb. His lodger told the police that V had believed that 'the Russians would come here', under whom 'he did not want to live'. Although there was no evidence at all that the Russians would occupy Hamburg, the criminal police commented: 'Supposedly, V could not adjust himself to the situation, since he was afraid of the Russians conquering [Hamburg].'[84]

Two West German psychiatrists wrote an article in 1949 in which they analysed the trend of the suicide rate in northern Baden and Bremen.

They noted a sharp increase in the suicide rate in 1945. Even so, levels were still lower than they had been in 1939.[85] In Frankfurt am Main, a largely Protestant city, there were fewer suicides per 100,000 people after the surrender of the city in March 1945 than during the war.[86]

In the small village of Södel in Hesse, occupied by the Americans, the 68-year-old businessman Hermann V was found hanged in his garden on 19 March 1945. He left a farewell letter to his wife and children that said: 'I am really very sorry to leave you, but you should not think badly of me, the war made me do it.'[87] Not far away, in Friedberg, the district town, a man aged 35 hanged himself on 4 February 1945. The cause, according to the local constabulary's report, was depression. His wife then killed her two young children before cutting her own wrists.[88] While there is considerably less evidence of suicides in this area than in the countryside surrounding Berlin, the two cases from the Friedberg area suggest that at least some Germans living in the West also thought that life was not worth living after the end of the war. Many Germans felt the absence of a future perspective, as though life would be insupportable after the destruction of the Nazi regime, regardless of the ideology of the occupier. Nevertheless, despite the rise in suicides that accompanied the hardships and chaos of the last months of the war and the first months of peace, western parts of Germany did not see a wave of suicides on the scale occurring in areas further east, where panic and fear of the Red Army caused people to kill themselves in extraordinary numbers. Fear of the Red Army was therefore one of the main motivations for suicides among German civilians at this time.

# IV

The suicide epidemic of 1945 took place in three overlapping phases. The first one began in the eastern territories of Germany as early as in January 1945 when the Red Army had already begun or was about to begin to occupy east Prussia and Silesia. The second one occurred around April and May 1945 when many Nazi officials, from the top to the bottom of the party hierarchy, took their lives. The final wave took place after the Allies' arrival. Nevertheless, while suicides had different individual motives, the sheer magnitude of this suicide wave suggests that many Germans had some common motivations for killing themselves. The suicide wave certainly sheds light on the collective emotions of fear and anxiety towards the end of the war.

Contemporaries were not slow to comment on this suicide epidemic. The Catholic psychiatrist Erich Menninger-Lerchenthal noted 'organized mass suicide on a large scale which had previously not occurred in the history of Europe'. He declared that 'there are suicides which do not have anything to do with mental illness or some moral and intellectual deviance, but predominantly with the continuity of a heavy political defeat and the fear of being held responsible'.[89] The Protestant August Knorr insisted that the suicides were directly caused by paganism and by the secular views of the Nazis. He evoked Goethe to demand an end to suicide as such: 'Will the bells of Easter Morning prevent the "Faustian man" from taking the bowl of poison...?'[90] Reinhold Schneider too, an influential Catholic writer, argued for a return to traditional religious values. He insisted in 1947 that 'suicide is the certain symbol of the confusion of all order, and it means sin and outrage'.[91]

Suicide in 1945 was not just about showing support for, or identification with the regime and its leaders, however. It resulted in many cases from the coming-together of many different motives, including nervousness and depression in the chaotic and destructive milieu of bombed-out cities and war-torn countryside, where survival often seemed difficult in the extreme. Needless to say, fear of the behaviour of Red Army soldiers should also not be underestimated, nor should the lurid warnings of Nazi propaganda. Women in particular resorted to suicide to avoid rape or because of shame after it had occurred. The belief that the Red Army posed a threat to life even led to many suicides among convinced Christians. Many contemporaries felt a complete breakdown of norms and values. To many people who committed suicide, politics, war, and everyday life were not perceived as separate things, but came together in a tremendously difficult time, where life seemed wholly deprived of any future purpose. Moral, psychological, and religious norms and values had collapsed. For the mass of Germans, life had been restructured to promote an eventually suicidal campaign of war, and when this failed, killing oneself became culturally and socially acceptable in a culture of suicide in defeat. The lack of a future was understood to apply to the German people in general, and found its expression by the common fears that they had and the common language they used to describe them. Each suicide had a profound impact on friends, families and relatives. They all had to come to terms with their losses on a very personal and emotional level. The chaos, misery and disorientation spanned the end of war and the beginning of the occupation. It would be some time before they were overcome.

# Conclusion

After the Nazi regime's collapse in 1945, Germans continued to commit suicide, but not in such high numbers as in the Third Reich. The low suicide rates (if compared to the socially and politically turbulent Weimar and Nazi years) mirrored the relative political stability and the slow beginning of the economic miracle in the new West German democracy. However, communist East Germany displayed much higher suicide rates than West Germany. East German rates were on average 150 per cent higher for men and 170 per cent for women than corresponding West German figures. One historian largely dismisses any significant impact of political factors on the suicide rate and explains the GDR's high suicide levels with East German society's Protestant heritage. Thuringia and Saxony had displayed very high suicide rates since the nineteenth century. Protestant regions, of course, generally display higher suicide rates than Catholic areas, where, under the impact of a strong cultural taboo, local and state institutions responsible for dealing with suicides tend to report suicides as accidents. Yet many Protestant East Germans increasingly opted out of the church. Moreover, such a deterministic explanation of suicide rates largely brushes over individual suicide motives, stripping those who took their lives of their individual agency.[1]

Suicide, at once the 'most private and impenetrable of human acts' as well as a social phenomenon can only be properly understood if one studies it simultaneously on macro-, micro-, and discourse levels. This book suggests a new history of Nazi Germany, one that combines traditional social history with cultural history, concerned with individual fates and circumstances. This history focuses on individual agency and experience within its wider social and political context. Individual attitudes and experiences towards suicide must be placed into their wider social and political context. Yet perceptions and representations of suicide give us a fascinating insight into the ways people responded to the social and political events in Weimar and Nazi Germany that had a profound emotional impact upon their everyday lives. Combining these distinct perspectives is difficult because public suicide discourse operated on a very different level. The public discourse on suicide concerned broader analytical diagnostic arguments which were frequently ideologically or politically motivated. Sometimes the macro- and the micro-level overlapped, as in cases where suicide notes incorporated the socio-economic diagnosis popularized in the daily press. In these cases suicides explicitly linked their own difficulties to wider social pressures.

This personal-social link was particularly clear in Weimar Germany. Suicide served as an ultimate means of ending people's personal misery, which they associated with the German defeat of 1918, the inflation of 1923, the Great Depression and the generally unstable political and social system of the Weimar Republic. At key moments of economic crisis, suicide rates increased sharply amongst the groups most affected. Theologians, scientists, statisticians, politicians, and newspapers referred to suicide to illustrate what they perceived as the Weimar Republic's miserable social and political conditions. This discourse helped to undermine the legitimacy of the Weimar Republic. The Nazis, and also the communists, promised to clamp down on suicide by overcoming the political and social factors that allegedly triggered it, notably unemployment. The Nazis blamed the suicide rate on the lack of living space, German reparations payments, and the economic misery that resulted from these factors. The communists stressed the evils of capitalist exploitation. Social and political difficulties clearly affected ordinary people to the extent that they killed themselves. Men in particular justified their suicide with the fact that they were unemployed and confronted with a collapse of their traditional environments. In Weimar Germany, state institutions, such as statistical offices, were concerned with rising suicide levels. However, Weimar state institutions did not really do much to prevent people from killing themselves. This they left to church institutions which, also following a nationalist, anti-Republican rhetoric, could not really prevent people from committing suicide since they had lost much of their moral authority in the wake of secularization.

In Nazi Germany, suicide levels failed to decline, despite Nazi claims to be building a people's community that would give no cause for suicide. Social dislocation and economic deprivation still prompted many people to commit suicide. In the Third Reich, discourses on suicide shifted from a largely socio-economic interpretation of suicide (which had been common in the Weimar Republic) to something more complicated and contradictory. Nazi thinking about suicide revolved around two main ideas which stood in some irreconcilable tension with each other: were suicides inferior people whose eradication from the racial body was to be encouraged; or were suicides irresponsible egotists who had the nerve to prioritize their own concerns before the national interest? Reports on suicides ostensibly motivated by unemployment or other socio-economic reasons disappeared from newspapers. But unpublished sources tell a different story.

Nazi politics had a direct impact on many suicides. Political opponents of the regime committed suicide in the wake of the Nazi seizure of power. Especially in 1933 and 1934, the Nazis 'suicided' political opponents, denying responsibility for killing or torturing them to their deaths. Some of those directly affected by Nazi policies, such as the Hereditary Health Law, the persecution of political opposition, and racial policies, committed suicide. Above all, German Jews committed suicide in their thousands during the Third Reich. The Jewish suicide rate dramatically increased after direct anti-Semitic actions such as the boycott of April 1933 and, most extremely, the *Anschluss* and the pogrom of November 1938.

The outbreak of war changed the everyday lives of ordinary people, including German Jews. From 1941, Jewish emigration became impossible, and deportations to the East began. Most of Germany's remaining Jews were middle aged or elderly and thus more likely than young people to commit suicide. They could not emigrate. Those German Jews who committed suicide were not simply passive victims. Suicide became the last means of maintaining their dignity and agency. The suicide rate among non-Jews fell after the outbreak of war, while suicide levels of German Jews dramatically increased. Those arrested for criminal offences such as listening to foreign radio stations, spreading 'malicious rumours', or undermining the German war effort also frequently committed suicide. These powerful individual case studies cast into doubt the now widely popular and largely simplistic hypothesis that the Nazis hardly needed to terrorize Germans who were allegedly enthusiastic Nazi supporters and collaborators right until the regime's downfall.[2]

Air raids also led many to kill themselves, and the suicide rate increased in 1942. Towards the war's end, Germany was hit by a wave of self-killings that was the culmination of an eventually suicidal war, led by a self-destructive Hitler and his regime. The Third Reich's end in an orgy of self-destruction was not altogether surprising. Stability and bureaucratic routine was impossible in a regime made up of myriad party and state institutions competing for power. The Third Reich was above all held together by Hitler's 'charismatic rule' and various institutions 'working towards the Führer'. Unlike Stalin's Soviet Union, the Third Reich could therefore not survive the dictator's death. In 1945, in the light of total defeat, Hitler's suicidal tendencies amalgamated with 'the incapacity of his form of authoritarian rule to reproduce itself and survive'.[3] There was a general feeling that everything was coming to an end. Many Germans experienced a complete breakdown of norms and values, an anomie, which cannot simply be reduced to the breakdown of the political structure of the Third Reich. The Third Reich created a society far more tightly bound by rules and regulations, far more closely organized, far more intrusively moulding of people's everyday lives and aspirations than anything previously experienced. Nazi ideology and propaganda shaped German society and culture in a way that gave many people the order and stability they craved in 1933. When it began to fall apart, when it eventually collapsed, the anomie which spread amongst those most loyal to the regime and most permeated by its values was correspondingly extreme. They were fortified in their decision to kill themselves by the Nazi cult of heroic self-sacrifice and by fear of the humiliation of arrest and trial—perhaps also, therefore, by an unconscious sense of guilt. For many less ideological Germans, fear of the Russians was a key motive. Desperation at the ruined state of Germany and the extreme difficulties of everyday life also played a role. For many people who committed suicide, politics, war, and everyday life did not come as separate events, but coalesced in a single, lethal cocktail. For a brief period in the spring of 1945, when the Third Reich came to its end, suicide lost its status as a taboo and became a routine phenomenon.

The Third Reich created a condition of anomie, a context in which many people thought that life was insupportable and therefore killed themselves. According to Durkheim, anomic suicide is typical of modern societies and occurs at times of socio-economic turmoil. It 'results from man's activity lacking regulation and his consequent sufferings' and 'springs from society's insufficient presence in individuals'.[4] Anomie could take on various forms. In the Weimar Republic, the anomie was of a largely socio-economic nature. In the Third Reich, socio-economic dislocation continued to prompt many suicides. Yet 1933 was an important caesura, leading to twelve years of political and racial persecution on an unprecedented scale. In the Nazi years, there was certainly a political anomie leading to several thousand suicides. From 1924 until the outbreak of the war, suicide levels in Germany were higher than they had been in Imperial Germany and than they would be in West Germany.

The Nazi regime deliberately transformed people's lives by enforcing policies that aimed to create a racially pure German society. The Nazis knew that their racial policies led many people, especially Jews, but also social outsiders and foreign workers, to kill themselves. The argument that suicide became a crucial part of Nazi extermination perhaps goes too far.[5] It ignores the fact that once the deportations of Jews had begun, the Nazis tried to prevent Jewish suicides, as the Nazis thought they should be the final arbiters of life and death; for many of those the Nazis targeted for political and, especially, racial reasons, suicide became the last resort for keeping one's dignity and controlling the timing and means of one's death and this the Nazis, in the end, would not accept.

In the Third Reich, state institutions spent little time on suicide prevention, since surely, the Nazis argued, people no longer had reason to kill themselves. Suicide, the Nazis and most contemporary social and psychological scientists thought, was a cowardly act that reflected personal weakness. Although re-criminalization failed (like the reform of the penal code altogether), the Nazis severely punished suicidal soldiers. Suicide was, after all, a crime against the people's community. Nazi discourse distinguished ordinary suicides from what the Nazis called heroic self-sacrifice or soldier's death (*Soldatentod*). This distinction was meant to brush over the allegedly 'honourable' behaviour of the Nazis in 1945, men whose radical policies had led to Germany's destruction. It would be a long time before the impact of this suicidal regime was overcome.

# Notes

## INTRODUCTION

1. Richard Cobb, *Death in Paris: The records of the Basse-Geôle de la Seine* (Oxford, 1978), 101. Important studies include Olive Anderson, *Suicide in Victorian and Edwardian England* (Oxford, 1987); Michael MacDonald and Terence R Murphy, *Sleepless Souls: Suicide in early modern England* (Oxford, 1990); Georges Minois, *History of Suicide: Voluntary death in Western culture* (Baltimore, 1999); Victor Bailey, *"This Rash Act": Suicide across the life cycle in the Victorian city* (Stanford, 1998); Alexander Murray, *Suicide in the Middle Ages* (2 vols, Oxford, 1998–2000); Vera Lind, *Selbstmord in der frühen Neuzeit: Diskurs, Lebenswelt und kultureller Wandel am Beispiel der Herzogtümer Schleswig und Holstein* (Göttingen, 1999); Ursula Baumann, *Vom Recht auf den eigenen Tod: Die Geschichte des Suizids vom 18. bis zum 20. Jahrhundert* (Weimar, 2001); Andreas Bähr, *Der Richter im Ich: Die Semantik der Selbsttötung in der Aufklärung* (Göttingen, 2002).

2. Susan K Morrissey, *Suicide and the Body Politic in Imperial Russia* (Cambridge, 2006), 1; for a medical-pathological approach see Kay Redfield Jamison, *Night Falls Fast: Understanding suicide* (New York, 1999).

3. Steven Lukes, *Emile Durkheim: His life and work. A historical and critical study* (Harmondsworth, 1973), 191–225.

4. Murray, *Suicide in the Middle Ages*, I, 15.

5. Emile Durkheim, *Suicide: A study in sociology* (London, 1952 [1897]), 95–258.

6. Peter Laslett, *The World We Have Lost* (2nd edn, London, 1971), 145.

7. Anderson, *Suicide*, 9–103.

8. Murray, *Suicide in the Middle Ages*, I, 348.

9. Murray, *Suicide in the Middle Ages*, I, 348.

10. MacDonald and Murphy, *Sleepless Souls*, 219–337.

11. VAC Gatrell, 'The Decline of Theft and Violence in Victorian and Edwardian England', in idem, Bruce Lehman and Geoffrey Parker (eds), *Crime and the Law: The social history of crime in Western Europe since 1500* (London, 1980), 238–337, 246.

12. Jack D Douglas, *The Social Meanings of Suicide* (Princeton, 1967), 163–340.

13. Dr Zahn, 'Die Methodik der Selbstmordstatistik', in *Archiv für die Erforschung und Bekämpfung des Selbstmordes*, 1 (1932), 25–8, 25; on Zahn see

J Adam Tooze, *Statistics and the German State: The making of modern economic knowledge* (Cambridge, 2001), 87–9; on confessional factors see David Lederer, 'Selbstmord im frühneuzeitlichen Deutschland: Klischee und Geschichte', in *Psychotherapie*, 4 (1999), 206–12.

14. Bailey, *'This Rash Act'*, 28–9.

15. Richard J Evans, *Tales from the German Underworld: Crime and Punishment in the Nineteenth Century* (New Haven, 1998), 1.

16. See generally Hans Medick and Andreas Bähr (eds), *Sterben von eigener Hand: Selbsttötung als kulturelle Praxis* (Cologne, 2005).

17. Susan K Morrissey, 'Suicide and civilization in late Imperial Russia', in *Jahrbücher für Geschichte Osteuropas*, 43 (1995), 201–17; and most recently Catharine Edwards, *Death in Ancient Rome* (New Haven, 2007), 6.

18. John Tosh, 'What Should Historians do with Masculinity? Reflections on Nineteenth-century Britain', in *History Workshop Journal*, 38 (1994), 179–202; George L. Mosse, *The Image of Man: The Creation of Modern Masculinity* (Oxford, 1996).

19. Catharine Edwards and Thomas Osborne, 'Scenographies of Suicide: an introduction', in *Economy and Society*, 34 (2005), 173–77, 174; see also Rebecca Flemming, 'Suicide, euthanasia and medicine: reflections ancient and modern', in *Economy and Society*, 34 (2005), 295–321, 298.

20. Günther Weisenborn, *Der lautlose Aufstand: Bericht über die Widerstandsbewegung des deutschen Volkes 1933–1945* (Frankfurt am Main, 1979 [1953]), 26; for an evaluation see Ian Kershaw, *The Nazi Dictatorship: Problems and perspectives of interpretation* (London, 2000), 190–1.

21. Susanne Hahn and Christina Schröder, 'Zur Einordnung des Suizids in das faschistische Konzept der "Vernichtung lebensunwerten Lebens"', in Sabine Fahrenbach and Achim Thom (eds), *Der Arzt als 'Gesundheitsführer': Ärztliches Wirken zwischen Ressourcenerschließung und humanitärer Hilfe im Zweiten Weltkrieg* (Frankfurt am Main, 1991), 109–16; see also Susanne Hahn, ' "Minderwertige, widerstandslose Individuen"—Der Erste Weltkrieg und das Selbstmordproblem in Deutschland', in Wolfgang Eckart and Christoph Gradmann (eds), *Die Medizin und der Erste Weltkrieg* (Pfaffenweiler, 1996), 273–98.

22. Baumann, *Vom Recht*, 323–79; see also Ursula Baumann, 'Suizid im "Dritten Reich": Facetten eines Themas', in Michael Grüttner, Rüdiger Hachtmann, and Heinz-Gerhard Haupt (eds), *Geschichte und Emanzipation: Festschrift für Reinhard Rürup* (Frankfurt am Main, 1999), 482–516.

23. Minois, *History of Suicide*, 302–28.

24. On suicide notes see Antoon A Leenars, *Suicide Notes: Predictive clues and patterns* (New York, 1988); Ronald W Maris, Alan L Berman, and Morton M Silverman, 'Suicide Notes and Communications', in eidem (eds), *Comprehensive Textbook of Suicidology* (New York, 2000), 266–83; Ian O'Donnell,

Richard Farmer and Jose Catalan, 'Suicide Notes', in *British Journal of Psychiatry*, 163 (1993), 45–8.

25. Jay W. Baird, *To Die For Germany: Heroes in the Nazi Pantheon* (Bloomington, 1990), xi.

## CHAPTER I

1. Jürg Schatzmann, 'Richard Semon (1859–1918) und seine Mnemotheorie' (MD diss, University of Zurich, 1968), 20; see also Emil Szittya, *Selbstmörder: Ein Beitrag zur Kulturgeschichte aller Zeiten und Völker* (Leipzig, 1925), 199.

2. Baldur von Schirach, *Ich glaubte an Hitler* (Hamburg, 1967), 15.

3. Quoted in Peter Fritzsche, *Reading Berlin 1900* (Cambridge, Mass, 1996), 121–2; see more generally Eric A Johnson, *Urbanization and Crime: Germany 1871–1914* (Cambridge, 1995), 55–61.

4. *Kölner Tageblatt*, 17 November 1925.

5. ADW, CA 1206 I, press clipping, *Der Westen*, no 481, 12 November 1925.

6. Durkheim, *Suicide*, 318–19. See Figure 3.

7. Hans W Gruhle, *Selbstmord* (Leipzig, 1940), 30.

8. August Busch, 'Der Freitod in Frankfurt a.M.', in *Bevölkerungs- und Wirtschaftszahlen. In zwangloser Folge herausgegeben vom Städtischen Statistischen Amt* (November 1932), 6.

9. See Dietmar Petzina, Werner Abelshauser and Anselm Faust (eds.), *Sozialgeschichtliches Arbeitsbuch Band III: Materialien zur Statistik des Deutschen Reiches 1914–1945* (Munich, 1978), 27–8.

10. Baumann, *Vom Recht*, 330. See also Julie Dorothea Wessinger, *Ueber den Selbstmord bei Frauen in den ersten zehn Jahren nach dem Kriege* (Berlin, 1933), 15.

11. Tosh, 'What Should Historians Do with Masculinity?, 185.

12. David F Crew, *Germans on Welfare: From Weimar to Hitler* (New York, 1998), 103.

13. Nils Retterstøl, *Suicide: A European perspective* (Cambridge, 1993), 83–4.

14. Retterstøl, *Suicide*, 76–9.

15. Karl Freudenberg, 'Wirtschaftslage und Selbstmordhäufigkeit', in *Zeitschrift für ärztliche Fortbildung*, 12 (1932), 371–2.

16. *Berliner Tageblatt*, no 48, 29 January 1932.

17. Retterstøl, *Suicide*, 76–9.

18. See Fig 5.

19. Richard J Evans, *The Coming of the Third Reich* (London, 2003), 114.

20. Helgard Kramer, 'Frankfurt's working women: Scapegoats or winners of the Great Depression?', in Evans and Geary (eds.), *The German Unemployed*, 108–41.

21. Kramer, 'Frankfurt's working women: Scapegoats or winners of the Great Depression?', 134.

22. Gruhle, *Selbstmord*, 54–5.

23. Gruhle, *Selbstmord*, 60; *Statistisches Jahrbuch für Bayern*, 16 (1924), 37. On suicides in Munich see also Claudia Brunner, *Arbeitslosigkeit in München 1927 bis 1933: Kommunalpolitik in der Krise* (Munich, 1992), 152–7.

24. Gruhle, *Selbstmord*, 63.

25. Helmut Beichel, 'Der Selbstmord in Baden in den Jahren 1927–1936', in *Beiträge zur gerichtlichen Medizin*, 15 (1939), 1–13, 6.

26. Beichel, 'Selbstmord in Baden', 4.

27. Gruhle, *Selbstmord*, 65.

28. Gruhle, *Selbstmord*, 64.

29. Gerhard Wilke, 'The sins of the fathers : Village society and social control in the Weimar Republic', in Richard J Evans (ed), *The German peasantry: Conflict and community in rural society from the eighteenth to the twentieth centuries* (London, 1986), 174–204.

30. Baumann, *Vom Recht*, 326–30.

31. *Statistik des Deutschen Reiches*, 336 (1924), 154.

32. Henry Morselli, *Suicide: An essay on comparative moral statistics* (London, 1881), 354; Richard J Evans, 'In search of German Social Darwinism', in idem (ed), *Rereading German History: From unification to reunification, 1800–1996* (London, 1997), 119–44, 121.

33. Baumann, *Vom Recht*, 331.

34. Karl Freudenberg, 'Die Selbstmorde in Deutschland nach dem Kriege', in *Klinische Wochenschrift*, 5 (1926), 29–33, 29.

35. Gerhard Füllkrug, *Der Selbstmord in der Kriegs- und Nachkriegszeit* (Schwerin, 1927), 99.

36. Gustav Donalies, 'Statistische Erhebungen an 3000 Fällen von vollendetem und versuchtem Selbstmord', in *Monatsschrift für Psychiatrie und Neurologie*, 69 (1928), 380–96, 389.

37. Evans, *The Coming of the Third Reich*, 109.

38. Busch, 'Der Freitod in Frankfurt a.M.', 9.

39. Donalies, 'Statistische Erhebungen', 389.

40. Alex Schackwitz, 'Selbstmordursachen', in *Deutsche Zeitschrift für die gesamte gerichtliche Medizin*, 10 (1927), 312–21, 316.

41. Donalies, 'Statistische Erhebungen', 384.

42. For examples see Richard J Evans, *Rituale der Vergeltung: Die Todesstrafe in deutschen Geschichte 1532–1987* (Berlin, 2001), 358–61; Baumann, *Vom Recht*, 256.

43. Karl Baumann, *Selbstmord und Freitod in sprachlicher und geistesgeschichtlicher Bedeutung* (Würzburg, 1934), 31–2.

44. Quoted in Baumann, *Selbstmord und Freitod*, 16–17.

45. Baumann, *Selbstmord und Freitod*, 32.

46. Quoted in Baumann, *Selbstmord und Freitod*, 15.

47. Quoted in Baumann, *Selbstmord und Freitod*, 24; see also David Daube, 'The linguistics of suicide', in *Philosophy and Public Affairs*, 1 (1971/72), 387–437, 432.

48. Quoted in Baumann, *Selbstmord und Freitod*, 23.

49. Baumann, *Selbstmord und Freitod*, 45.

50. Baumann, *Selbstmord und Freitod*, 31.

51. Roderich von Ungern-Sternberg, *Die Ursachen der Steigerung der Selbst-mordhäufigkeit in Westeuropa während der letzten hundert Jahre* (Berlin, 1935), 55.

52. Karl Freudenberg, 'Die Selbstmorde in Deutschland nach dem Kriege', in *Klinische Wochenschrift*, 5 (1926), 29–33, 30.

53. BAB R 8034 II/5538, Bl 19: *Deutsche Zeitung*, no 104a, 5 May 1931.

54. BAB R 8034 II/5538, Bl 27: *Abend*, no 116, 9 March 1931.

55. Josef Maria Frank, *Unus multorum: Die Geschichte eines Selbstmordes* (Berlin, 1925).

56. Reinhold Happel, 'Kuhle Wampe oder Wem gehört die Welt—eine exemplarische Analyse', in Helmut Korte (ed), *Film und Realität in der Weimarer Republik: Mit Analysen der Filme 'Kuhle Wampe' und 'Mutter Krausens Fahrt ins Glück'* (Munich, 1978), 169–212, 175.

57. On Münzenberg see Babette Gross, *Willi Münzenberg: Eine politische Biographie* (Stuttgart, 1967); and most recently the hatchet job by Sean McMeekin, *The Red Millionaire: A political biography of Willi Münzenberg, Moscow's secret propaganda Tsar in the West* (New Haven, 2003).

58. *Die Welt am Abend*, no 33, 12 July 1924.

59. *Die Welt am Abend*, no 11, 14 January 1931; see David F Crew, 'Gewalt auf dem "Amt": Wohlfahrtsbehörden und ihre Klienten in der Weimarer Republik', in Thomas Lindenberger and Alf Lüdtke (eds), *Physische Gewalt: Studien zur Geschichte der Neuzeit* (Frankfurt am Main, 1995), 213–37.

60. *Die Welt am Abend*, no 75, 31 March 1932.

61. *Die Welt am Abend*, no 124, 30 May 1932.

62. *Statistik für das Deutsche Reich*, 495 (1932–1934), I, 170.

63. Evans, *The Coming of the Third Reich*, 305.

64. *Die Welt am Abend*, no 153, 2 July 1932.

65. Hans von Hentig, 'Der Selbstmord in Sowjet-Rußland 1922–1925', in *Archiv für Kriminologie*, 80 (1927), 252–3.

66. Thomas Mergel, *Parlamentarische Kultur in der Weimarer Republik: Politische Kommunikation, symbolische Politik und Öffentlichkeit im Reichstag* (Düsseldorf, 2002), 319.

67. *Verhandlungen des Reichstags, IV. Wahlperiode 1928*, Band 425, 2614.

68. See numbers in Eckart Elsner, 'Selbstmord in Berlin', in *Berliner Statistik*, 37 (1983), 218–39, 220.

69. *Verhandlungen des Reichstags, IV. Wahlperiode 1929*, Band 425, 3095.

70. *Die Rote Fahne*, no 3, 4 January 1933. For a similar case see 'Erwerbsloser Angesteller wirft sich unter U-Bahn', in *Die Rote Fahne*, no 28, 2 February 1930.

71. On the press in the Weimar Republic see Bernhard Fulda, 'Press and Politics in Berlin, 1924–1930' (unpublished PhD thesis, University of Cambridge, 2003); for a survey see Kurt Koszyk, *Deutsche Presse 1914–1945: Geschichte der deutschen Presse, Teil III* (Berlin, 1972).

72. Ludwig Preller, *Sozialpolitik in der Weimarer Republik* (Düsseldorf, 1978 [1949]), 446.

73. *8 Uhr-Abendblatt*, no 118, 23 May 1932.

74. Gabriele Tergit, *Blüten der Zwanziger Jahre: Gerichtsreportagen und Feuilletons 1923–1933*, Jens Brüning (ed) (Berlin, 1984), 199–201, 200.

75. Evans, *Rituale*, 731–6.

76. *8-Uhr Abendblatt*, no 97, 26 April 1932; see also *Berliner Illustrierte Nachtausgabe*, no 97, 26 April 1932.

77. Erich Frey, *Ich beantrage Freispruch Aus den Erinnerungen des Strafverteidigers Prof Dr Dr Frey* (Gütersloh, 1960), 269–384.

78. *Völkischer Beobachter*, 12 February 1928, quoted in Wilhelm Carlé, *Weltanschauung und Presse: Eine soziologische Untersuchung* (Leipzig, 1931), S 19–S 22.

79. GStA, HA I Rep 84a, no 53183, Bl 4: *Vossische Zeitung*, no 93, 24 February 1931; ibid, Bl 6: *Berlin am Morgen*, no 47, 25 February 1931; ibid, Bl 8: Büro des Reichspräsidenten—Der Staatssekretär an den Preußischen Minister der Justiz, 9 March 1931; ibid, Bl 12-15: Gründe, 26 August 1931.

80. *Der Angriff*, 15 January 1931. I owe this document to Dr Moritz Föllmer.

81. Evans, *The Coming of the Third Reich*, 211–12.

82. *Völkischer Beobachter* (Reichsausgabe), no 106, 15 April 1932.

83. Speech on 13 July 1928 on 'Deutsche Außenpolitik', in Bärbel Dusik and Klaus A Lankheit (eds), *Hitler: Reden, Schriften, Anordnungen. Februar 1925 bis Januar 1933* (Munich, 1994), III/1, 11–22, 15.

84. *Statistik des Deutschen Reiches*, 441 (1931), 105.

85. Interview with Ward Price, 18 October 1933, printed in Max Domarus (ed), *Hitler: Reden und Proklamationen. Kommentiert von einem deutschen Zeitgenossen* (Stuttgart, 1965), I/1, 323.

86. *Statistik des Deutschen Reiches*, 495 (1932–1934), I, 170.

87. On the Inner Mission see generally Jochen-Christoph Kaiser, *Sozialer Protestantismus im 20. Jahrhundert: Beiträge zur Geschichte der Inneren Mission 1914–1945* (Munich, 1989). On Füllkrug's crusade against suicide see the brief treatment by Baumann, *Vom Recht*, 333–5.

88. Gerhard Füllkrug, *Der Selbstmord: Eine moralstatistische und volkspsychologische Untersuchung* (Schwerin, 1919), 153, 162.

89. Gerhard Füllkrug, *Der Selbstmord in der Kriegs- und Nachkriegszeit: Eine moralstatistische Untersuchung* (Schwerin, 1927), 119–20.

90. Füllkrug, *Der Selbstmord: Eine moralstatistische und volkspsychologische Untersuchung*, 188–9.

91. Kaiser, *Sozialer Protestantismus*, 13.

92. Anderson, *Suicide in Victorian and Edwardian England*, 334–44.

93. Martin Olpe, *Selbstmord und Seelsorge* (Halle, 1913), 63.

94. Young-Sun Hong, *Welfare, Modernity and the Weimar State, 1918–1933* (Princeton, 1998), 72.

95. Baumann, *Vom Recht*, 145.

96. M Julier, 'Die Mitwirkung der Polizei bei der Selbstmordbekämpfung', in *Caritas: Zeitschrift für Caritas und Caritaswissenschaft*, 34 (October 1929), 387–92, 390.

97. Sace Elder, 'Murder Scenes: Criminal violence in the public culture and private lives of Weimar Berlin' (unpublished PhD thesis, University of Illinois at Urbana-Champaign, 2002).

98. On the wider context of this argument see Moritz Föllmer, 'Der "kranke Volkskörper": Industrielle, hohe Beamte und der Diskurs der nationalen Regeneration in der Weimarer Republik', in *Geschichte und Gesellschaft*, 27 (2001), 41–67; and idem, 'The problem of national solidarity in inter-war Germany', in *German History* 23 (2005), 202–31.

99. ADW, EREV, Nr 161, Abschrift Der Polizeipräsident an den CA für Innere Mission, 12 September 1930. For Füllkrug's account of his own work see his 'Der Kampf gegen den Selbstmord: Bericht über die Arbeit der Ständigen Kommission zur Bearbeitung der Selbstmordfrage in Berlin', in *Archiv für die Erforschung und Bekämpfung des Selbstmordes*, 1 (1932), 51–4.

100. ADW, CA 1206 I, draft letter, undated, but probably from 1925.

101. Hugh McLeod, *European Religion in the Age of the Great Cities: 1830–1930* (London, 1995), 15.

102. Gerhard Füllkrug, *Die Flucht vor dem Leben: Erläuternder Text zur Lichtbildreihe mit gleichem Titel* (Berlin-Dahlem, 1928).

103. Füllkrug, *Flucht vor dem Leben*, 3.

104. See Hong, *Welfare*, 185–94.

105. Hans Rost, *Der Selbstmord als sozialstatistische Erscheinung* (Cologne, 1905), 57.

106. Rost, *Selbstmord als sozialstatistische Erscheinung*, 115.

107. EZAB, EZA 1/906, Vermerk (undated but probably from 1928).

108. Hans Rost, *Bibliographie des Selbstmordes* (Augsburg, 1927); idem, *Archiv für die Erforschung und Bekämpfung des Selbstmordes*, 1 (1932). See Figs 1 and 2.

109. Hans Rost, 'Der Selbstmord in den Kulturstaaten der Erde', in *Archiv für die Erforschung und Bekämpfung des Selbstmordes*, 1 (1932), 5–12, 5, 10.

110. Hans Rost, 'Wie kann man die Selbstmordneigung bekämpfen?', printed in *Archiv für die Erforschung und Bekämpfung des Selbstmordes*, 1 (1932), 40–5.

111. Richard Detlev Loewenberg, *Ueber den Selbstmord in Hamburg in den letzten fünfzig Jahren (1880–1930)* (Berlin, 1932), 39.

112. ADW, CA 1206 I, Preisausschreiben, 1 May 1926; ADW, CA 1206aI, Preußischer Minister für Volkswohlfahrt to Füllkrug, 22 December 1925.

113. ADW, CA 1206aII, Füllkrug to Ricarda Huch, 5 March 1926.

114. ADW, CA 1206aII, Walter von Molo to Fräulein Werner, 2 May 1927.

115. ADW, CA 1206aI, Alois U, Amtsrat, to CA, 12 March 1927.

116. ADW, CA 1206aII, Maria Kohn, Die Nacht auf der Brücke.

117. ADW, CA 1206aI, An den Zentralausschuß für innere Mission, 25 May 1926.

118. ADW, CA 1206bI, Erich S to Füllkrug, 15 April 1930; Füllkrug to S, undated (probably April 1930).

119. ADW, CA 1206bI, Karl L to Herr Hartmann, 14 April 1930.

120. ADW, CA 1206bI, Hermann L to Dr Schildkrug (sic!), 17 April 1930; Füllkrug to L, 25 April 1930.

121. Paul Lerner, *Hysterical Men: War, psychiatry and the politics of trauma in Germany, 1890–1930* (Ithaca, 2003).

122. ADW, CA 1206 bI, Fritz Reppo, 'Erlebnisse eines Selbstmordkandidaten', in: *Berlin am Morgen*, no 218, 18 September 1930.

123. ADW; CA 1206bI, Hermann E to Füllkrug, 22 April 1930 and undated; Füllkrug to E, 23 May 1930.

124. Quoted in Robert Weldon Whalen, *Bitter Wounds: German victims of the Great War, 1914–1939* (Ithaca, 1984), 190.

125. ADW, CA 1206bI, Füllkrug to Otto U, 2 May 1930.

126. LAB, A Rep 358–01, no 539, Vermerk, 5 March 1931; Polizei-Direktion Wien, Sicherheits-Bureau, 9 March 1931; on con men see Evans, *Tales from the German Underworld*, 136–65.

127. LAB, A Rep 358-01, no 539, *Berliner Börsen-Kurier*, 6 March 1931; ibid, *BZ am Mittag*, 5 March 1931.

128. Ibid., Anni M to Gennat, 5 March 1931.

129. LAB, A Pr Br, Rep 030, Tit 198B, no 1942.

130. For a similar argument see Fulda, 'Press and politics', 257.

131. On Harmsen see Atina Grossmann, *Reforming Sex: The German movement for birth control and abortion reform, 1920–1950* (New York, 1995) and Sabine Schleiermacher, *Sozialethik im Spannungsfeld von Sozial- und Rassenhygiene: Der Mediziner Hans Harmsen im Centralausschuß für die Innere Mission* (Husum, 1998).

132. ADW, CA/G 350, protocol, 24 January 1933.

133. Kaiser, *Sozialer Protestantismus*.

134. ADW, CA/G 350, 'Hilfe für Lebensmüde' (undated, but probably from 1933); on the Protestant church after 1933 see generally Richard J Evans, *The Third Reich in Power* (New York, 2005), 220–60.

135. ADW, CA/G 350, protocol, 9 June 1937.

136. These documents survived in the Potsdam State Archives of the former GDR and are now kept in the Landesarchiv Berlin. Before being passed on

to the archives, a colonel of the Berlin branch of the GDR *Volkspolizei* called Großmann compiled a list of these documents, which he wanted to use for criminological research. This seems to suggest that GDR police authorities were interested in a typology of suicide and murder, and helps explain why the collection was preserved.

137. Univ Prof Dr Strauch quoted in Krim-Kom Willy Finke, 'Mord oder Selbstmord', in *Kriminalistische Monatshefte*, 1 (1927), 117; see also Polizeioberinspektor Schneble, 'Ein interessanter Beitrag zum Problem "Mord oder Selbstmord"', in *Kriminalistische Monatshefte*, 2 (1928), 153–8.

138. Elder, 'Murder Scenes', 71–2; Patrick Wagner, *Volksgemeinschaft ohne Verbrecher. Konzeptionen und Praxis der Kriminalpolizei in der Zeit der Weimarer Republik und des Nationalsozialismus* (Hamburg, 1996), 79–96. On Gennat see Evans, *Rituale,* 697; and the anecdotal account by Regina Stürickow, *Der Kommissar vom Alexanderplatz* (Berlin, 1998), 119–29.

139. Regierungsdirektor Dr Weiß, Leiter der Berliner Kriminalpolizei, 'Die Beziehungen zwischen Presse und Kriminalpolizei', in *Polizei und Presse: Sondernummer der 'Deutschen Presse': Organ des Reichsverbandes der Deutschen Presse e.V.*, 16 (9 October 1926), no 40/41, 4–5.

140. Paul Schmidt, *Der praktische Dienst der Straßenpolizei: Ein Handbuch für den Unterricht und Selbstunterricht der Beamten der Schutzpolizei* (Berlin, 1922), 65.

141. *Vorwärts*, no 144, 26 March 1932.

142. *Die Rote Fahne*, no 65, 27 March 1932. As late as 1982, the GDR economic historian Jürgen Kuczynski, quoting the article from *Die Rote Fahne* without consulting any other source, declared this simplistic communist orthodoxy to be true. See Jürgen Kuczynski, *Geschichte des Alltags des Deutschen Volkes: Studien* (East-Berlin, 1982), V, 141–3.

143. *Berliner Morgenpost*, no 74, 26 March 1932.

144. LAB, A Pr Br, Rep 030, Tit 198B, no 494, Abschlussvermerk, 29 March 1932.

145. LAB, A Pr Br, Rep 030, Tit 198B, no 523, Bl 3–4: Gennat to Herrn Regierungsdirektor Scholtz, 29 December 1932.

146. LAB, A Pr Br, Rep 030, Tit 198B, no 523, Bl 37: Vermerk, 29 December 1932.

147. LAB, A Pr Br, Rep 030, Tit 198B, no 523, Bl 48, 52: 29 December 1932.

148. LAB, A Pr Br, Rep 030, Tit 198B, no 523, Bl 79: Vermerk Gennat, 17 March 1933.

149. LAB, A Pr Br, Rep 030, Tit 198B, no 1631, Bl 19–22: Für den Tagesbericht, 12 February 1926.

150. LAB, A Pr Br, Rep 030, Tit 198B, no 1270, Bl 138a–149: Aktenmässige Darstellung der Todesermittlungssache Dr Barckhausen, Berlin, den 15 September 1931, geschrieben am 12.3.1932.

151. R Weichbrodt, *Der Selbstmord* (Basle, 1937), 89–90.

152. Meinhard Böhme, 'Selbstmord als Unfallfolge im versicherungsrechtlichen Sinne', *Veröffentlichungen aus dem Gebiete der Medizinalverwaltung*, 42 (1934), 261–336, 267.

153. Carl Bennewitz, 'Die Selbstmordsterblichkeit deutscher Lebensversicherter', in *Zeitschrift für das gesamte Versicherungswesen*, 31 (1931), 68–83, 82–3; Dr Alfred Schwöner, 'Die Selbstmörder: Alarmstatistiken der Lebensversicherungs-Gesellschaften', in *BZ am Mittag*, no 163, 16 July 1931; for further cases see Weichbrodt, *Der Selbstmord*, 163–4.

154. LAB, A Pr Br, Rep 030, Tit 198B, no 1270, Bl 138a–149: Aktenmässige Darstellung der Todesermittlungssache Dr. Barckhausen. Berlin, den 15 September 1931, geschrieben am 12 März 1932.

155. 'Der Fall Dr Barckhausen: Das Leben schreibt einen Kriminalroman', in *Vossische Zeitung*, Erste Beilage, no 176, 25 July 1931. On the crash of the *Danatbank* see Evans, *The Coming of the Third Reich*, 253.

156. Loewenberg, *Ueber den Selbstmord in Hamburg*, 34.

157. Eve Rosenhaft, *Beating the Fascists? The German Communists and political violence, 1929–1933* (Cambridge, 1983); Evans, *The Coming of the Third Reich*, 266–88.

158. LAB, A Pr Br, Rep 030, Tit 198B, no 463, Bl 30: Bericht, Abteilung IA, 30 September 1930.

159. Peter Longerich, *Die braunen Bataillone: Geschichte der SA* (Munich, 1989), 115–51.

160. LAB, A Pr Br, Tit 198B, no 463, Bl 55–61: Verhandelt: Paul G, 4 October 1930; Pamela E Swett, *Neigbors and Enemies: The culture of radicalism in Berlin, 1929–1933* (Cambridge, 2004), 294.

161. See generally Richard Bessel, *Political Violence and the Rise of Nazism: The storm troopers in eastern Germany 1925–1934* (New Haven, 1984), 75–96; Evans, *The Coming of the Third Reich*, 296.

162. GStA, I HA, Rep 84a, no 57804, Bl 1: *Völkischer Beobachter*, no 243, 30 August 1932; Bl 3: Oberstaatsanwalt als Leiter der Anklagebehörde beim Sondergericht an Herrn Preußischen Justizminister, 17 October 1932.

163. GStA, I HA, Rep 84a, no 57804, Bl 4: Vermerk, 17 January 1939.

164. LAB, A Pr Br, Rep 030, Tit 198B, no 1939, Verfügung, gez Gennat, 4 May 1926.

165. Most of these suicide notes are from Berlin. Despite many hours spent in other archives, I have not found similar collections of such files from rural areas. There are 417 suicide notes altogether kept in 14 folders in the Landesarchiv Berlin, ranging from 1888 until 1944. For the Weimar years, there are some 200 farewell letters, ranging from 1925 until 1932. LAB, A Pr Br, Rep 030, Tit 198B, Findbuch, Bl 415.

166. See Baumann, *Vom Recht*, 339–47, 340, 347.

167. LAB, A Pr Br Rep 030, Tit 198B, no 1940; see also Moritz Föllmer, ' "Good-bye diesem verfluchten Leben": Kommunikationskrise und Selbstmord in der Weimarer Republik', in idem (ed), *Sehnsucht nach Nähe: Interpersonale Kommunikation in Deutschland seit dem 19. Jahrhundert* (Stuttgart, 2004), 109–25, 122.

168. LAB, A Pr Br, Rep 030, Tit 198B, no 1939.

169. LAB, A Pr Br, Rep 030, Tit 198B, no 1939 (original emphasis).

170. LAB, A Pr Br, Rep 030, no 1939 (original emphasis).

171. LAB, A Pr Br, Rep 030, no 1939.

172. LAB, A Pr Br, Rep 030, Tit 198B, no 1945.

173. LAB, A Pr Br, Rep 030, Tit 198B, no 1943.

174. LAB, A Pr Br, Rep 030, Tit 198B, no 1944, Bitterling, Kriminal-Assistent, 24 March 1931.

175. Durkheim, *Suicide*, 201–39.

CHAPTER 2

1. Printed in Domarus (ed), *Hitler*, I/1, 279.

2. Calculated from numbers in Ernst Roesner, 'Selbstmord: Statistik', in Alexander Elster and Heinrich Lingemann (eds), *Handwörterbuch der Kriminologie und der anderen strafrechtlichen Hilfswissenschaften* (Berlin, 1936), II, 546–76, 551.

3. *Der Stürmer*, no 30 (July 1933).

4. Domarus, *Hitler*, II/1, 1408.

5. Kurt Helpap, 'Statistische Erhebungen über 485 versuchte und vollendete Selbstmorde, die auf der I. Inneren Abteilung des Horst-Wessel-Krankenhauses, Berlin, in den Jahren 1935 1937 beobachtet wurden', in *Deutsche Zeitschrift für die gesamte gerichtliche Medizin*, 30 (1938), 73–89, 88.

6. Albrecht Graf zu Münster, 'Ursachen des Selbstmordes in Deutschland: Eine zusammenfassende Darstellung', (unpublished MD thesis, University of Berlin, 1940), 6, 21, 34.

7. Entry on 'Selbstmord', in *Meyers Lexikon* (8th edn, Leipzig, 1942), IX, 1514–15.

8. Ernst Schäfer, 'Die Schuldlehre', in Franz Gürtner (ed), *Das kommende deutsche Strafrecht: Allgemeiner Teil: Bericht über die Arbeit der amtlichen Strafrechtskommission* (Berlin, 1934), 37–55, 37.

9. Roland Freisler, 'Willensstrafrecht: Versuch und Vollendung', in Gürtner (ed), *Das kommende deutsche Strafrecht*, 9–36, 11–12.

10. Evans, *Rituale*, 762–3.

11. Lothar Gruchmann, *Justiz im Dritten Reich 1933–1940: Anpassung und Unterwerfung in der Ära Gürtner* (Munich, 1987), 498, 761.

12. Hans-Walter Schmuhl, *Rassenhygiene, Nationalsozialismus, Euthanasie: Von der Verhütung zur Vernichtung 'lebensunwerten Lebens'* (Göttingen, 1987), 294–7.

13. Michael Burleigh, *Death and Deliverance: 'Euthanasia' in Germany, c 1900–1945* (Cambridge, 1994), 180; Beth Griech-Pollele, 'Bishop von Galen, the Euthanasia Project and the Sermons of Summer 1941', in *Journal of Contemporary History*, 36 (2001), 43–64.

14. BAB, R 8034 II/1774, Bl 13: *Völkischer Beobachter*, 25 June 1936.

15. Quoted in Kenneth M Pinnow, 'Violence against the collective self and the problem of social integration in early Bolshevik Russia', in *Kritika*, 4 (2003), 653–77 , 660–1.

16. Quoted in Baumann, *Vom Recht*, 351; on Gleispach, see Evans, *Rituale*, 762.

17. BAB, R 8034 II/1774, Bl 1: *Rhein-Westfälische Zeitung*, 2 February 1936.

18. Gruchmann, *Justiz im Dritten Reich*, 786; see also Jürgen Regge and Werner Schubert (eds), *Quellen zur Reform des Straf- und Strafprozeßrechts, II. Abteilung, NS-Zeit (1933–1939)-Strafgesetzbuch, Band 1: Entwürfe eines Strafgesetzbuches, 1. Teil* (Berlin, 1988), 133.

19. Evans, *Rituale*, 783–91.

20. BAB, R 3001/alt/R 22/1314, Bl 20–5: Abschrift aus 'Völkischer Beoachter' vom 5 Januar 1929: Strafe oder Vernichtung? Von Ludwig Binz; see also Evans, *Rituale*, 785.

21. BAB, R 3001/R 22 alt/1314, Bl 14-19: Protokoll der 17 Sitzung vom 1 März 1934.

22. StA Darmstadt, G 24, no 335, Der Generalstaatsanwalt an Hessisches Staatsministerium, Abt 1c Justiz, 12 September 1934.

23. BAB, R 3001/alt/R 22/1314, Bl 14-19: Stellungnahme der Strafrechtskommission zu der Frage der Vollziehung der Todesstrafe (Protokoll der 17. Sitzung vom 1. März 1934); see also, ibid, Bl 26: *Neue Berliner Zeitung: Das 12 Uhr-Blatt*, 25 October 1934.

24. Quoted in Bradley F Smith and Agnes F Peterson (eds), *Heinrich Himmler: Geheimreden 1933 bis 1945 und andere Ansprachen* (Frankfurt am Main, 1974), 90.

25. BAB, R 1501/127177/9, Bl 3: Der Reichsführer SS, Verteiler V, Betr: Selbstmorde von SS-Angehörigen, 1 April 1939; ibid, Bl 1: Der Reichsführer SS-Hauptamt SS-Gericht, 8 November 1944.

26. StA Darmstadt G 15 Friedberg, Q 1117, Abschrift Der Reichsführer SS und Chef der deutschen Polizei im Reichsministerium des Innern an den Reichsstatthalter in Hessen-Landesregierung Darmstadt, 11 January 1938, signed by Kurt Daluege; Betrifft: Häufung der Selbstmordfälle in der uniformierten Ordnungspolizei und Fürsorge der Dienstvorgesetzten.

27. BAB, NS 19/2291, Namentliche Aufstellung der in den Monaten Juli bis September 1942 durch Selbstmorde verstorbenen SS-Angehörigen, 19 November 1942.

28. BAB, NS 19/1181, Bl 2: Der Reichsführer SS to SS-Gruppenführer Winkelmann, 8 January 1944; see also Heinz Höhne, *Der Orden unter dem Totenkopf: Die Geschichte der SS* (Gütersloh, 1967), 140–1.

29. BAB, NS 19/1048, Bl 84: Der Reichsführer SS to HSSPF Elbe, 29 April 1944.

30. Gottfried Benn, 'Über Selbstmord im Heer (1940)', in *Neue Rundschau*, 87 (1976), 669–74, 674; see also his autobiographical sketch: Gottfried Benn, *Doppelleben: Zwei Selbstdarstellungen* (Stuttgart, 1984), 119–20.

31. Quoted in Evans, 'In search of German Social Darwinism', 138.

32. Gruhle, *Selbstmord*, 149.

33. Weichbrodt, *Der Selbstmord*, 133–44.

34. Gustav Donalies, review in *Der Nervenarzt*, 1938, Heft 2, copy in Institut für Stadtgeschichte Frankfurt am Main, Rep 553 Nachlaß Quint, S 1/150–532.

35. See Karl Binding and Alfred Hoche, *Die Freigabe der Vernichtung lebensunwerten Lebens: Ihr Maß und ihre Form* (Leipzig, 1920), 5.

36. Binding and Hoche, *Die Freigabe*, 8, 27, 34; Burleigh, *Death and Deliverance*, 11–42.

37. David Welch, *Propaganda and the German Cinema* (Oxford, 1983), 125–32, 127; Burleigh, *Death and Deliverance*, 212; Karl-Ludwig-Rost, ' "Euthanasie" -Filme im NS-Staat: Sozial- und filmhistorische Hintergründe einer Verführung zum Töten', in *Zeitgeschichte*, 28 (2001), 214–27.

38. Heinz Boberach (ed), *Meldungen aus dem Reich: Die geheimen Lageberichte des Sicherheitsdienstes der SS* (Herrsching, 1984), IX, 3174–8, 3178.

39. See for example Robert Gaupp, *Ueber den Selbstmord* (2nd edn, Munich, 1910).

40. Evans, 'In search of German Social Darwinism', 137–8.

41. BAB, R 58/483, Bl 86: Ein Selbstmörder und seine Vorfahren, undated but probably from 1935.

42. Johannes Schottky, 'Ueber den Mordversuch eines Jugendlichen bei geplantem Selbstmord', in *Monatschrift für Kriminologie und Strafrechtsreform*, 32 (1941), 1–32, 14, 25, 22, 31.

43. Alexander Elster, 'Der Selbstmord in kriminologischer, ethischer und sozialer Beurteilung', in idem and Lingemann (eds), *Handwörterbuch der Kriminologie und der anderen strafrechtlichen Hilfswissenschaften*, II, 538–42, 540; see also Arthur Hübner, 'Selbstmord: Forensisch-medizinische Erfahrungen', in Elster and Lingemann (eds), *Handwörterbuch der Kriminologie*, II, 543–6, 545.

44. Hans FK Günther, *Rassenkunde des deutschen Volkes* (Munich, 1926), 433; Wolfgang Damus, 'Der Selbstmord unter besonderer Berücksichtigung der Juden' (med diss, University of Vienna, 1942), 7, 49.

45. *BZ am Mittag*, no 99, 25 April 1935.

46. Weichbrodt, *Selbstmord*, 143.

47. Pinnow, 'Violence against the collective self', 676.

48. Karen Peter (ed), *NS-Presseanweisungen der Vorkriegszeit: Edition und Dokumentation* (Munich, 1998), V/1, 255.

49. Peter (ed), *NS-Presseanweisungen*, VI/1, 375.

50. Gerhard Füllkrug, 'Sozialer und gesundheitlicher Fürsorgedienst: Fürsorge für die Lebensmüden' in *Gesundheitsfürsorge: Zeitschrift der evangelischen Kranken- und Pflegeanstalten*, 7 (May 1933), 101–3.

51. Dr Ernst March, 'Die Not der Lebensmüden', in *Deutsche Volksmission*, 1 (1935), copy in ADW, CA/G 350.

52. Adolf Senff, 'Analyse von 1000 Selbstmordfällen unter besonderer Berücksichtigung bevölkerungspolitischer und versicherungspolitischer Belange' (unpublished PhD thesis, University of Berlin, 1936), 23.

53. See Figs 7 and 8. A consistent set of statistics detailing the relative age of those committing suicide is not available.

54. See Figs 9 and 10 in the appendix to this volume.

55. BAB, R 8034 II/5538, Bl 144: *Wirtschaftspolitischer Dienst*, 31 March 1936.

56. Claudia Brunner, *Arbeitslosigkeit im NS-Staat: Das Beispiel München* (Pfaffenweiler, 1997), 277–9.

57. Timothy W Mason, *Sozialpolitik im Dritten Reich: Arbeiterklasse und Volksgemeinschaft* (Opladen, 1977), 127, 166.

58. Petzina, Abelshauser and Faust, *Sozialgeschichtliches Arbeitsbuch Band III*, 96–7.

59. Richard Grunberger, *A Social History of the Third Reich* (London, 1971), 224.

60. LAB, A Pr Br, Rep 030, Tit 198B, no 1628, Bl 3: Vermerk, 2 September 1935.

61. BAB, NS 18/1371, Bl 3–4: Führerinformation, 6 November 1941.

62. Sheila Fitzpatrick, *Everyday Stalinism: Ordinary Life in Extraordinary Times. Soviet Russia in the 1930s* (New York, 1999), 172–5.

63. GStA, I HA, Rep 84a, Rep 90, Annex P, Bd 10,3, Bl 192–3: Regierungspräsident Magdeburg an Herrn Preußischen Ministerpräsidenten, 24 March 1936; on corruption in the Third Reich see Frank Bajohr, *Parvenüs und Profiteure: Korruption in der NS-Zeit* (Frankfurt am Main, 2001).

64. GStA, I HA, Rep 90, Annex P, Bd 10,4, Bl 26: Regierungspräsident an den Herrn Preußischen Ministerpräsidenten, 6 January 1937.

65. LAB, A Pr Br, Rep 030, Tit 198B, no 816, Bl 178–90: Bericht KJMI3, 12 November 1938. His wife was acquitted of charges of manslaughter on 7 June 1939.

66. Peter (ed), *NS-Presseanweisungen der* Vorkriegszeit, VI/3, 997.

67. Der Oberstaatsanwalt Limburg (18.7.1938), in Thomas Klein (ed), *Die Lageberichte der Justiz aus Hessen* (Darmstadt, 1999), 623.

68. Ian Kershaw, *Popular Opinion and Political Dissent in the Third Reich. Bavaria, 1933–1945* (Oxford, 1983), 17.

69. *Statistisches Jahrbuch für Bayern*, 21 (1936), 44.

70. BAB, R 58/473, Bl 97–8: Abschrift: Polizeiliche Ermittlungen bei Selbstmorden und Selbstmordversuchen. Statistik über Selbstmorde und Selbstmordversuche. RdErl d RFSSuChdDtPol im RMdI vom 28.2.1939.

71. Karlheinz Perl, 'Die psychiatrische Bedeutung der Selbsttötung in Westfalen im Vergleich zu anderen deutschen Gauen', in *Archiv für Psychiatrie und Nervenkrankheiten*, 110 (1939), 253–90, 264.

72. BAB, R 58/483, Bl 102–106: Die Notwendigkeit der Einführung einer obligatorischen Leichenschau, 1936.

73. BAB, NS 18/1371, Bl 3: Die aufgeführten neuen Zahlen für die deutsche Bevölkerung, 6 November 1941.

74. Durkheim, *Suicide*, 352; see also Retterstøl, *Suicide*, 85–6.

75. Cf Karl-Heinz Janssen and Fritz Tobias, *Der Sturz der Generäle: Hitler und die Blomberg-Fritsch Krise 1938* (Munich, 1994), 249.

76. BAB, R 58/158, Bl 43–4: Betr Statistik über die im 3 Vierteljahr 1940 im Reichsgebiet verübten Selbstmorde und Selbstmordversuche, 10 March 1941. Unfortunately this statistic is not available for other periods.

77. Erich Schmahl, 'Statistik der Selbstmorde und Selbstmordversuche', in Friedrich Burgdörfer (ed), *Die Statistik in Deutschland nach ihrem heutigen Stand: Ehrengabe für Friedrich Zahn* (Berlin, 1940), I, 333–8, 338.

78. LAB, A Pr Br, Rep 030, Tit 198B, no 1631, Bl 161: Zusammenfassung, 5 November 1938; see also Wagner, *Volksgemeinschaft ohne Verbrecher*, 191–8.

79. Evans, *The Coming of the Third Reich*, 310–27.

80. LAB, A Pr Br, Rep 030, Tit 198B, no 1228, Bericht, 27 March 1933.

81. Evans, *The Coming of the Third Reich*, 339.

82. GStA, I HA, Rep 84a, no 53422, Bl 1–2: Oberstaatsanwalt Bochum an den Herrn Preußischen Minister der Justiz, 16 June 1934; ibid, Bl 4: 24 October 1934; on the background see Gruchmann, *Justiz im Dritten Reich*, 334–6.

83. Willy Brandt, *Erinnerungen* (Frankfurt am Main, 1989), 96; on the context see Heinrich August Winkler, *Der Weg in die Katastrophe: Arbeiter und Arbeiterbewegung in der Weimarer Republik 1930 bis 1933* (Bonn, 1989), 901–6; Evans, *The Coming of the Third Reich*, 351–4.

84. *Berliner illustrierte Nachtausgabe*, no 96, 25 April 1933; LAB, A Pr Br, Rep 030, Tit 198B, no 1804, Bl 101: *Deutsche Allgemeine Zeitung*, no 191, 25 April 1933.

85. Entry in Martin Schumacher (ed), *M.d.R.: Die Reichstagsabgeordneten der Weimarer Republik in der Zeit des Nationalsozialismus. Politische Verfolgung, Emigration und Ausbürgerung 1933–1945* (Düsseldorf, 1994), 364–6.

86. Evans, *The Coming of the Third Reich*, 370–1; *Braunbuch über Reichstagsbrand und Hitler-Terror. Vorwort von Lord Marley* (Basle, 1933), 78, 116–18.

87. *Berliner Illustrierte Nachtausgabe*, no 88, 13 April 1933; on violence following the Nazi seizure of power see Evans, *The Coming of the Third Reich*, 333–49; *Braunbuch*, 182–221.

88. Cf Hugo Weidenhaupt, *Kleine Geschichte der Stadt Düsseldorf* (Düsseldorf, 1993), 170.

89. Evans, *Rituale*, 748.

90. Quoted in Friedrich Schlotterbeck, *The Darker the Night, the Brighter the Stars: A German worker remembers (1933–1945)* (London, 1947), 29.

91. Landeshauptstadt Düsseldorf (ed), *Verfolgung und Widerstand in Düsseldorf, 1933–1945* (Düsseldorf, 1990), 34.

92. Klaus Drobisch and Günther Wieland, *System der NS-Konzentrationslager 1933–1939* (Berlin, 1993), 71–5; 131; on early camps see Jane Caplan, 'Political detention and the origin of the concentration camps in Nazi Germany', in Neil Gregor (ed), *Nazism, War and Genocide: Essays in honour of Jeremy Noakes* (Exeter, 2005), 22–41, 23.

93. Evans, *The Coming of the Third Reich*, 409–10; cf Chris Hirte, *Erich Mühsam: 'Ihr seht mich nicht feige'* (East-Berlin, 1985), 447.

94. Gruchmann, *Justiz im Dritten Reich*, 653.

95. Gruchmann, *Justiz im Dritten Reich*, 646.

96. Klaus Behnken (ed), *Deutschland-Berichte der Sopade* (Frankfurt am Main, 1980), IV, 697.

97. Nikolaus Wachsmann, *Hitler's Prisons: Legal terror in Nazi Germany* (New Haven, 2004), 136–7.

98. *Braunbuch*, 325.

99. Evans, *The Third Reich in Power*, 68–73.

100. Allan Merson, *Communist Resistance in Nazi Germany* (London, 1985), 138–9.

101. BAB, R 3001/20603, Bl 54–6: Diensttagebuch des Reichsjustizministers, 2 April 1935.

102. Quoted in Volker Kühn (ed), *Deutschlands Erwachen: Kabarett unterm Hakenkreuz 1933–1945* (Weinheim, 1989), 335.

103. Quoted in Evans, *The Third Reich in Power*, 175.

104. Behnken (ed), *Deutschland-Berichte der Sopade*, I, 19.

105. Longerich, *Die braunen Bataillone*, 179–206.

106. GStA, I HA, Rep 84a, no 54767, Bl 2–5: Generalstaatsanwalt bei dem Landgericht an den Herrn Preussischen Justizminister, 15 September 1934; ibid, Bl 8: Beglaubigte Abschrift, Angriff vom Februar 1934; ibid, Bl 10–15: Der Generalstaatsanwalt bei dem Landgericht, 18 December 1934. See Longerich, *Die Braunen Bataillone*, 224–30.

107. Peter H Merkl, *Political Violence under the Swastika: 581 early Nazis* (Princeton, 1975), 665.

108. LAB, A Pr Br, Rep 030, Tit 198B, no 1281, Bl 9: interrogation of Bruno L, 19 April 1935.

109. LAB, A Pr Br, Rep 030, Tit 198B, no 1281, Bl 29–32: Schlussbericht, 3 May 1935.

110. On the institutional context see Robert Gellately, *The Gestapo and German Society: Enforcing racial terror, 1933–1945* (Oxford, 1990), 22–43.

111. GStA, I HA, Rep 84a, no 54761, Bl 1–13: Anklage auf Mordverdacht gegen Unbekannt, 26 July 1933 (original emphasis).

112. GStA, I HA, Rep 84a, no 54761, Bl 24–31: Tatsachenbericht Helmuth U, 10 March 1933.

113. Ibid, Bl 31: U to SA-Führung, 28 February 1933.

114. Ibid, Bl 1: Adolf Hitler, Kanzlei to Ministerialrat Diels, 20 January 1934; ibid, Bl, 52–4: III. Geheimdienst, 14 March 1934.

115. Ibid, Bl 9: Julius U an Herrn Staatsanwaltschaftsrat von Haacke, 16 October 1934.

116. Kevin P Spicer, *Resisting the Third Reich: The Catholic clergy in Hitler's Berlin* (DeKalb, Ill, 2004), 38–41; Lothar Gruchmann, 'Erlebnisbericht Werner Pünders über die Ermordung Klauseners am 30. Juni 1934 und ihre Folgen', in *Vierteljahrshefte für Zeitgeschichte*, 19 (1971), 404–31.

117. Gruchmann, *Justiz im Dritten Reich*, 479–80.

118. Quoted in Ian Kershaw, *Hitler, 1889–1936: Hubris* (London, 1998), 516.

119. Robert Gellately, *Backing Hitler: Consent and coercion in Nazi Germany* (Oxford, 2001), 15.

120. Quoted in Evans, *The Third Reich in Power*, 110–11.

121. GStA, I HA, Rep 84a, no 54818, Der Oberstaatsanwalt bei dem Landgericht Königsberg an den Herrn Preußischen Minister der Justiz, Bl 2–3: 29 August 1934; ibid, Bl 4–6: 31 August 1934; ibid, Bl 7–8: 12 September 1934, ibid: Bl 13: 15 January 1935; cf Gellately, *Backing Hitler*, 15–16.

122. For a similar argument see Wachsmann, *Hitler's Prisons*, 372.

123. See more generally Robert Gellately and Nathan Stoltzfus (eds), *Social Outsiders in the Third Reich* (Princeton, 2001).

124. StA Hamburg, Bestand 331–5 Polizeibehörde—Unnatürliche Sterbefälle.

125. StA Hamburg, 331–5 Polizeibehörde—Unnatürliche Sterbefälle, no 70/38, Polizei an die Direktion Farmsen, 4 January 1938.

126. Ernst Klee, *'Euthanasie' im NS-Staat: Die 'Vernichtung lebensunwerten Lebens'* (Frankfurt am Main, 1985), 36–8.

127. Wolfgang Ayass, *'Asoziale' im Nationalsozialismus* (Stuttgart, 1995); Evans, *The Third Reich in Power*, 88–9.

128. Evans, *The Third Reich in Power*, 532.

129. StA Würzburg, Gestapostelle no 1627, Haftbefehl, Untersuchungsrichter Würzburg, 17 July 1935.

130. Geoffrey J Giles, 'The institutionalization of homosexual panic in the Third Reich', in Gellately and Stoltzfus (eds), *Social Outsiders*, 233–55, 240.

131. Burkhard Jellonnek, *Homosexuelle unter dem Hakenkreuz: Die Verfolgung von Homosexuellen im Dritten Reich* (Paderborn, 1990), 113, 328.

132. LAB, A Rep 358–02, no 132128, Bl 2: Abschrift, 3 March 1937; also quoted in Gabriele Roßbach, '*Sie sahen das Zwecklose ihres Leugnens ein*: Verhöre bei Gestapo und Kripo', in Andreas Pretzel and Gabriele Roßbach (eds), *Wegen der zu erwartenden hohen Strafe: Homosexuellenverfolgung in Berlin 1933–1945* (Berlin, 2000), 74–98, 91.

133. LAB, A Rep 358–02, no 132128, Bl 28: Gründe, 7 April 1937.

134. Quoted in Roßbach, '*Sie sahen das Zwecklose ihres Leugnens ein*', 91.

135. Wachsmann, *Hitler's Prisons*, 144.

136. StA Hamburg, 331−5 Polizeibehörde—Unnatürliche Sterbefälle, no 375/38, Vermerk, 15 January 1938.

137. LAB, A Pr Br, Rep 030, Tit 198B, Findbuch, Bl 415.

138. LAB, A Pr Br, Rep 030, Tit 198B, no 1948.

139. LAB, A Pr Br, Rep 030, Tit 198B, no 1949.

140. StA Darmstadt, G 15 Friedberg, no P 483, Bericht des Hessischen Polizei-Amts Bad Nauheim an Hessisches Kreisamt Friedberg, Abschrift, 14 April 1935.

141. LAB, A Pr Br, Rep 030, Tit 198B, no 1948, 171. Polizei-Revier Schöneberg, 4 February 1935.

142. LAB, A Pr Br, Rep 030, Tit 198B, no 1949.

143. Robert Proctor, *The Nazi War on Cancer* (Princeton, 1999), 173−247.

144. LAB, A Pr Br, Rep 030, Tit 198B, no 1947.

145. On sacrifice in the Third Reich see Baird, *To Die For Germany*; Sabine Behrenbeck, 'The transformation of sacrifice: German identity between heroic narrative and economic success', in Paul Betts and Greg Eghigian (eds), *Pain and prosperity: Reconsidering twentieth-century German history* (Stanford, 2003), 110−36.

146. LAB, A Pr Br, Rep 030, Tit 198B, no 1950.

147. LAB, A Pr Br, Rep 030, Tit 198B, no 1951 (original emphases).

148. LAB, A Pr Br, Rep 030, Tit 198B, no 1951 (original emphases).

149. LAB, A Pr Br, Rep 030, Tit 198B, no 1953.

150. LAB, A Pr Br, Rep 030, Tit 198B, no 1954, Kriminal-Inspektion Neukölln-Treptow, 27 May 1939.

151. LAB, A Pr Br, Rep 030, Tit 198B, no 1952.

152. Durkheim, *Suicide*, 201−39.

153. Philippe Ariès, *The Hour of Our Death* (New York, 1981), 559−601.

CHAPTER 3

1. For a summary see Janet Schenk McCord, 'A study of the suicides of eight Holocaust survivors/writers' (PhD thesis, Boston University, 1995); Lisa Lieberman, *Leaving You: The cultural meaning of suicide* (Chicago, 2003), 148.

2. Konrad Kwiet and Helmut Eschwege, *Selbstbehauptung und Widerstand: Deutsche Juden im Kampf um Existenz und Menschenwürde 1933−1945* (Hamburg, 1984), 194−215, 196−7.

3. Marion Kaplan, *Between Dignity and Despair: Jewish life in Nazi Germany* (New York, 1998), 179−84.

4. *Der Gelbe Fleck: Die Ausrottung von 500000 deutschen Juden, mit einem Vorwort von Lion Feuchtwanger* (Paris, 1936), 261. See also Comité des Délégations

Juives (ed), *Das Schwarzbuch: Tatsachen und Dokumente. Die Lage der Juden in Deutschland 1933* (reprint Frankfurt am Main, 1983 [1934]).

5. Kwiet and Eschwege, *Selbstbehauptung und Widerstand*, 200.

6. Diary of Max Reiner (1940), printed in Monika Richarz, *Jüdisches Leben in Deutschland: Selbstzeugnisse zur Sozialgeschichte, 1918–1945* (Stuttgart, 1982), 106–19, 116.

7. Comité des Délégations Juives (ed), *Schwarzbuch*, 521; *Der Gelbe Fleck*, 263; Michael Kater, *Doctors under Hitler* (Chapel Hill, 1989), 188.

8. *Jüdische Rundschau*, 25 April 1933, quoted in Comité des Délégations Juives (ed), *Schwarzbuch*, 522.

9. *Der Stürmer*, no 30 (July 1933).

10. Cf Kwiet and Eschwege, *Selbstbehauptung und Widerstand*, 200.

11. For background see Alexandra Przyrembel, *'Rassenschande': Reinheitsmythos und Vernichtungslegitimation im Nationalsozialismus* (Göttingen, 2003), 185–488.

12. Gestapa Sachsen, Bericht für Oktober 1935, Document 1342, in Otto Dov Kulka and Eberhard Jäckel (eds), *Die Juden in den geheimen NS-Stimmungsberichten 1933–1945* (Düsseldorf, 2004), CD-Rom.

13. Hertha Nathorff, *Das Tagebuch der Hertha Nathorff: Berlin-New York. Aufzeichnungen 1933 bis 1945*, Wolfgang Benz (ed) (Munich, 1987), 74; Hans Robinsohn, *Justiz als politische Verfolgung: Die Rechtsprechung in 'Rassenschandefällen' beim Landgericht Hamburg 1936–1943* (Stuttgart, 1977), 142.

14. StA Würzburg, Gestapostelle Würzburg no. 15591, Schutzmannschaft Würzburg, Meldung (22 March 1936).

15. Evans, *The Third Reich in Power*, 570–3.

16. Paul A Nisbet, Ronald W Maris, Alan L Berman and Morton M Silverman, 'Age and the lifespan', in idem (eds), *Comprehensive Textbook of Suicidology* (New York, 2000), 127–44.

17. WL, PC 3, reel 33, Joodsche Perscommissie voor Bijzondere Berichtgeving, 3 November 1937; see also Kwiet and Eschwege, *Selbstbehauptung und Widerstand*, 201.

18. Quoted in Peter Gay, *Freud: A life for our time* (London, 1988), 622.

19. Gerhard Botz, *Wien vom 'Anschluß' zum Krieg: Nationalsozialistische Machtübernahme und politisch-soziale Umgestaltung am Beispiel der Stadt Wien 1938/39* (Vienna, 1978), 98–105; Evan Burr Bukey, *Hitler's Austria: Popular sentiment in the Nazi era, 1938–1945* (Chapel Hill, 2000), 142.

20. Elke Fröhlich (ed), *Die Tagebücher von Joseph Goebbels: Sämtliche Fragmente* (Munich, 1987), I/5, 225.

21. Quoted in Herbert Rosenkranz, *Verfolgung und Selbstbehauptung: Die Juden in Österreich, 1938–1945* (Vienna, 1978), 40.

22. WL, Testaments to the Holocaust: Atrocities, 1933–39, reel 72.

23. G Warburg, *Six Years of Hitler: The Jews under the Nazi regime* (London, 1939), 247.

24. WL, PC 4, reel 73, *Daily Herald*, 28 May 1938.

25. Evans, *The Third Reich in Power*, 605.

26. Kwiet and Eschwege, *Selbstbehauptung und Widerstand*, 202.

27. Evans, *The Third Reich in Power*, 590.

28. Kater, *Doctors under Hitler*, 200–1.

29. There is no explicit ban on suicide in either the Bible or the Talmud. The Halakha bans suicide, but makes some exceptions. When forced to murder someone, to convert to another faith, or to commit incest, suicide becomes acceptable. See *Jüdisches Lexikon* (Berlin, 1930), V, 350–2.

30. StA Hamburg, 331–5 Polizeibehörde—Unnatürliche Sterbefälle, no 57/39. On Jews in Hamburg during the Third Reich see Ina Lorenz, 'Das Leben der Hamburger Juden im Zeichen der "Endlösung" (1942–1945)', in Arno Herzig and Ina Lorenz (eds), *Verdrängung und Vernichtung der Juden unter dem Nationalsozialismus* (Hamburg, 1992), 207–47.

31. Michael Wildt, 'Violence against Jews in Germany, 1933–1939', in David Bankier (ed), *Probing the Depths of German Anti-Semitism: German society and the persecution of the Jews, 1933–1941* (New York, 2000), 181–209, 202–4.

32. StA Hamburg, 331–5 Polizeibehörde—Unnatürliche Sterbefälle, no 170/39, Geheime Staatspolizei, Staatspolizeileitstelle Hamburg, 10 November 1938.

33. SD-Außenstelle Hofgeismar. Judenaktion, 17 November 1938, printed in Kulka and Jäckel (eds), *Die Juden in den geheimen NS-Stimmungsberichten*, 320.

34. LAB, A Pr Br Rep 030, Tit 198B, no 1943. Cf Baumann, *Vom Recht auf den eigenen Tod*, 373–6.

35. Evans, *The Third Reich in Power*, 575.

36. Evans, *The Third Reich in Power*, 594–5.

37. In June 1933, there had been 160,564 *Glaubensjuden* in Berlin. In May 1939, this number had dropped to 78,713 including *Rassejuden*, according to Wolf Gruner, 'Die Reichshauptstadt und die Verfolgung der Berliner Juden 1933–1945', in Reinhard Rürup (ed), *Jüdische Geschichte in Berlin: Essays und Studien* (Berlin, 1995), 229–66, 256; for national figures see 'Jüdische Bevölkerungsstatistik', in Benz (ed), *Die Juden in Deutschland*, 733; see also 'Die Juden und jüdischen Mischlinge in den Reichsteilen und nach Gemeindegrößenklassen 1939', in *Statistisches Jahrbuch für das Deutsche Reich*, 59 (1941/42), 27.

38. Kaplan, *Between Dignity and Despair*, 129–44.

39. LAB, A Pr Br, Rep 030, Tit 198B, no 787, Schlußbericht der Aktiven Mordkommission, 27 July 1939.

40. See Rosi Cohen, *Das Problem des Selbstmordes in Stefan Zweigs Leben und Werk* (Bern, 1982); Martin Jay, 'Against consolation: Walter Benjamin and the refusal to mourn', in Jay Winter and Emmanuel Sivan (eds), *War and Remembrance in the Twentieth Century* (Cambridge, 1999), 221–39.

41. Leo Baeck Institute Berlin, MM 33, Lini G to Julius G, 9 December 1939.

42. Leo Baeck Institute Berlin, MM 31, Julius Guggenheim Memoirs, undated.

43. Kwiet and Eschwege, *Selbstbehauptung und Widerstand*, 202–3.

44. Marion Kaplan, 'Jewish daily life in wartime Germany', in Bankier (ed), *Probing the Depths*, 395–412, 395; Kaplan, *Between Dignity and Despair*, 184.

45. Kwiet and Eschwege, *Selbstbehauptung und Widerstand*, 56.

46. Martin Riesenburger, *Das Licht erlösche nicht: Dokumente aus der Nacht des Nazismus* (East-Berlin, 1960), 39–40.

47. Hildegard Henschel, 'Aus der Arbeit der Jüdischen Gemeinde Berlin während der Jahre 1941–1943: Gemeindearbeit und Evakuierung von Berlin, 16. Oktober 1941–16 Juni 1943', in *Zeitschrift für die Geschichte der Juden*, 9 (1972), 33–52, 44. See also Rivka Elkin, *Das Jüdische Krankenhaus in Berlin zwischen 1938 und 1945* (Berlin, 1993), 42–3.

48. WL, Eye Witness Accounts, P.III.a. no 1095.

49. Herbert Schott, 'Die ersten drei Deportationen mainfränkischer Juden 1941/42', in Albrecht Liess (ed), *Wege in die Vernichtung: Die Deportation der Juden aus Mainfranken 1941–1943* (Munich, 2003), 73–166, 139.

50. Quoted in Richarz, *Jüdisches Leben*, 431; see also Kwiet and Eschwege, *Selbstbehauptung und Widerstand*, 206–7.

51. Kwiet and Eschwege, *Selbstbehauptung und Widerstand*, 199.

52. BAB, NS 18/1371, Bl 4: 'Führerinformation', undated; ibid, Bl 5: 'Dem Herrn Minister', 7 April 1942.

53. Bruno Blau, 'The last days of German Jewry in the Third Reich', in *Yivo Annual of Jewish Social Science*, 8 (1953), 197–204, 200.

54. LAB, A Pr Br Rep 030, Tit 198B, no 1623–1626. See Figs 11 and 12 in the appendix to this volume.

55. Wolf Gruner, *Judenverfolgung in Berlin 1933–1945: Eine Chronologie der Behördenmaßnahmen in der Reichshauptstadt* (Berlin, 1996), 80.

56. Henschel, 'Aus der Arbeit der Jüdischen Gemeinde Berlin während der Jahre 1941–1943', 35.

57. Gruner, *Judenverfolgung*, 88, 98–101.

58. Eric A Johnson and Karl-Heinz Reuband, *What We Knew: Terror, mass murder, and everyday life in Nazi Germany* (Cambridge, Mass., 2005), 364.

59. Victor Klemperer, *Ich will Zeugnis ablegen bis zum letzten: Tagebücher 1942–1945* (Berlin, 1995), II, 92.

60. LAB, A Pr Br Rep 030, Tit 198B, no 1623, 'Zusammenstellung der Selbstmorde und Selbstmordversuche für das Kalenderjahr 1941'; ibid, no 1624, 'Zusammenstellung der Selbstmorde und Selbstmordversuche für das Kalenderjahr 1942'; ibid no 1625, 'Zusammenstellung der Selbstmorde und Selbstmordversuche für das Kalenderjahr 1943'; on gender and suicide see Kushner, 'Women and suicide in historical perspective', 537–52. See Figs 11 and 12 in the appendix to this volume.

61. Richarz, *Jüdisches Leben*, 433.

62. Ilse Rewald, *Berliner, die uns halfen, die Hitlerdiktatur zu überleben* (Berlin, 1975), 4.

63. Howard K Smith, *Last Train from Berlin* (London, 1942), 140.

64. Quoted in Eric A Johnson, *Nazi Terror: The Gestapo, Jews and ordinary Germans* (New York, 2000), 444–7, 446. On the BBC broadcasting of the Holocaust see David Bankier, *The Germans and the Final Solution: Public opinion under Nazism* (Oxford, 1992), 113.

65. LAB, A Rep 358-02, no 142671.

66. LAB, A Rep 358-02, no 142676 (original emphasis).

67. Kwiet and Eschwege, *Selbstbehauptung und Widerstand*, 212; Kaplan, *Between Dignity and Despair*, 181.

68. Kaplan, *Between Dignity and Despair*, 183.

69. LAB, A Rep 358-02, no 143148, Leichensache, Schlafmittelvergiftung, 15 March 1943.

70. LAB, A Rep 358-02, no 141883.

71. LAB, A Pr Br, Rep 030, Tit 198B, no 1596, Bl 5: Oberbürgermeister als Ortspolizeibehörde, 12 January 1943.

72. LAB, A Rep 358-02, no 137482, Selbstmord durch Sprung aus dem Fenster, 26 August 1943.

73. Kaplan, 'Jewish daily life', 406.

74. LAB, A Rep 358-02, no 142565, Kriminal-Inspektion Mitte, 9 March 1943.

75. Kwiet and Eschwege, *Selbstbehauptung und Widerstand*, 199.

76. Wolfgang Benz, *Überleben im Dritten Reich: Juden im Untergrund und ihre Helfer* (Munich, 2003).

77. LAB, A Rep 358-02, no 4305.

78. On mixed marriages see Beate Meyer, 'The mixed marriage: A guarantee of survival or a reflection of German society during the Nazi regime?', in David Bankier (ed), *Probing the Depths of German Anti-Semitism: German society and the persecution of the Jews, 1933–1941* (New York, 2000), 54–77.

79. Hans-Jürgen Brandt, 'Erinnerungen an die Tragödie einer Künstlerehe: Meta und Joachim Gottschalk', in *Frankfurter Hefte: Zeitschrift für Kultur und Politik*, 37 (1982), 5–8. On Mischehen see also Ursula Büttner, 'The persecution of Christian-Jewish families in the Third Reich', in *Year Book of the Leo Baeck Institute*, 34 (1989), 267–89.

80. LAB, A Rep 358-02, no 141660, Krim Pol Rev 101, 3 November 1944.

81. Klemperer, *Ich will Zeugnis ablegen bis zum letzten*, II, 653–4.

82. Gruner, *Judenverfolgung*, 91.

83. LAB, A Rep 358-02, no 143652, Pol Rev 294, Krim Pol Hermsdorf to Generalstaatsanwalt, 6 January 1945 (emphases in the original).

84. StA Hamburg, 331–5, Polizeibehörde—Unnatürliche Sterbefälle, no. 224/45.

85. LAB, A Rep 358-02, no 144354, Suicide note of Natalie G, 11 March 1945.

86. Kwiet and Eschwege, *Selbstbehauptung und Widerstand*, 209. On the camps see generally Ulrich Herbert, Karin Orth and Christoph Dieckmann (eds), *Die nationalsozialistischen Konzentrationslager—Entwicklung und Struktur* (Göttingen, 1998).

87. Wolfgang Sofsky, *Die Ordnung des Terrors: Das Konzentrationslager* (Frankfurt am Main, 1993), 73.
88. Thomas Bronisch, 'Suicidality in German concentration camps', in *Archives of Suicide Research*, 2 (1996), 129–44, 142.
89. Forschungsstelle für Zeitgeschichte Hamburg 6262, Konzentrationslager Mauthausen, Kommandantur to Frau Gertrud B, 14 September1942.
90. Paul Martin Neurath, *Die Gesellschaft des Terrors: Innenansichten der Konzentrationslager Dachau und Buchenwald* (Frankfurt am Main, 2004), 134.
91. Jean Améry, *Jenseits von Schuld und Sühne* (Munich, 1988 [1977]), 32. See also Irene Heidelberger-Leonard, *Jean Améry: Revolte in der Resignation: Biographie* (Stuttgart, 2004).
92. Bruno Bettelheim, *The Informed Heart: The human condition in modern mass society* (London, 1961), 250–1.
93. Hermann Langbein, *Menschen in Auschwitz* (Vienna, 1972), 144–9, 144.
94. Yitzhak Arad, *Belzec, Sobibor, Treblinka: The Operation Reinhard death camps* (Bloomington, 1987), 223–5.
95. Kaplan, *Between Dignity and Despair*, 183.
96. Volker Dahm, 'Kulturelles und geistiges Leben', in Benz (ed), *Die Juden in Deutschland*, 75–267, 258.
97. Hannah Arendt, 'We refugees', in eadem, *The Jew as Pariah: Jewish identity and politics in the modern age*, Ron H Feldman (ed) (New York, 1978), 55–66, 59.
98. Kwiet and Eschwege, *Selbstbehauptung und Widerstand*, 196.

# CHAPTER 4

1. *Statistisches Jahrbuch für das Deutsche Reich*, 59 (1941/42).
2. BAB, NS 18/1371, Bl 5: Dem Herrn Minister, 7 April 1942. See Fig 13.
3. Richard Bessel, *Nazism and War* (New York, 2004), 95, 106–7.
4. Bessel, *Nazism and War*, 117–18. See Fig 14.
5. Cf Gellately, *Backing Hitler*, 253; Nicholas Stargardt, *Witnesses of War: Children's lives under the Nazis* (London, 2005), 13; for a critique see Peter Longerich, *"Davon haben wir nichts gewußt": Die Deutschen und die Judenverfolgung 1933–1945* (Munich, 2006), 317; Richard J. Evans, 'Coercion and consent in Nazi Germany', in *Proceedings of the British Academy*, 151 (2006), 53–81.
6. Peter Hüttenberger, 'Heimtückefälle vor dem Sondergericht München, 1933–1939', in Martin Broszat, Elke Fröhlich, and Anton Grossmann (eds), *Bayern in der NS-Zeit: Herrschaft und Gesellschaft im Konflikt* (7 vols, Munich, 1981), IV, 435–526, 436; Bernward Dörner, *'Heimtücke': Das Gesetz als Waffe. Kontrolle, Abschreckung und Verfolgung in Deutschland 1933–1945* (Paderborn, 1998), 20–5, 62–5.

7. StA Würzburg, Gestapostelle Würzburg, no 11227; on the wider context see Johnson, *The Nazi Terror*, 333–46.

8. Norbert Frei, *Der Führerstaat: Nationalsozialistische Herrschaft 1933 bis 1945* (Munich, 1987), 137. StA Würzburg, Gestapostelle Würzburg, no 15241.

9. Gellately, *Backing Hitler*, 193; Vandana Joshi, *Gender and Power in the Third Reich: Female denouncers and the Gestapo (1933–1945)* (London, 2003).

10. For a similar case see Gellately, *Backing Hitler*, 192.

11. Bessel, *Nazism and War*, 112.

12. StA Würzburg, Gestapostelle Würzburg, no 7402, Stapo AD Stelle Würzburg, 7 July 1941; Wachsmann, *Hitler's Prisons*, 284–8.

13. LAB, A Pr Br Rep 030, Tit 198B, no 1592, Bl 3: Der Amtsvorsteher als Ortspolizeibehörde, Kriminalpolizei, 27 February 1942.

14. Ayass, *'Asoziale' im Nationalsozialismus*, 175–9; see also Gabriele Lotfi, *KZ der Gestapo: Arbeitserziehungslager im Dritten Reich* (Stuttgart, 2000).

15. LAB, A Pr Br, Rep 030, Tit 198B, no 1592, Bl 49: Der Bürgermeister als Ortspolizeibehörde, Kriminalpolizei, 6 September 1943.

16. StA Hamburg, 331–5 Polizeibehörde—Unnatürliche Sterbefälle, no 86/44, Kriminalbereitschaftsdienst für unnatürliche Todesfälle, 19 December 1943.

17. Evans, *Rituale*, 826.

18. Wachsmann, *Hitler's Prisons*, 210.

19. Evans, *Rituale*, 840–3.

20. Printed in Heinz Boberach (ed), *Richterbriefe: Dokumente zur Beeinflussung der deutschen Rechtssprechung 1942–1944* (Boppard, 1975), 9.

21. Quoted in Wachsmann, *Hitler's Prisons*, 303–4.

22. StA Darmstadt, G 24, no 1189, Bl 238, Bl 240: copy of suicide note of Johannes R, filed on 10 August 1944.

23. StA Würzburg, Gestapostelle Würzburg, no 603, NSDAP Gauleitung Mainfranken, Der Stellvertretende Gauleiter to Geheime Staatspolizei, Aussendienststelle Würzburg, 3.3.1943; ibid, SD des Reichsführers SS to Gestapostelle Würzburg, 5 June 1943; ibid., Staatspolizeileitstelle Karlsruhe to Gestapostelle Würzburg, 10 September 1943; ibid, Gestapostelle Würzburg to Gauleitung Mainfranken, 24 September 1943.

24. Wachsmann, *Hitler's Prisons*, 191–226.

25. Evans, *Rituale*, 880.

26. Bessel, *Nazism and War*, 178.

27. LAB, A Rep 358-02, no 144060, Revierkriminalbüro 256, Karlshorst, 18 February 1945; on the increasing terror against Germans in the last months of the war see Evans, *Rituale*, 878–90.

28. Geoffrey J Giles, ' "The Most Unkindest Cut of All": Castration, homosexuality and Nazi justice', in *Journal of Contemporary History*, 27 (1991), 41–61, 42, 51.

29. Wachsmann, *Hitler's Prisons*, 146.

30. Andreas Pretzel, '*Ich wünsche meinem schlimmsten Feind nicht, daß er das durchmacht, was ich da durchgemacht habe*: Vorfälle im Konzentrationslager Sachsenhausen vor Gericht in Berlin', in idem and Roßbach, *Wegen der zu erwartenden hohen Strafe*, 119–68, 135.

31. LAB, A Rep 358-02, no 110562, Bl 4-5, 10–12: Verhandelt, 24 February 1942.

32. LAB, A Rep 358-02, no 110562, Bl 36: Verhandelt, 13 May 1942.

33. Giles, 'The institutionalization of homosexual panic', 248.

34. LAB, A Rep 358-02, no 140794, Bericht, 29 July 1944.

35. LAB, A Rep 358-02, no 108079, Der Generalstaatsanwalt bei dem Land-gericht, 23 February 1945.

36. LAB, A Rep 358-02, no 141448, Krim Gruppe S I, betr Entziehung der Festnahme durch Selbstmordversuch, 13 December 1943.

37. On the treatment of homosexuals in the Wehrmacht see Geoffrey J Giles, 'A gray zone among the field gray men: Confusion in the discrimination against homosexuals in the Wehrmacht', in Jonathan Petropoulos and John K Roth (eds), *Gray Zones: Ambiguity and compromise in the Holocaust and its aftermath* (New York, 2005), 127–46.

38. Giles, ' "The Most Unkindest Cut of All" ', 43, 57.

39. StA Hamburg, 331–5 Polizeibehörde—Unnatürliche Sterbefälle, no 111/40, 74. Polizeirevier, 7 December 1939; on popular reactions to the war's outbreak, see Evans, *The Third Reich in Power*, 704–5.

40. Ursula Büttner, ' "Gomorrha" und die Folgen: Der Bombenkrieg', in Forschungsstelle für Zeitgeschichte (ed), *Hamburg im 'Dritten Reich'*, 613–32, 613.

41. Bessel, *Nazism and War*, 107.

42. Büttner, 'Gomorrha', 613.

43. On the bombings see the controversial book by Jörg Friedrich, *Der Brand: Deutschland im Bombenkrieg 1940–1945* (Berlin, 2002); and the review by Nicholas Stargardt, 'Victims of Bombing and Retaliation', in *German Historical Institute London Bulletin*, 16 (November 2004), 57–70.

44. Ian Kershaw, *The 'Hitler Myth': Image and reality in the Third Reich* (Oxford, 1987), 202.

45. Statistisches Landesamt (ed), *Statistisches Jahrbuch für die Freie und Hansestadt Hamburg* (Hamburg, 1955), 61.

46. Hessisches Hauptstaatsarchiv Wiesbaden, Abt, 407/867, K I—1, 12 April 1944. On the bombings of Frankfurt see Dieter Rebentisch, 'Frankfurt am Main in der Weimarer Republik und im Dritten Reich', in Frankfurter Historische Kommission (ed), *Frankfurt am Main: Die Geschichte der Stadt in neun Beiträgen* (Sigmaringen, 1991), 423–519, 514.

47. Büttner, 'Gomorrha', 616–20.

48. Boberach (ed), *Meldungen aus dem Reich*, XIV, 5542 (original emphasis).

49. Boberach (ed), *Meldungen aus dem Reich*, XIV, 5563.

50. Kershaw, 'Hitler Myth', 203; Büttner, 'Gomorrha', 623.

51. Gerald Kirwin, 'Waiting for retaliation: A study in Nazi propaganda behaviour and German civilian morale', in *Journal of Contemporary History*, 16 (1981), 565–83, 579.

52. LAB, A Pr Br, Rep 030, Tit 198B, no 1592, Bl 36: Der Amtsvorsteher als Ortspolizeibehörde, Kriminalpolizei, Falkensee, 23 March 1943.

53. StA Hamburg, 331–5 Polizeibehörde—Unnatürliche Sterbefälle, no 119/44, Universitäts-Krankenhaus Eppendorf, 16 December 1943.

54. Büttner, 'Gomorrha', 630.

55. StA Hamburg, 331–5 Polizeibehörde—Unnatürliche Sterbefälle, no 113/44, 3. Krim Komm, Hamburg, am 8.1.43 (sic! This must read 1944).

56. StA Hamburg, 331–5 Polizeibehörde—Unnatürliche Sterbefälle, no 234/44, 3 KK, 7 January 1944.

57. LAB, A Pr Br, Rep 030, Tit 198B, no 844, Verhandelt, 29 January 1944.

58. Ulrich Herbert, *Fremdarbeiter: Politik und Praxis des 'Ausländer-Einsatzes' in der Kriegswirtschaft des Dritten Reiches* (Bonn, 1985), 271.

59. Quoted in Birthe Kundrus, 'Forbidden company: Romantic relationships between Germans and foreigners, 1939 to 1945', in Dagmar Herzog (ed), *Sexuality and German Fascism* (New York, 2005), 201–22, 201.

60. Quoted in Boberach (ed), *Meldungen aus dem Reich*, IX, 3200–1.

61. Kundrus, 'Forbidden company', 208–10.

62. Gellately, *Backing Hitler*, 177–8.

63. Quoted in Kundrus, 'Forbidden company', 217.

64. StA Hamburg, 331–5 Polizeibehörde—Unnatürliche Sterbefälle, no 29/42, Der Polizeipräsident Hamburg, Bericht, 5 January 1942.

65. Joshi, *Gender and Power in the Third Reich*, 148–51.

66. LAB, A Pr Br, Rep 030, Tit 198B, no 416, Bl 59–61: Schlussbericht, 2 April 1942.

67. Gellately, *The Gestapo and German Society*, 243.

68. Quoted in Kundrus, 'Forbidden company', 205.

69. LAB, A Pr Br, Rep 030, Tit 198B, no 1590, Bl 56: Staatliche Kriminalpolizei, Der Polizeipräsident in Potsdam, 19 April 1943.

70. Bessel, *Nazism and War*, 158.

71. BAB, R 3001/IIIg2 340/41, Der Oberstaatsanwalt Halle an den Herrn Vorsitzer des Sondergerichts Halle (Saale), 19 August 1941; ibid, Der Oberstaatsanwalt Halle an den Herrn Reichsminister der Justiz, 11 September 1941 (original emphasis). On the *Sondergerichte* see also Gruchmann, *Justiz im Dritten Reich*, 946–56; 1102–12. Legal discrimination against Poles was formalized in the Polish decrees of December 1941. On context see Hans Wüllenweber, *Sondergerichte im Dritten Reich: Vergessene Verbrechen der Justiz* (Frankfurt am Main, 1990), 24.

72. LAB, A Pr Br, Rep 030, Tit 198B, no 1604, Bl 4: Der Oberbürgermeister als Ortspolizeibehörde—Kriminalpolizei, 5 June 1942.

73. LAB, A Pr Br, Rep 030, Tit 198B, no 1592, Bl 32: Der Amtsvorsteher als Ortspolizeibehörde, Kriminalpolizei, 7 January 1943.

74. LAB, A Pr Br, Rep 030, Tit 198B, no 1583, Bl 57: Bericht, 15 February 1945; Evans, *Rituale*, 869–78.

75. LAB, A Rep 358–02, no 145363, Kommandeur der Sipo und des SD Außenposten Strausberg, 9 April 1945. On foreign workers see generally Herbert, *Fremdarbeiter*; Evans, *Rituale*, 869–78.

76. Kershaw, '*Hitler Myth*', 192.

77. Bessel, *Nazism and War*, 137.

78. Quoted in Joachim Szodrynski, 'Die "Heimatfront" zwischen Stalingrad und Kriegsende', in Forschungsstelle für Zeitgeschichte (ed), *Hamburg im Dritten Reich*, 633–85, 633.

79. Boberach (ed), *Meldungen*, XII, 4750.

80. Hans Mommsen, 'Die Rückkehr zu den Ursprüngen—Betrachtungen zur inneren Auflösung des Dritten Reiches nach der Niederlage von Stalingrad', in Michael Grüttner, Rüdiger Hachtmann, and Heinz-Gerhard Haupt (eds), *Geschichte und Emanzipation: Festschrift für Reinhard Rürup* (Frankfurt am Main, 1999), 418–34, 421–2.

81. LAB, A Pr Br, Rep 030, Tit 198B, no 1954, Kripoleitstelle—Chef des Reichssicherheitshauptamtes, 13 February 1943. The suicide note itself is not in the file.

82. Peter Jahn, '"Russenfurcht" und Antibolschewismus: Zur Entstehung und Wirkung von Feindbildern', in idem and Reinhard Rürup (eds), *Erobern und Vernichten: Der Krieg gegen die Sowjetunion 1941–1945* (Berlin, 1991), 47–64.

83. LAB, A Pr Br, Rep 030, Tit 198B, no 1954, Anzeige über einen Selbstmord durch Erschießen, 9 March 1943.

84. Michael H Kater, *Hitler Youth* (Cambridge, MA, 2004), 44–8.

85. LAB, A Pr Br, Rep 030, Tit 198B, no 1954, Abschrift, Kommissariat Berlin-Pankow, 21 August 1943.

86. LAB, A Pr Br, Rep 030, Tit 198B, no 1594, Bl 64: Bericht, 2 May 1944.

87. Bessel, *Nazism and War*, 150.

88. LAB, A Pr Br, Rep 030, Tit 198B, no 1583, Bl 49: Außendienststelle Eberswalde to Kriminalpolizei Berlin, 1 February 1945.

89. Frei, *Führerstaat*, 153–64.

90. Cf Gellately, *Backing Hitler*, 253.

91. Neil Gregor, 'Nazism: a political religion? Rethinking the voluntarist turn', in *Journal of Modern History*, in idem (ed), *Nazism, War and Genocide: Essays in honour of Jeremy Noakes* (Exeter, 2005), 1–21.

92. Eric D Weitz, *Creating German Communism, 1890–1990: From popular protests to socialist state* (Princeton, 1997), 304; Merson, *Communist Resistance*, 255.

93. Shareen Blair Brysac, *Resisting Hitler: Mildred Harnack and the Red Orchestra* (Oxford, 2000), 9, 337, 342.

94. Hans Mommsen, 'Social views and constitutional plans of the resistance', in Hermann Graml (ed), *The German Resistance to Hitler* (London, 1970), 55–147.

95. Peter Hoffmann, *Widerstand, Staatsstreich, Attentat: Der Kampf der Opposition gegen Hitler* (2nd edn, Munich, 1970), 602–4.

96. Joachim C Fest, *Staatsstreich: Der lange Weg zum 20. Juli* (Berlin, 1994), 399.

97. Hoffmann, *Widerstand*, 608–9.

98. Quoted in Hoffmann, *Widerstand*, 613.

99. Hoffmann, *Widerstand*, 616.

100. Hoffmann, *Widerstand*, 630.

101. LAB, F Rep 280, LAZ 9803, Aktennotiz, 26 June 1957. On Plettenberg see Peter Steinbach and Johannes Tuchel (eds), *Lexikon des Widerstandes, 1933–1945* (Munich, 1998), 156.

102. Jan C Nedoschill, 'Suizide deutscher Soldaten im Zweiten Weltkrieg', in *Österreichische Zeitschrift für Soziologie*, 23 (1998), 60–81; Georg Berger, *Die Beratenden Psychiater des deutschen Heeres, 1939–1945* (Frankfurt am Main, 1998), 166; see also Angelika Ebbinghaus, 'Soldatenselbstmord im Urteil des Psychiaters Bürger-Prinz', in eadem and Karsten Linne (eds), *Kein abgeschlossenes Kapitel: Hamburg im 3. Reich* (Hamburg, 1997), 486–537, 518.

103. Baumann, *Vom Recht*, 358.

104. Hoover Institution Archives, Stanford, D Lerner Collection, Box 7, Folder 4, 'Increase in suicides, attempted suicides and absence without leave since the Invasion', 18 September 1944 (the German document is dated 1 August 1944).

105. BAB, NS 19/2768, Bl 2–3: Blitz Partei-Kanzlei München to RFSS, 25 May 1944; see also Bl 5: 'Rundschreiben 166/44g: Betrifft: Freitod', 17 July 1944.

106. BAB, NS 19/2768, Bl 2–3: 'Blitz Partei-Kanzlei München an RSHA, betr Freitod von Soldaten', 26 May 1944; ibid, Bl 5: 'Der Leiter der Partei-Kanzlei, Rundschreiben 166/44g, betr Freitod', 17 July 1944.

107. Helmut Heiber (ed), *Akten der Partei-Kanzlei* (Munich, 1983), fiche 102–015 91: 'Blitz-Fernschreiben SS-Standartenführer Brandt to SS-Sturmbannführer Dr Beyer', 27 May 1944.

108. Printed in Helmut Heiber (ed), *Hitlers Lagebesprechungen: Die Protokollfragmente seiner militärischen Konferenzen, 1942–1945* (Munich, 1963), 79.

109. On Nazi ideas of heroic death see Baird, *To Die For Germany*, 202–42.

110. Printed in Heiber (ed), *Hitlers Lagebesprechungen*, 73.

111. Printed in Heiber (ed), *Hitlers Lagebesprechungen*, 75.

112. Fröhlich (ed), *Die Tagebücher*, VII, 234 (1 February 1943); ibid, 240 (2 February 1943); see also *Völkischer Beobachter* (Berlin edn), 24 January 1943, 'Heldenhafter Widerstand unter Auftreten aller Kräfte'; ibid, 27 January 1943, 'Heroischer Widerstand in den Ruinen Stalingrads'; ibid, 1 February 1943, 'Der Führer ehrt die Heldenschar von Stalingrad'.

113. See the anecdotal account by Walter Görlitz, *Paulus und Stalingrad: Lebensweg des Generalfeldmarschalls Friedrich Paulus* (Frankfurt am Main, 1964).

114. *Das Schwarze Korps*, no 48 (30 November 1944).

115. LAB, A Rep 009, no 234, Bl 55: Sonderabdruck aus dem Dienstblatt Teil III vom 9. April 1937: Bestattung gefallener Wehrmachtsangehöriger; on Nazi views on heroic death see Sabine Behrenbeck, *Der Kult um die toten Helden in Deutschland: Nationalsozialistische Mythen, Riten und Symbole* (Vierow, 1996).

116. LAB, A Rep 009, no 234, Bl 104: Der Oberbürgermeister Hauptplanungs-samt. Betrifft: Unterrichtung der NSDAP über Selbstmörder innerhalb der Wehrmacht, undated.

117. Berger, *Die Beratenden Psychiater des deutschen Heeres*, 170; Ebbinghaus, 'Sol-datenselbstmord', 497–502.

118. Quoted in Ebbinghaus, 'Soldatenselbstmord', 522. For a full version see Hoover Institution Archives, Stanford, D Lerner Collection, Box 6, Folder 3, 'Suicide and suicide attempts of German soldiers', 17 July 1944 (original document dated 17 January 1942).

119. On de Crinis see Günter Komo, *'Für Volk und Vaterland': Die Militärpsychiatrie in den Weltkriegen* (Münster, 1992), 147–9.

120. Archiv der Humboldt-Universität Berlin, Best. Nervenklinik, no 11, Gutach-ten, 8 February 1943; cf Baumann, *Vom Recht*, 361–3.

121. Christopher R Browning, *Ordinary Men: Reserve Police Battalion 101 and the Final Solution in Poland* (New York, 1992); see also Christian Streit, *Keine Kameraden: Die Wehrmacht und die sowjetischen Kriegsgefangenen 1941–1945* (Stuttgart, 1978).

122. Manfred Messerschmidt, *Die Wehrmachtsjustiz 1933–1945* (Paderborn, 2005); Ebbinghaus, 'Soldatenselbstmord', 502–4.

123. Printed in Ebbinghaus, 'Soldatenselbstmord', 513.

124. Ebbinghaus, 'Soldatenselbstmord', 510–1.

125. Bessel, *Nazism and War*, 150.

126. Bernd Wegner, 'Hitler, der Zweite Weltkrieg und die Choreographie des Untergangs', in *Geschichte und Gesellschaft*, 26 (2000), 493–518.

127. Gerhard L Weinberg, 'Unexplored questions about the German military during World War II', in *Journal of Military History*, 62 (1998), 371–80; see also Peter Hall, 'Kamikaze', in Diego Gambetta (ed), *Making Sense of Suicide Missions* (Oxford, 2005), 1–42.

128. Willi A Boelcke (ed), *Deutschlands Rüstung im Zweiten Weltkrieg: Hitlers Konferenzen mit Albert Speer 1942–1945* (Frankfurt am Main, 1969), 371, 389–90.

129. Fröhlich (ed), *Die Tagebücher*, XIII, 356 (29 August 1944), see also 582 (28 September 1944) and ibid, XIV, 262 (23 November 1944).

130. BAB, NS 19/2936, Bl 1–2: Bernhard B to Schwarzes Korps, November 1944; for the article see *Das Schwarze Korps*, no 46 (16 November 1944).

131. Fröhlich (ed), *Die Tagebücher*, XIV, 495 (30 December 1944).

132. Fröhlich (ed), *Die Tagebücher*, XV, 513 (15 March 1945), 658 (1 April 1945), 684 (8 April 1945).

133. Quoted in Antony Beevor, *Berlin: The Downfall 1945* (London, 2002), 238.

134. Weinberg, 'Unexplored Questions', 379.

135. Behrenbeck, *Der Kult um die toten Helden*, 520–32; Baird, *To Die For Germany*, 202–42.


CHAPTER 5

1. Michael Geyer, '"There is a land where everything is pure: Its name is land of death": Some observations on catastrophic nationalism', in Greg Eghigian and Matthew Paul Berg (eds), *Sacrifice and National Belonging in Twentieth-Century Germany* (Arlington, 2002), 118–47, 123. For a narrative account see Joachim Fest, *Der Untergang: Hitler und das Ende des Dritten Reiches* (Berlin, 2002).

2. As an example among many see the debate in Jörg Friedrich, *Der Brand: Deutschland im Bombenkrieg* (Berlin, 2002); Lothar Kettenacker (ed), *Ein Volk von Opfern? Die neue Debatte um den Bombenkrieg 1940–45* (Berlin, 2003).

3. Thomas Mann, *Tagebücher 1944–1.4.1946*, Inge Jens (ed) (Frankfurt am Main, 1986), 192, 196.

4. William L Shirer, *End of a Berlin Diary* (London, 1947), 50.

5. Theo Findahl, *Letzter Akt—Berlin, 1939–1945* (Hamburg, 1946), 155.

6. Anton Joachimsthaler, *Hitlers Liste: Ein Dokument persönlicher Beziehungen* (Munich, 2003), 330–5.

7. Kershaw, *Hitler,* I, 351–5; Joachimsthaler, *Hitlers Liste*, 440–2, 448.

8. Quoted in Fröhlich (ed), *Die Tagebücher*, I/2, 295–8, 297 (8 December 1932); see also Sebastian Haffner, *Germany: Jekyll and Hyde* (London, 1940), 24.

9. Haffner, *Germany*, 24; see also Kershaw, *Hitler*, I, xxviii.

10. Domarus (ed), *Hitler*, II/1, 1316.

11. Ian Kershaw, *Hitler (Profiles in Power)* (Harlow, 2001 [1991]), 216–17.

12. Walter C Langer, *The Mind of Adolf Hitler: The secret wartime report* (London, 1973), 211–12.

13. Domarus, (ed), *Hitler*, II/2, 2146.

14. A good study of Hitler's suicide is Anton Joachimsthaler, *Hitlers Ende: Legenden und Dokumente* (2nd edn, Munich, 2003), 201–87.

15. Quoted in Richard Overy, *Interrogations: The Nazi elite in Allied hands 1945* (London, 2001), 312.

16. IWM, 63/34/1, PE von Stemann, 'Himmler's last minutes in the hands of an English country doctor', unpaginated; IWM PP/MCR/292/reel 1: 'The Second World War papers of Major N Whittaker'.

17. Evans, *Rituale*, 901.

18. Bessel, *Nazism and War*, 187.

19. Joseph Goebbels, *Tagebücher 1945: Die letzten Aufzeichnungen* (Hamburg, 1977), 548.

20. Numbers based on Peter Hüttenberger, *Die Gauleiter: Studie zum Wandel des Machtgefüges in der NSDAP* (Stuttgart, 1969), 213–20; Ruth Bettina Birn, *Die Höheren SS- und Polizeiführer: Himmlers Vertreter im Reich und in den besetzten Gebieten* (Düsseldorf, 1986), 330–88. On suicides within the Wehrmacht leadership see *Frankfurter Allgemeine Zeitung*, 16 August 1950; and more generally, Klaus-Jürgen Preuschoff, *Suizidales Verhalten in deutschen Streitkräften* (Regensburg, 1988).

21. Stephanie Zibell, 'Der Gauleiter Jakob Sprenger und sein Streben nach staatlicher Macht im Gau Hessen-Nassau', in *Zeitschrift für Geschichtswissenschaft*, 49 (2001), 389–408, 408.

22. Martin Broszat (ed), *Kommandant in Auschwitz: Autobiographische Aufzeichnungen von Rudolf Höß* (Stuttgart, 1961), 143. See also Hüttenberger, *Die Gauleiter*, 213–20.

23. Gitta Sereny, *Albert Speer: His battle with truth* (New York, 1995), 543.

24. Domarus, *Hitler*, II/2, 2204–5.

25. Domarus, *Hitler*, II/2, 2213–14.

26. Timothy W Mason, 'Introduction to the English edition', in idem, *Social Policy in the Third Reich: The working class and the 'National Community'* (Oxford, 1993), 1–18, 12.

27. Behrenbeck, *Kult um die toten Helden*, 71, 75, 587–8.

28. *Völkischer Beobachter* (Munich edn), 28 March 1945.

29. *Völkischer Beobachter* (Munich edn), 16 April 1945.

30. Welch, *Propaganda and the German Cinema*, 221–37; see also *Völkischer Beobachter* (Berlin edn), 31 January 1945.

31. Ian Kershaw, *Hitler: Nemesis* (London, 2000), 783.

32. *Völkischer Beobachter* (Berlin edn), 1 March 1945.

33. Jacob Kronika, *Der Untergang Berlins* (Flensburg, 1946), 39–40.

34. Wegner, 'Hitler, der Zweite Weltkrieg und die Choreographie des Untergangs', 508.

35. Jeffrey Herf, *The Jewish Enemy: Nazi propaganda during World War II and the Holocaust* (Cambridge, MA, 2006), 262.

36. Quoted in Jeremy Noakes and Geoffrey Pridham (eds), *Nazism 1919–1945: A documentary reader* (Exeter, 1998), IV, 667–71, 670.

37. Quoted in Goebbels, *Tagebücher 1945*, 557.

38. Quoted in Overy, *Interrogations*, 477–98, 498.

39. Overy, *Interrogations*, 148–9, 205.

40. Quoted in Emmy Göring, *My Life with Göring* (London, 1972), 157.

41. Joachim C Fest, *Hitler* (Harmondsworth, 1982), 747.

42. Hannah Arendt, 'Organisierte Schuld', in *Die Wandlung*, 1 (1945/46), 333–44, 343. See also Klaus-Dietmar Henke, *Die amerikanische Besetzung Deutschlands* (Munich, 1995), 964.

43. Boberach (ed), *Meldungen aus dem Reich*, XVII, 6737.

44. Kronika, *Untergang*, 41.

45. LAB, F Rep 240 neu, A 0382, *Der Panzerbär*, 26 April 1945.

46. David Welch, *The Third Reich: Politics and propaganda* (London, 1993), 120–4. As an example among many see *Völkischer Beobachter* (Berlin edn), 8 March 1945.

47. BAB, NS 26/2127, Proklamation, 22 February 1945 (original emphasis). Cf Wolfram Wette, 'Das Rußland-Bild in der NS-Propaganda: Ein Problemaufriß', in Hans-Erich Volkmann (ed), *Das Rußlandbild im Dritten Reich* (Cologne, 1994), 55–78, 72.

48. Norman Naimark, *The Russians in Germany: A history of the Soviet zone of occupation, 1945–1949* (Cambridge, Mass, 1997), 69–140; see also Catherine Merridale, *Ivan's War: Life and death in the Red Army* (London, 2006), 268–71.

49. Magret Boveri, *Tage des Überlebens: Berlin 1945* (Munich, 1969), 111.

50. Helke Sander und Barbara Johr, *BeFreier und Befreite: Krieg, Vergewaltigung, Kinder* (Munich, 1992), 17; see also Atina Grossmann, 'A question of silence: The rape of German women by occupation soldiers', in *October*, 72 (1995), 43–64. See also eadem, *Jews, Germans, and Allies: Close encounters in occupied Germany* (Princeton, 2007), 53.

51. Printed in Susanne zur Nieden, *Alltag im Ausnahmezustand: Frauentagebücher im zerstörten Deutschland 1943–1945* (Berlin, 1993), 160; see also Bessel, *Nazism and War*, 188.

52. Boveri, *Tage des Überlebens*, 137.

53. Sereny, *Albert Speer*, 507.

54. LAB, F Rep 240, Acc 2651, no 2, Bl 131/1-131/10: Bericht von Gertrud S.

55. Ruth Andreas-Friedrich, *Battleground Berlin: Diaries 1945–1948* (New York, 1990), 16; see also anon, *A Woman in Berlin*, (London 1955), 27.

56. LAB, A Rep 358–02, no 144165, 196. Kriminalinspektion Schöneberg, 22 February 1945.

57. Richard Bessel, ''Leben nach dem Tod'—Vom Zweiten Weltkrieg zur zweiten Nachkriegszeit', in Bernd Wegner (ed), *Wie Kriege enden: Wege zum Frieden von der Antike bis in die Gegenwart* (Paderborn, 2002), 239–58, 246.

58. LAB, A Rep 358–02, no 144165, Abschrift des von Frau von B hinterlassenen Briefes, 16 February 1945.

59. Richard Bessel, 'Hatred after war: Emotion and the post-war history of East Germany', in *History and Memory*, 17 (2005), 195–216, 199–203.

60. LAB, LAZ 10678, Tagebuch Hertha v Gebhardt.

61. LAB, A Rep 358–02, no 145161, Leichensache. Polizeirevier 153, Kriminal-Polizei Schmargendorf to Generalstaatsanwalt, 1 April 1945.

62. StA Hamburg, 331–5 Polizeibehörde—Unnatürliche Sterbefälle, no 233/45, Der Polizeipräsident, 25./20. Polizeirevier, 16 February 1945; on the end of the war in Hamburg see Szodrzynski, 'Die ''Heimatfront'' ', 672–85.

63. National statistics are not available. See Fig 14 in the appendix to this volume.

64. Hauptamt für Statistik (ed), *Berlin in Zahlen 1947* (Berlin, 1949), 158; Elsner, 'Selbstmord in Berlin', 220, 224. See Fig 15 in the appendix to this volume.

65. LAB, A Rep 358–02, no 145391, Kriminalpolizeileitstelle Berlin, Kriminal-inspektion Mitte to Generalstaatsanwalt, 22 April 1945.

66. LAB, A Rep 358–02, no 143769, Krim-Bez Zehlendorf, 6 February 1945.

67. LAB, A Pr Br, Rep 030, Tit 198B, no 1590, Bl 150: Meldung, 10 February 1945.

68. Ibid, Bl 158–9: Meldung, 27 March 1945.

69. LAB, A Pr Br, Rep 030, Tit 198B, no 1604, Bl 27: Meldung, 4 April 1945.

70. Theodor Schieder (ed), *Die Vertreibung der Deutschen Bevölkerung aus den Gebieten östlich der Oder-Neiße* (Bonn, 1953). On the political intentions behind this edition see Robert G Moeller, *War Stories: The search for a usable past in the Federal Republic of Germany* (Berkeley, 2001), 51–87.

71. Schieder (ed), *Die Vertreibung*, I/2, 214–7, 214. On background see Norman M Naimark, *Fires of Hatred: Ethnic cleansing in twentieth-century Europe* (Cambridge, Mass, 2001), 126.

72. Schieder (ed), *Die Vertreibung*, I/2, 248–53, 249.

73. Only around 15,000 people lived there in 1933, but population numbers rose as refugees from further east arrived in 1945. See Norbert Buske (ed), *Das Kriegsende 1945 in Demmin: Berichte, Erinnerungen, Dokumente* (Schwerin, 1995), 43–4.

74. Damian van Melis, *Entnazifizierung in Mecklenburg-Vorpommern: Herrschaft und Verwaltung 1945–1948* (Munich, 1999), 23–4.

75. On suicides of refugees see H Bayreuther, 'Über den Selbstmord in der Nachkriegszeit: Eine Untersuchung von 1200 Fällen aus einer süddeutschen Großstadt', in *Zeitschrift für die gesamte Neurologie und Psychiatrie*, 195 (1956), 264–84, 282.

76. See Neil Gregor, '"Is he still alive, or long since dead?" Loss, absence and remembrance in Nuremberg, 1945–1956', in *German History*, 21 (2003), 183–203.

77. StA Darmstadt, H 14 DA F 1940, Bl 5: Beschluss Amtsgericht Darmstadt, 21 October 1954.

78. StA Darmstadt, H 14, F 306, Bl 3: Zur Sache, 1 October 1946.

79. LAB, A Rep 358–02, no 145187, Polizei-Bericht, 2 April 1945.

80. Goebbels, *Tagebücher 1945*, 549–50.

81. Bessel, 'Leben nach dem Tod', 251.

82. *Statistisches Jahrbuch für Bayern*, 23 (1947), 69; see also Bernd Martin, 'Die deutsche Kapitulation: Versuch einer Bilanz des Zweiten Weltkrieges', in *Freiburger Universitätsblätter* 34, 130 (1995), 45–70, 48.

83. The National Archives/PRO, FO 1050/314, Report on Kripoleitstelle Hamburg, June 1945.

84. StA Hamburg, 331–5 Polizeibehörde—Unnatürliche Sterbefälle, no 237/45, 11 Pol Revier, 5 February 1945.

85. Berthold Mueller and Johann Sitka, 'Untersuchungen über das Verhalten des Selbstmordes unter dem Einfluss der Verhältnisse der letzten Jahre', in *Ärztliche Wochenschrift*, 4 (1949), 663–7, 666.

86. Rudolf Krämer-Badoni, 'Zustand einer Großstadtbevölkerung am Beispiel Frankfurts', in *Die Wandlung*, 2 (1946), 812–41, 825; Anon, 'Der freiwillige Tod (Ein Beitrag zur Entwicklung der Selbstmordhäufigkeit in Frankfurt a. M.)', in *Statistische Monatsberichte Frankfurt am Main*, 3 (1955), 39–46, 40.

87. StA Darmstadt, G 15 Friedberg, Q 1014, Gend.-Posten Södel an den Herrn Oberstaatsanwalt in Gießen, 20 March 1945.

88. StA Darmstadt, G 15 Friedberg, Q 1006, Gendarmerieposten Friedberg, betr Mord und Selbstmord, 4 February 1945; on the end of war in this area see Herfried Münkler, *Machtzerfall: Die letzten Tage des Dritten Reiches dargestellt am Beispiel der hessischen Kreisstadt Friedberg* (Berlin, 1985), 199.

89. Erich Menninger-Lerchenthal, *Das europäische Selbstmordproblem: Eine zeitgemäße Betrachtung* (Vienna, 1947), 9, 13.

90. August Knorr, *Zum Problem des Selbstmordes* (Tübingen, 1948), 4, 37.

91. Reinhold Schneider, *Über den Selbstmord* (Baden-Baden, 1947), 40.

## CONCLUSION

1. Cf Udo Grashoff, '*In einem Anfall von Depression . . .*': *Selbsttötungen in der DDR* (Berlin, 2006), 50–4 and 27, 30 for East and West German suicide figures.

2. See among others, Gellately, *Backing Hitler*; Frank Bajohr, 'Die Zustimmungsdiktatur: Grundzüge nationalsozialistischer Herrschaft in Hamburg', in Forschungsstelle für Zeitgeschichte (ed), *Hamburg im 'Dritten Reich'*, 69–121. For a judicious critique see Evans, 'Coercion and consent'; Geoff Eley, 'Hitler's silent majority? Conformity and resistance under the Third Reich', in *Michigan Quarterly Review*, 42 (2003), 550–83; Gregor, 'Nazism: A political religion?', 1–21.

3. Kershaw, *Hitler (Profiles in Power)*, 217; Ian Kershaw, ' "Working towards the Führer": Reflections on the nature of the Hitler dictatorship', in *Contemporary European History*, 2 (1993), 103–18.

4. Durkheim, *Suicide*, 219.

5. Hahn and Schröder, 'Zur Einordnung des Suizids in das faschistische Konzept der "Vernichtung lebensunwerten Lebens" ', 109–16.

# Statistical Appendix

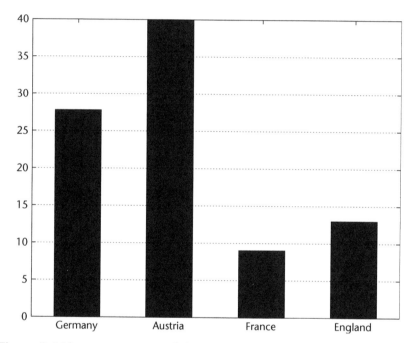

**Fig. 1.** Suicides per 100,000 population in Germany, Austria, France, and England and Wales, calculated as an annual average for 1919–30 (compiled from Gruhle, *Selbstmord*, 17)

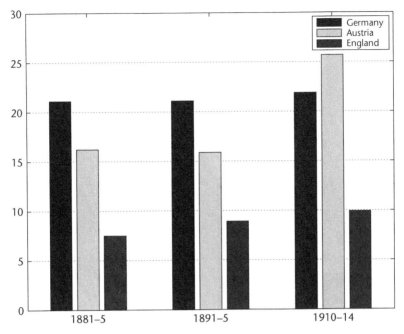

Fig. 2. Average suicide rates per 100,000 population in Germany, Austria-Hungary, England and Wales, 1881–5, 1891–5, 1910–14 (compiled from Howard Kushner, *Self-Destruction in the Promised Land: A psychocultural biology of American Suicide* (New Brunswick, 1989), 156)

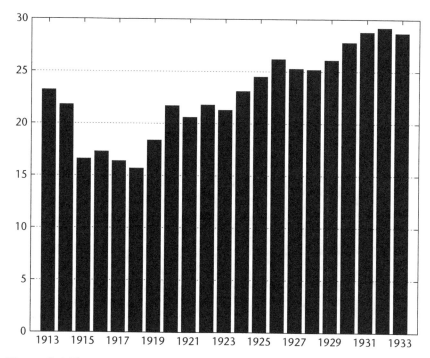

**Fig. 3.** Suicides per 100,000 population in Germany, 1913–33; numbers for after 1918 exclude territories ceded to France and Poland (compiled from *Statistik des Deutschen Reiches*, 307 (1923), 57, ibid, 316 (1924), 34, ibid, 336 (1925), 40; ibid, 360 (1928), 301; ibid, 393 (1929), 137; ibid, 441 (1931), 105; ibid, 495 (1932–34), I, 170)

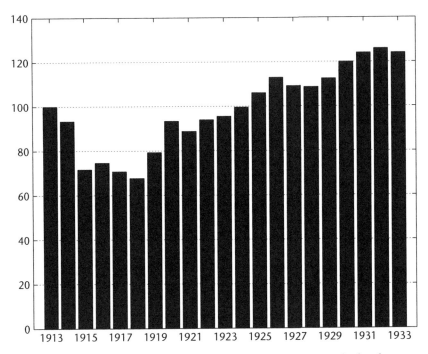

**Fig. 4.** Suicide per 100,000 population in Germany, 1913–33, calculated as an index 1913 = 100; numbers for after 1918 exclude those territories ceded to France and Poland (calculated from source as in Fig 3)

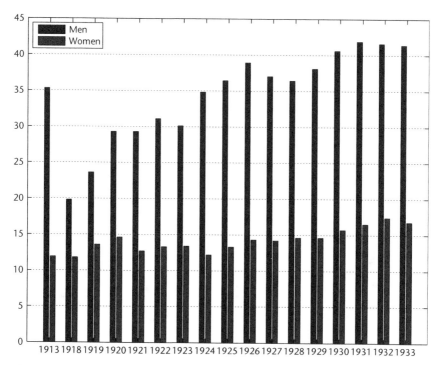

**Fig. 5.** Suicides in Germany per 100,000 population by sex, 1913, 1918–1933;
German numbers for after 1918 exclude territories ceded to France and Poland
(compiled from *Statistik des Deutschen Reiches*, 307 (1923), 57, ibid, 316 (1924), 34,
ibid, 336 (1925), 40; ibid, 360 (1928), 301; ibid, 393 (1929), 137; ibid, 441 (1931),
105; ibid, 495 (1932–4), I, 170)

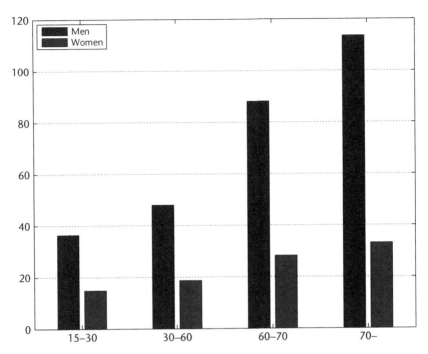

Fig. 6. Average annual suicide rates in Germany per 100,000 population, 1921–33, by age group and by sex (compiled from source as in Fig 5)

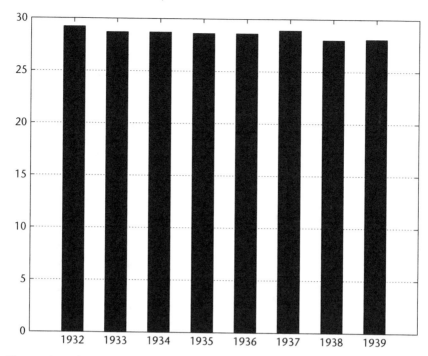

**Fig. 7.** Suicides in Germany per 100,000 population, 1932–9, excluding Austria and annexed territories (compiled from *Statistik für das Deutsche Reich*, 495 (1932–4), I, 170; *Statistisches Jahrbuch für das Deutsche Reich*, 56 (1937), 58 (1939/40))

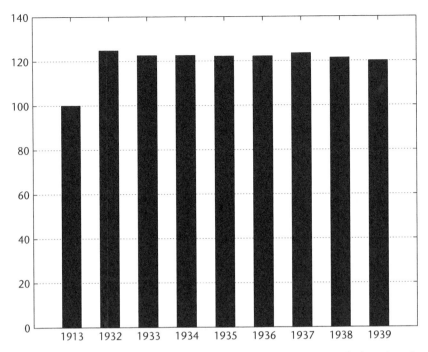

Fig. 8. Suicides in Germany per 100,000 population, 1932–9, excluding Austria and annexed territories, calculated as an index 1913 = 100 (source as in Fig 7)

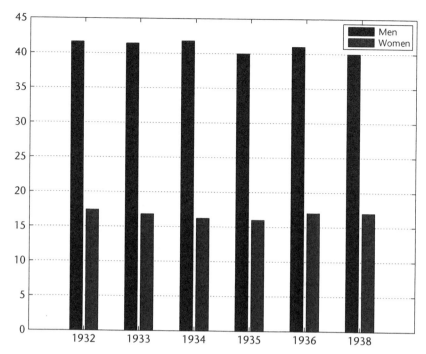

**Fig. 9.** Sex-specific suicide rate per 100,000 population in Germany, 1932–6, 1938, excluding annexed territories (source as in Fig 7)

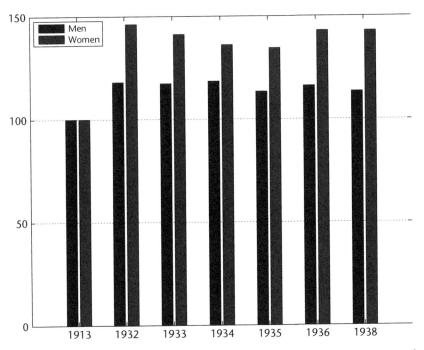

Fig. 10. Suicides per 100,000 population in Germany, 1932–6, 1938, by sex, calculated as an index 1913 = 100, excluding annexed territories (source as in Fig 7)

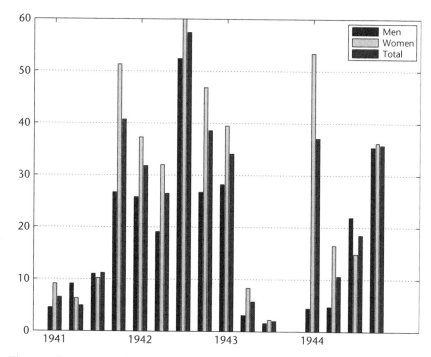

**Fig. 11.** Percentage of suicides in Berlin that were classified Jewish, quarterly figures 1941 to 1944 (numbers unavailable for fourth quarter of 1943) (compiled from LAB, A Pr Br, Tit 198B Rep 030, no 1623−6)

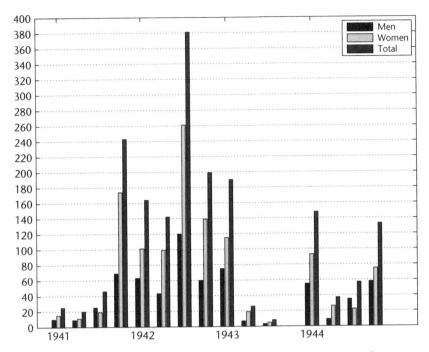

**Fig. 12.** Suicides in Berlin, classified Jewish, 1941–4, by quarter (numbers unavailable for fourth quarter of 1943) (source as in Fig 11)

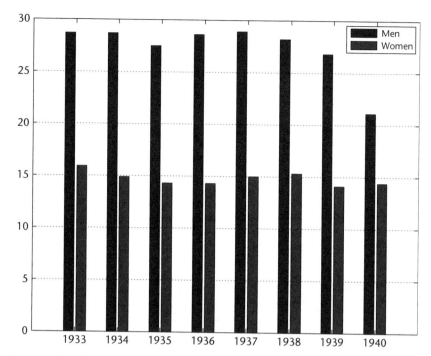

Fig. 13. Suicides in Germany per 100,000 population, 1934–40 (excluding
Austria and annexed territories and Jewish suicides) (compiled from BAB, NS
18/1371, Bl 8: 'Selbstmorde ab 1933')

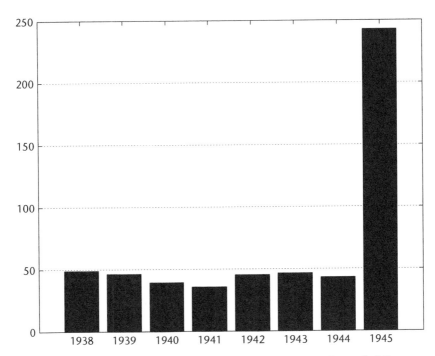

**Fig. 14.** Suicides in Berlin per 100,000 population, 1938–45 (compiled from Elsner, 'Selbstmord in Berlin', 220)

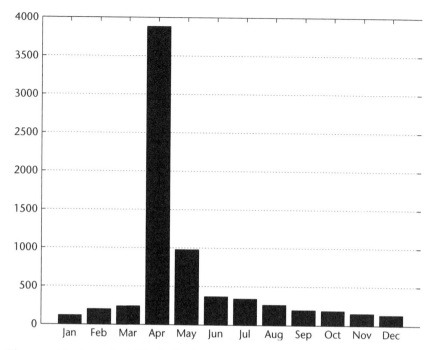

Fig. 15. Number of suicides in Berlin in 1945 (compiled from Hauptamt für Statistik (ed), *Berlin in Zahlen 1947* (Berlin 1949), 158)

# Bibliography

I MANUSCRIPT SOURCES

**I Archiv der Humboldt-Universität, Berlin**
Bestand Nervenklinik.

**II Bundesarchiv, Berlin-Lichterfelde**
NS 18 Reichspropagandaleiter.
NS 19 Persönlicher Stab Reichsführer SS.
NS 26 Hauptarchiv der NSDAP.
R 58 Reichssicherheitshauptamt.
R 1501 Reichsministerium des Innern.
R 3001 Reichsjustizministerium.
R 8034 II Reichslandbund—Pressearchiv.

**III Geheimes Staatsarchiv Preußischer Kulturbesitz, Berlin-Dahlem**
I HA Rep 84a Justizministerium.
I HA Rep 90, Annex P Geheime Staatspolizei; Lageberichte und Ereignismeldungen.

**IV Landesarchiv, Berlin**
A Rep 009 Magistrat der Stadt Berlin, Deputation für das Siedlungs- und Wohnungswesen/Amt für Siedlungs- und Wohnungswesen.
A Pr Br, Rep 030 Polizeipräsidium Berlin, Tit 198B Zentralkartei für Mordsachen.
A Rep 358-01 Generalstaatsanwaltschaft bei dem Landgericht Berlin, Strafverfahren, 1919–1933.
A Rep 358-02 Generalstaatsanwaltschaft bei dem Landgericht Berlin, Strafverfahren, 1933–1945.
F Rep 240 Zeitgeschichtliche Sammlung.
F Rep 280 Quellensammlung zur Berliner Zeitgeschichte (Sammlung der ehemaligen Forschungsstelle für Berliner Zeitgeschichte).

**V Hessisches Hauptstaatsarchiv, Wiesbaden**
Abt 407 Preußisches Polizeipräsidium Frankfurt a. M.

**VI Hessisches Staatsarchiv, Darmstadt**
G 15 Friedberg Kreisamt Friedberg.
G 24 Generalstaatsanwalt beim Oberlandesgericht Darmstadt.

H 14 Darmstadt Amtsgericht Darmstadt.
H 14 Dieburg Amtsgericht Dieburg.

## VII Staatsarchiv, Würzburg
Gestapostelle Würzburg. Gestapoakten.

## VIII Staatsarchiv der Freien und Hansestadt Hamburg
331–5 Polizeibehörde—Unnatürliche Sterbefälle.

## IX Forschungsstelle für Zeitgeschichte, Hamburg
6262 Judenverfolgung, Berichte, 1933–1945.

## X Archiv des Diakonischen Werks, Berlin
CA Centralausschuß für Innere Mission.
EREV Evangelischer Reichs-Erziehungsverband e.V.

## XI Leo Baeck Institute Archives, Berlin
MM 31 Guggenheim, Julius, Memoirs.

## XII The National Archives, Public Records Office, London
FO 1050 Foreign Office.

## XIII Imperial War Museum, London
IWM PP/MCR/292/reel 1: The Second World War papers of Major N Whittaker.
63/34/1, PE von Stemann, Himmler's last minutes in the hands of an English
   country doctor.

## XIV Wiener Library, London
Eyewitness Accounts.
PC Press Clippings Collection.

## XV Hoover Institution Archives, Stanford
D Lerner Collection.

## XVI Evangelisches Zentralarchiv, Berlin
EZA 1 Kirchenbundesamt.

## XVII Institut für Stadtgeschichte, Frankfurt am Main
Rep 553 Nachlaß Quint.

### II PRINTED PRIMARY SOURCES

*8 Uhr-Abendblatt.*
Améry, Jean, *Jenseits von Schuld und Sühne* (Munich, 1988 [1977]).
Andreas-Friedrich, Ruth, *Battleground Berlin: Diaries 1945–1948* (New York, 1990).
Anon., 'Der freiwillige Tod (Ein Beitrag zur Entwicklung der Selbstmordhäufigkeit
   in Frankfurt a. M.)', in *Statistische Monatsberichte Frankfurt am Main*, 3 (1955),
   39–46.
Anon, *A Woman in Berlin* (London, 1955).

Baumann, Karl, *Selbstmord und Freitod in sprachlicher und geistesgeschichtlicher Bedeutung* (Würzburg, 1934).

Bayreuther, H, 'Über den Selbstmord in der Nachkriegszeit: Eine Untersuchung von 1200 Fällen aus einer süddeutschen Großstadt', in *Zeitschrift für die gesamte Neurologie und Psychiatrie*, 195 (1956), 264–84.

Behnken, Klaus (ed), *Deutschland-Berichte der Sopade* (7 vols, Frankfurt am Main, 1980).

Beichel, Helmut, 'Der Selbstmord in Baden in den Jahren 1927–1936', in *Beiträge zur gerichtlichen Medizin*, 15 (1939), 1–13.

Benn, Gottfried, 'Über Selbstmord im Heer (1940)', in *Neue Rundschau*, 87 (1976), 669–74.

—— *Doppelleben: Zwei Selbstdarstellungen* (Stuttgart, 1984).

Bennewitz, Carl, 'Die Selbstmordsterblichkeit deutscher Lebensversicherter', in *Zeitschrift für das gesamte Versicherungswesen*, 31 (1931), 68–83.

*Berliner Illustrierte Nachtausgabe.*

*Berliner Morgenpost.*

*Berliner Tageblatt.*

Bettelheim, Bruno, *The Informed Heart: The human condition in modern mass society* (London, 1961).

Binding, Karl and Alfred Hoche, *Die Freigabe der Vernichtung lebensunwerten Lebens: Ihr Maß und ihre Form* (Leipzig, 1920).

Blau, Bruno, 'The last days of German Jewry in the Third Reich', in *Yivo Annual of Jewish Social Science*, 8 (1953), 197–204.

Boberach, Heinz (ed), *Meldungen aus dem Reich: Die geheimen Lageberichte des Sicherheitsdienstes der SS* (Herrsching, 1984).

—— *Richterbriefe: Dokumente zur Beeinflussung der deutschen Rechtssprechung 1942–1944* (Boppard, 1975).

Boelcke, Willi A (ed), *Deutschlands Rüstung im Zweiten Weltkrieg: Hitlers Konferenzen mit Albert Speer 1942–1945* (Frankfurt am Main, 1969).

Böhme, Meinhard, 'Selbstmord als Unfallfolge im versicherungsrechtlichen Sinne', in *Veröffentlichungen aus dem Gebiete der Medizinalverwaltung*, 42 (1934), 261–336.

Boveri, Magret, *Tage des Überlebens: Berlin 1945* (Munich, 1969).

Brandt, Willy, *Erinnerungen* (Frankfurt am Main, 1989).

*Braunbuch über Reichstagsbrand und Hitler-Terror. Vorwort von Lord Marley* (Basle, 1933).

Broszat, Martin (ed), *Kommandant in Auschwitz: Autobiographische Aufzeichnungen von Rudolf Höß* (Stuttgart, 1961).

Busch, August, 'Der Freitod in Frankfurt a. M.', in *Bevölkerungs- und Wirtschaftszahlen. In zwangloser Folge herausgegeben vom Städtischen Statistischen Amt* (November 1932).

*BZ am Mittag.*

Comité des Délégations Juives (ed), *Das Schwarzbuch: Tatsachen und Dokumente. Die Lage der Juden in Deutschland 1933* (reprint Frankfurt am Main, 1983 [1934]).

*Der gelbe Fleck: Die Ausrottung von 500000 deutschen Juden, mit einem Vorwort von Lion Feuchtwanger* (Paris, 1936).

*Die Rote Fahne.*

*Die Welt am Abend.*

Domarus, Max, *Hitler: Reden und Proklamationen. Kommentiert von einem deutschen Zeitgenossen* (2 vols, each in 2 parts, Munich, 1965).

Donalies, Gustav, 'Statistische Erhebungen an 3000 Fällen von vollendetem und versuchtem Selbstmord', in *Monatsschrift für Psychiatrie und Neurologie*, 69 (1928), 380–96.

Dr. Zahn, 'Die Methodik der Selbstmordstatistik', in *Archiv für die Erforschung und Bekämpfung des Selbstmordes*, 1 (1932), 25–8.

Dusik, Bärbel and Klaus A Lankheit (eds), *Hitler: Reden, Schriften, Anordnungen. Februar 1925 bis Januar 1933* (Munich, 1994).

Elster, Alexander, 'Der Selbstmord in kriminologischer, ethischer und sozialer Beurteilung', in idem and Heinrich Lingemann (eds), *Handwörterbuch der Kriminologie und der anderen strafrechtlichen Hilfswissenschaften* (2 vols, Berlin, 1936), II, 538–42.

Findahl, Theo, *Letzter Akt—Berlin, 1939–1945* (Hamburg, 1946).

Finke, Willy, 'Mord oder Selbstmord', in *Kriminalistische Monatshefte*, 1 (1927), 117.

Frank, Josef Maria, *Unus multorum: Die Geschichte eines Selbstmordes* (Berlin, 1925).

Freisler, Roland, 'Willensstrafrecht: Versuch und Vollendung', in Franz Gürtner (ed), *Das kommende deutsche Strafrecht: Allgemeiner Teil: Bericht über die Arbeit der amtlichen Strafrechtskommission* (Berlin, 1934), 9–36.

Freudenberg, Karl, 'Die Selbstmorde in Deutschland nach dem Kriege', in *Klinische Wochenschrift*, 5 (1926), 29–33.

_____ 'Wirtschaftslage und Selbstmordhäufigkeit', in *Zeitschrift für ärztliche Fortbildung*, 12 (1932), 371–2.

Frey, Erich, *Ich beantrage Freispruch: Aus den Erinnerungen des Strafverteidigers Prof. Dr. Dr. Frey* (Gütersloh, 1960).

Füllkrug, Gerhard, 'Der Kampf gegen den Selbstmord: Bericht über die Arbeit der Ständigen Kommission zur Berarbeitung der Selbstmordfragen in Berlin', in *Archiv für die Erforschung und Bekämpfung des Selbstmordes*, 1 (1932), 51–4.

_____ 'Sozialer und gesundheitlicher Fürsorgedienst: Fürsorge für die Lebensmüden', in *Gesundheitsfürsorge: Zeitschrift der evangelischen Kranken- und Pflegeanstalten*, 7 (May 1933), 101–3.

_____ *Der Selbstmord in der Kriegs- und Nachkriegszeit* (Schwerin, 1927).

_____ *Der Selbstmord: Eine moralstatistische und volkspsychologische Untersuchung* (Schwerin, 1919).

_____ *Die Flucht vor dem Leben: Erläuternder Text zur Lichtbildreihe mit gleichem Titel* (Berlin-Dahlem, 1928).

Fröhlich, Elke (ed), *Die Tagebücher von Joseph Goebbels: Sämtliche Fragmente* (15 vols, Munich, 1987–1998).

Gaupp, Robert, *Ueber den Selbstmord* (2nd edn, Munich, 1910).

Goebbels, Joseph, *Tagebücher 1945: Die letzten Aufzeichnungen* (Hamburg 1977).

Goering, Emmy, *My Life with Goering* (London, 1972).

Gruhle, Hans W, *Selbstmord* (Leipzig, 1940).

Günther, Hans F K, *Rassenkunde des deutschen Volkes* (Munich, 1926).

Hauptamt für Statistik (ed), *Berlin in Zahlen 1947* (Berlin, 1949).

Heiber, Helmut (ed), *Akten der Partei-Kanzlei der NSDAP* (Munich, 1983).

——*Hitlers Lagebesprechungen: Die Protokollfragmente seiner militärischen Konferenzen, 1942–1945* (Munich, 1963).

Helpap, Kurt, 'Statistische Erhebungen über 485 versuchte und vollendete Selbstmorde, die auf der I. Inneren Abteilung des Horst-Wessel-Krankenhauses, Berlin, in den Jahren 1935–1937 beobachtet wurden', in *Deutsche Zeitschrift für die gesamte gerichtliche Medizin*, 30 (1938), 73–89.

Henschel, Hildegard, 'Aus der Arbeit der Jüdischen Gemeinde Berlin während der Jahre 1941–1943: Gemeindearbeit und Evakuierung von Berlin, 16. Oktober 1941–16. Juni 1943', in *Zeitschrift für die Geschichte der Juden*, 9 (1972), 33–52.

Hentig, Hans von, 'Der Selbstmord in Sowjet-Rußland 1922–1925', in *Archiv für Kriminologie*, 80 (1927), 252–3.

Hübner, Arthur, 'Selbstmord: Forensisch-medizinische Erfahrungen', in Elster and Lingemann (eds), *Handwörterbuch der Kriminologie*, vol II, 543–6.

*Jüdisches Lexikon* (Berlin, 1930), V.

Julier, M, 'Die Mitwirkung der Polizei bei der Selbstmordbekämpfung', in *Caritas: Zeitschrift für Caritas und Caritaswissenschaft*, 34 (October 1929), 387–92.

Klein, Thomas (ed), *Die Lageberichte der Justiz aus Hessen* (Darmstadt, 1999).

Klemperer, Victor, *Ich will Zeugnis ablegen bis zum letzten* (2 vols, 5th edn, Berlin, 1995).

Knorr, August, *Zum Problem des Selbstmordes* (Tübingen, 1948).

*Kölner Tageblatt.*

Krämer-Badoni, Rudolf, 'Zustand einer Großstadtbevölkerung am Beispiel Frankfurts', in *Die Wandlung*, 2 (1946), 812–41.

Kronika, Jacob, *Der Untergang Berlins* (Flensburg, 1946).

Kulka, Otto Dov and Eberhard Jäckel (eds), *Die Juden in den geheimen NS-Stimmungsberichten 1933–1945* (Düsseldorf, 2004).

Langer, Walter C, *The Mind of Adolf Hitler: The secret wartime report* (London, 1973).

Langbein, Hermann, *Menschen in Auschwitz* (Vienna, 1972).

Litten, Irmgard, *Die Hölle sieht Dich an: Der Fall Litten mit einem Vorwort von Rudolf Olden* (Paris, 1940).

Loewenberg, Richard Detlev, *Ueber den Selbstmord in Hamburg in den letzten fünfzig Jahren (1880–1930)* (Berlin, 1932).

Mann, Thomas, *Tagebücher 1944–1.4.1946*, Inge Jens (ed) (Frankfurt am Main, 1986).

Menninger-Lerchenthal, Erich, *Das europäische Selbstmordproblem: Eine zeitgemäße Betrachtung* (Vienna 1947).

*Meyers Lexikon* (9 vols, Leipzig, 1942).

Morselli, Henry, *Suicide: An essay on comparative moral statistics* (London, 1881).

Mueller, Berthold and Johann Sitka, 'Untersuchungen über das Verhalten des Selbstmordes unter dem Einfluss der Verhältnisse der letzten Jahre', in *Ärztliche Wochenschrift*, 4 (1949), 663–7.

Nathorff, Hertha, *Das Tagebuch der Hertha Nathorff: Berlin–New York. Aufzeichnungen 1933 bis 1945*, Wolfgang Benz (ed) (Munich, 1987).

Neurath, Paul Martin, *Die Gesellschaft des Terrors: Innenansichten der Konzentrationslager Dachau und Buchenwald* (Frankfurt am Main, 2004).

Noakes, Jeremy and Geoffrey Pridham (eds), *Nazism 1919–1945: A documentary reader* (vol IV, Exeter, 1998).

Olpe, Martin, *Selbstmord und Seelsorge* (Halle, 1913).

Perl, Karlheinz, 'Die psychiatrische Bedeutung der Selbsttötung in Westfalen im Vergleich zu anderen deutschen Gauen', in *Archiv für Psychiatrie und Nervenkrankheiten*, 110 (1939), 253–90.

Peter, Karen and Gabriele Toepser-Ziegert (ed), *NS-Presseanweisungen der Vorkriegszeit: Edition und Dokumentation* (7 vols, Munich, 1984–2001).

Polizeioberinspektor Schneble, 'Ein interessanter Beitrag zum Problem "Mord oder Selbstmord"', in *Kriminalistische Monatshefte*, 2 (1928), 153–8.

Regge, Jürgen and Werner Schubert (eds), *Quellen zur Reform des Straf- und Strafprozeßrechts, II. Abteilung, NS-Zeit (1933–1939) Strafgesetzbuch, Band 1: Entwürfe eines Strafgesetzbuches, 1. Teil* (Berlin, 1988).

Regierungsdirektor Dr Weiß, Leiter der Berliner Kriminalpolizei, 'Die Beziehungen zwischen Presse und Kriminalpolizei', in *Polizei und Presse: Sondernummer der 'Deutschen Presse': Organ des Reichsverbandes der Deutschen Presse e.V.*, 16 (9 October 1926), no 40/41, 4–5.

Rewald, Ilse, *Berliner, die uns halfen, die Hitlerdiktatur zu überleben* (Berlin, 1975).

Richarz, Monika (ed), *Jüdisches Leben in Deutschland: Selbstzeugnisse zur Sozialgeschichte, 1918–1945* (Stuttgart, 1982).

Riesenburger, Martin, *Das Licht erlösche nicht: Dokumente aus der Nacht des Nazismus* (East-Berlin, 1960).

Rost, Hans, 'Der Selbstmord in den Kulturstaaten der Erde', in *Archiv für die Erforschung und Bekämpfung des Selbstmordes*, 1 (1932), 5–12.

_____'Wie kann man die Selbstmordneigung bekämpfen?', in *Archiv für die Erforschung und Bekämpfung des Selbstmordes* 1 (1932), 40–5.

_____*Bibliographie des Selbstmordes* (Augsburg, 1927).

_____*Der Selbstmord als sozialstatistische Erscheinung* (Cologne, 1905).

Schackwitz, Alex, 'Selbstmordursachen', in *Deutsche Zeitschrift für die gesamte gerichtliche Medizin*, 10 (1927), 312–21.

Schäfer, Ernst, 'Die Schuldlehre', in Franz Gürtner (ed), *Das kommende deutsche Strafrecht: Allgemeiner Teil: Bericht über die Arbeit der amtlichen Strafrechtskommission* (Berlin, 1934), 37–55.

Schieder, Theodor (ed), *Die Vertreibung der Deutschen Bevölkerung aus den Gebieten östlich der Oder-Neiße* (Bonn, 1953).

Schirach, Baldur von, *Ich glaubte an Hitler* (Hamburg, 1967).

Schlotterbeck, Friedrich, *The Darker the Night, the Brighter the Stars: A German worker remembers (1933–1945)* (London, 1947).

Schmahl, Erich, 'Statistik der Selbstmorde und Selbstmordversuche', in Friedrich Burgdörfer (ed), *Die Statistik in Deutschland nach ihrem heutigen Stand: Ehrengabe für Friedrich Zahn* (2 vols, Berlin, 1940), I, 333–8.

Schmidt, Paul, *Der praktische Dienst der Straßenpolizei: Ein Handbuch für den Unterricht und Selbstunterricht der Beamten der Schutzpolizei* (Berlin, 1922).

Schneider, Reinhold, *Über den Selbstmord* (Baden-Baden, 1947).

Schottky, Johannes, 'Ueber den Mordversuch eines Jugendlichen bei geplantem Selbstmord', in *Monatsschrift für Kriminologie und Strafrechtsreform*, 32 (1941), 1–32.

Schwöner, Alfred, 'Die Selbstmörder: Alarmstatistiken der Lebensversicherungs-Gesellschaften', in *BZ am Mittag*, no 163, 16 July 1931.

Shirer, William L, *End of a Berlin Diary* (London, 1947).

Smith, Bradley F and Agnes F Peterson (eds), *Heinrich Himmler: Geheimreden 1933 bis 1945 und andere Ansprachen* (Frankfurt am Main, 1974).

Smith, Howard K, *Last Train from Berlin* (London, 1942).

*Das Schwarze Korps*.

Statistisches Landesamt (ed), *Statistisches Jahrbuch für die Freie und Hansestadt Hamburg* (Hamburg, 1955).

*Statistik des Deutschen Reiches*.

*Statistisches Jahrbuch für Bayern*.

*Statistisches Jahrbuch für das Deutsche Reich*.

*Der Stürmer*.

Szittya, Emil, *Selbstmörder: Ein Beitrag zur Kulturgeschichte aller Zeiten und Völker* (Leipzig, 1925).

Tergit, Gabriele, *Blüten der Zwanziger Jahre: Gerichtsreportagen und Feuilletons 1923–1933*, Jens Brüning (ed) (Berlin, 1984).

Ungern-Sternberg, Roderich von, *Die Ursachen der Steigerung der Selbstmordhäufigkeit in Westeuropa während der letzten hundert Jahre* (Berlin, 1935).

*Verhandlungen des Reichstags*.

*Völkischer Beobachter*.

*Vorwärts*.

*Vossische Zeitung*.

Warburg, G, *Six Years of Hitler: The Jews under the Nazi regime* (London, 1939).

Weichbrodt, R, *Der Selbstmord* (Basle, 1937).

Weisenborn, Günther, *Der lautlose Aufstand: Bericht über die Widerstandsbewegung des deutschen Volkes 1933–1945* (Frankfurt am Main, 1979 [1953]).

Wessinger, Julie Dorothea, *Ueber den Selbstmord bei Frauen in den ersten zehn Jahren nach dem Kriege* (Berlin, 1933).

Zur Nieden, Susanne, *Alltag im Ausnahmezustand: Frauentagebücher im zerstörten Deutschland 1943–1945* (Berlin, 1993).

### III SECONDARY WORKS

Anderson, Olive, *Suicide in Victorian and Edwardian England* (Oxford, 1987).

Arad, Yitzhak, *Belzec, Sobibor, Treblinka: The Operation Reinhard death camps* (Bloomington, 1987).

Arendt, Hannah, 'Organisierte Schuld', in *Die Wandlung*, 1 (1945/46), 333−44.

_____ 'We refugees', in eadem, *The Jew as Pariah: Jewish identity and politics in the modern age*, Ron H Feldman (ed) (New York, 1978), 55−66.

Ariès, Philippe, *The Hour of Our Death* (London, 1981 [1977]).

Ayass, Wolfgang, *'Asoziale' im Nationalsozialismus* (Stuttgart, 1995).

Bähr, Andreas, *Der Richter im Ich: Die Semantik der Selbsttötung in der Aufklärung* (Göttingen, 2002).

Bailey, Victor, *'This Rash Act': Suicide across the life cycle in the Victorian city* (Stanford, 1998).

Baird, Jay W, *To Die For Germany: Heroes in the Nazi pantheon* (Bloomington, 1990).

Bajohr, Frank, *Parvenüs und Profiteure: Korruption in der NS-Zeit* (Frankfurt am Main, 2001).

_____ 'Die Zustimmungsdiktatur: Grundzüge nationalsozialistischer Herrschaft in Hamburg', in Forschungsstelle für Zeitgeschichte (ed), *Hamburg im 'Dritten Reich'* (Göttingen, 2005), 69−131.

Bankier, David, *The Germans and the Final Solution: Public opinion under Nazism* (Oxford, 1992).

Baumann, Ursula, 'Suizid im 'Dritten Reich': Facetten eines Themas', in Michael Grüttner, Rüdiger Hachtmann and Heinz-Gerhard Haupt (eds), *Geschichte und Emanzipation: Festschrift für Reinhard Rürup* (Frankfurt am Main, 1999), 482−516.

_____ *Vom Recht auf den eigenen Tod: Die Geschichte des Suizids vom 18. bis zum 20. Jahrhundert* (Weimar, 2001).

Beevor, Antony, *Berlin: The Downfall 1945* (London, 2002).

Behrenbeck, Sabine, 'The Transformation of Sacrifice: German identity between heroic narrative and economic success', in Paul Betts and Greg Eghigian (eds), *Pain and prosperity: Reconsidering twentieth-century German history* (Stanford, 2003), 110−36.

_____ *Der Kult um die toten Helden in Deutschland: Nationalsozialistische Mythen, Riten und Symbole* (Vierow, 1996).

Benz, Wolfgang (ed), *Die Juden in Deutschland 1933−1945: Leben unter nationalsozialistischer Herrschaft* (Munich, 1989).

_____ *Überleben im Dritten Reich: Juden im Untergrund und ihre Helfer* (Munich, 2003).

_____ 'Der Novemberpogrom 1938', in idem (ed), *Die Juden in Deutschland*, 499−544.

Berger, Georg, *Die Beratenden Psychiater des deutschen Heeres, 1939−1945* (Frankfurt am Main, 1998).

Bessel, Richard, 'Hatred after War: Emotion and the post-war history of East Germany', in *History and Memory*, 17 (2005), 195–216.

——— ' 'Leben nach dem Tod'—Vom Zweiten Weltkrieg zur zweiten Nachkriegszeit', in Bernd Wegner (ed), *Wie Kriege enden: Wege zum Frieden von der Antike bis in die Gegenwart* (Paderborn, 2002), 239–58.

——— *Germany after the First World War* (Oxford, 1993).

——— *Nazism and War* (New York, 2004).

——— *Political Violence and the Rise of Nazism: the storm troopers in Eastern Germany, 1925–1934* (New Haven, 1984).

Birn, Ruth Bettina, *Die Höheren SS- und Polizeiführer: Himmlers Vertreter im Reich und in den besetzten Gebieten* (Düsseldorf, 1986).

Botz, Gerhard, *Wien vom 'Anschluß' zum Krieg: Nationalsozialistische Machtübernahme und politisch-soziale Umgestaltung am Beispiel der Stadt Wien 1938/39* (Vienna, 1978).

Brandt, Hans-Jürgen, 'Erinnerungen an die Tragödie einer Künstlerehe: Meta und Joachim Gottschalk', in *Frankfurter Hefte: Zeitschrift für Kultur und Politik*, 37 (1982), 5–8.

Bronisch, Thomas, 'Suicidality in German concentration camps', in *Archives of Suicide Research*, 2 (1996), 129–44.

Broszat, Martin, 'Resistenz und Widerstand', in Martin Broszat, Elke Frölich and Falk Wiesemann (eds), *Bayern in der NS-Zeit* (6 vols, Munich, 1977–83), vol IV, 691–709.

——— Klaus-Dietmar Henke and Hans Woller (eds), *Von Stalingrad zur Währungsreform: Zur Sozialgeschichte des Umbruchs in Deutschland* (Munich, 1988).

Browning, Christopher R, *Ordinary Men: Reserve Police Battalion 101 and the Final Solution in Poland* (New York, 1992).

Brunner, Claudia, *Arbeitslosigkeit im NS-Staat: Das Beispiel München* (Pfaffenweiler, 1997).

——— *Arbeitslosigkeit in München 1927 bis 1933: Kommunalpolitik in der Krise* (Munich, 1992).

Brysac, Shareen Blair, *Resisting Hitler: Mildred Harnack and the Red Orchestra* (Oxford, 2000).

Bukey, Evan Burr, *Hitler's Austria: Popular sentiment in the Nazi era, 1938–1945* (Chapel Hill, 2000).

Burleigh, Michael, *Death and Deliverance: 'Euthanasia' in Germany, c1900–1945* (Cambridge, 1994).

Buske, Norbert (ed), *Das Kriegsende 1945 in Demmin: Berichte, Erinnerungen, Dokumente* (Schwerin, 1995).

Büttner, Ursula, 'The persecution of Christian-Jewish families in the Third Reich', in *Year Book of the Leo Baeck Institute*, 34 (1989), 267–89.

——— ' 'Gomorrha'' und die Folgen: Der Bombenkrieg', in Forschungsstelle für Zeitgeschichte (ed), *Hamburg im 'Dritten Reich'* (Göttingen, 2005), 613–32.

Caplan, Jane, *Government Without Administration: State and civil service in Weimar and Nazi Germany* (Oxford, 1988).

Caplan, Jane, 'Political detention and the origin of the concentration camps in Nazi Germany', in Neil Gregor (ed), *Nazism, War and Genocide: Essays in honour of Jeremy Noakes* (Exeter, 2005), 22–41.

Carlé, Wilhelm, *Weltanschauung und Presse: Eine soziologische Untersuchung* (Leipzig, 1931).

Cobb, Richard, *Death in Paris: The records of the Basse-Geôle de la Seine* (Oxford, 1978).

Cohen, Rosi, *Das Problem des Selbstmordes in Stefan Zweigs Leben und Werk* (Bern, 1982).

Crew, David F, 'Gewalt auf dem "Amt": Wohlfahrtsbehörden und ihre Klienten in der Weimarer Republik', in Thomas Lindenberger and Alf Lüdtke (eds), *Physische Gewalt: Studien zur Geschichte der Neuzeit* (Frankfurt am Main, 1995), 213–37.

_____ *Germans on Welfare: From Weimar to Hitler* (New York, 1998).

Dahm, Volker, 'Kulturelles und geistiges Leben', in Benz (ed), *Die Juden in Deutschland*, 75–267.

Daube, David, 'The linguistics of suicide', in *Philosophy and Public Affairs*, 1 (1971/72), 387–437.

Dölling, Dieter, 'Kriminologie im Dritten Reich', in Ralf Dreier and Wolfgang Sellert (eds), *Recht und Justiz im Dritten Reich* (Frankfurt am Main, 1989), 194–225.

Dörner, Bernward, *'Heimtücke': Das Gesetz als Waffe. Kontrolle, Abschreckung und Verfolgung in Deutschland 1933–1945* (Paderborn, 1998).

Douglas, Jack D, *The Social Meanings of Suicide* (Princeton, 1967).

Drobisch, Klaus and Günther Wieland, *System der NS-Konzentrationslager 1933–1939* (Berlin, 1993).

Durkheim, Emile, *Suicide: A study in sociology* (London, 1952 [1897]).

Ebbinghaus, Angelika, 'Soldatenselbstmord im Urteil des Psychiaters Bürger-Prinz', in eadem and Karsten Linne (eds), *Kein abgeschlossenes Kapitel: Hamburg im 3. Reich* (Hamburg, 1997), 486–537.

Edwards, Catharine, *Death in Ancient Rome* (New Haven, 2007).

_____ and Thomas Osborne, 'Scenographies of suicide: An introduction', in *Economy and Society*, 34 (2005), 173–77

Eghigian, Greg, 'Pain, entitlement, and social citizenship in modern Germany', in idem and Paul Betts (eds), *Pain and Prosperity: Reconsidering twentieth-century German history* (Stanford, 2003), 16–34.

_____ 'The politics of victimization: Social pensioners and the German social state in the inflation of 1914–1924', in *Central European History*, 26 (1993), 375–404.

Eley, Geoff, 'Hitler's silent majority? Conformity and resistance under the Third Reich', in *Michigan Quarterly Review*, 42 (2003), 550–83.

Elkin, Rivka, *Das Jüdische Krankenhaus in Berlin zwischen 1938 und 1945* (Berlin, 1993).

Elsner, Eckart, 'Selbstmord in Berlin', in *Berliner Statistik*, 37 (1983), 218–39.

Evans, Richard J, 'In search of German Social Darwinism', in idem (ed), *Rereading German History: From unification to reunification, 1800–1996* (London, 1997), 119–44.

—— 'Introduction: The experience of unemployment in the Weimar Republic', in idem and Dick Geary (eds), *The German Unemployed: Experiences and consequences of mass unemployment from the Weimar Republic to the Third Reich* (London, 1987), 1–22.

—— *In Defence of History* (London, 1998).

—— *Rituale der Vergeltung: Die Todesstrafe in der deutschen Geschichte, 1532–1987* (Berlin, 2001 [1996]).

—— *Tales from the German Underworld: Crime and punishment in the nineteenth century* (New Haven, 1998).

—— *The Coming of the Third Reich* (London, 2003).

—— *The Third Reich in Power* (New York, 2005).

—— 'Coercion and consent in Nazi Germany', in *Proceedings of the British Academy*, 151 (2006), 53–81.

Fest, Joachim C, *Hitler* (Harmondsworth, 1982 [1973]).

Fest, Joachim, *Der Untergang: Hitler und das Ende des Dritten Reiches* (Berlin, 2002).

—— *Staatsstreich: Der lange Weg zum 20. Juli* (Berlin, 1994).

Fitzpatrick, Sheila, *Everyday Stalinism—Ordinary life in extraordinary times. Soviet Russia in the 1930s* (New York, 1999).

Flemming, Rebecca, 'Suicide, euthanasia and medicine: Reflections ancient and modern', *Economy and Society*, 34 (2005), 295–321.

Föllmer, Moritz, ' "Good-bye diesem verfluchten Leben": Kommunikationskrise und Selbstmord in der Weimarer Republik', in idem (ed), *Sehnsucht nach Nähe: Interpersonale Kommunikation in Deutschland seit dem 19. Jahrhundert* (Stuttgart, 2004), 109–25.

—— 'Der "kranke Volkskörper": Industrielle, hohe Beamte und der Diskurs der nationalen Regeneration in der Weimarer Republik', in *Geschichte und Gesellschaft*, 27 (2001), 41–67.

—— 'The problem of national solidarity in inter-war Germany', in *German History* 23 (2005), 202–31.

*Frankfurter Allgemeine Zeitung.*

Frei, Norbert, *Der Führerstaat: Nationalsozialistische Herrschaft 1933 bis 1945* (Munich, 1987).

Friedländer, Saul, *Nazi Germany and the Jews, volume I: The years of persecution* (New York, 1997).

Friedrich, Jörg, *Der Brand: Deutschland im Bombenkrieg 1940–1945* (Berlin, 2002).

Fritzsche, Peter, *Reading Berlin 1900* (Cambridge, Mass., 1996).

Gatrell, VAC, 'The decline of theft and violence in Victorian and Edwardian England', in idem, Bruce Lehman and Geoffrey Parker (eds), *Crime and the Law: The social history of crime in Western Europe since 1500* (London, 1980), 238–339.

Gay, Peter, *Freud: A life for our time* (London, 1988).

Gedenkstätte Buchenwald (ed), *Konzentrationslager Buchenwald 1937–1945: Begleit-buch zur ständigen historischen Ausstellung* (Göttingen, 1999).

Gellately, Robert *Backing Hitler: Consent and coercion in Nazi Germany* (Oxford, 2001).

——— *The Gestapo and German Society: Enforcing racial terror, 1933–1945* (Oxford, 1990).

Geyer, Michael, ' "There is a land where everything is pure: Its name is Land of Death": Some observations on catastrophic nationalism', in Greg Eghigian and Matthew Paul Berg (eds), *Sacrifice and National Belonging in Twentieth-Century Germany* (Arlington, 2002), 118–47.

Giles, Geoffrey J, 'The institutionalization of homosexual panic in the Third Reich', in Gellately and Stoltzfus (eds), *Social Outsiders*, 233–55.

——— ' "The most unkindest cut of all": Castration, homosexuality and Nazi Justice', in *Journal of Contemporary History*, 27 (1991), 41–61.

——— 'A gray zone among the field gray men: Confusion in the discrimination against homosexuals in the Wehrmacht', in Jonathan Petropoulos and John K Roth (eds), *Gray Zones: Ambiguity and compromise in the Holocaust and its aftermath* (New York, 2005), 127–46.

Görlitz, Walter, *Model: Der Feldmarschall und sein Endkampf an der Ruhr* (Frankfurt am Main, 1992).

Graf, Christoph, 'Kontinuitäten und Brüche: Von der Politischen Polizei der Weimarer Republik zur Geheimen Staatspolizei', in Gerhard Paul and Klaus-Michael Mallmann (eds), *Die Gestapo: Mythos und Realität* (Darmstadt, 1995), 73–83.

Grashoff, Udo, *'In einem Anfall von Depression…': Selbsttötungen in der DDR* (Berlin, 2006).

Gregor, Neil, ' "Is he still alive, or long since dead?": Loss, absence and remembrance in Nuremberg, 1945–1956', in *German History*, 21 (2003), 183–203.

——— 'Nazism: A political religion? Rethinking the voluntarist turn', in idem (ed), *Nazism, War and Genocide: Essays in honour of Jeremy Noakes* (Exeter, 2005), 1–21.

Griech-Polelle, Beth, 'Bishop von Galen, the euthanasia project and the sermons of summer 1941', in *Journal of Contemporary History*, 36 (2001), 43–64.

Gross, Babette, *Willi Münzenberg: Eine politische Biographie* (Stuttgart, 1967).

Grossmann, Atina, 'A question of silence: The rape of German women by occupation soldiers', in *October*, 72 (1995), 43–64.

——— *Reforming Sex: The German movement for birth control and abortion reform, 1920–1950* (New York, 1995).

——— *Jews, Germans, and Allies: Close encounters in occupied Germany* (Princeton, 2007).

Gruchmann, Lothar, *Justiz im Dritten Reich 1933–1940: Anpassung und Unterwerfung in der Ära Gürtner* (Munich, 1987).

—— 'Erlebnisbericht Werner Pünders über die Ermordung Klauseners am 30. Juni 1934 und ihre Folgen', in *Vierteljahrshefte für Zeitgeschichte*, 19 (1971), 404–31.

Grunberger, Richard, *A Social History of the Third Reich* (London, 1971).

Gruner, Wolf, 'Die Reichshauptstadt und die Verfolgung der Berliner Juden 1933–1945', in Reinhard Rürup (ed), *Jüdische Geschichte in Berlin: Essays und Studien* (Berlin, 1995), 229–66.

——*Judenverfolgung in Berlin: Eine Chronologie der Behördenmaßnahmen in der Reichshauptstadt* (Berlin, 1996).

Haffner, Sebastian, *Germany: Jekyll and Hyde* (London, 1940).

Hahn, Susanne, ' "Minderwertige, widerstandslose Individuen"—Der Erste Weltkrieg und das Selbstmordproblem in Deutschland', in Wolfgang Eckart and Christoph Gradmann (eds), *Die Medizin und der Erste Weltkrieg* (Pfaffenweiler, 1996), 273–98.

Hahn, Susanne and Christina Schröder, 'Zur Einordnung des Suizids in das faschistische Konzept der "Vernichtung lebensunwerten Lebens" ', in Sabine Fahrenbach and Achim Thom (eds), *Der Arzt als 'Gesundheitsführer': Ärztliches Wirken zwischen Ressourcenerschließung und humanitärer Hilfe im Zweiten Weltkrieg* (Frankfurt am Main, 1991), 109–16.

Halbwachs, Maurice, *The Causes of Suicide* (London, 1978 [1930]).

Hall, Peter, 'Kamikaze', in Diego Gambetta (ed), *Making Sense of Suicide Missions* (Oxford, 2005), 1–42.

Happel, Reinhold, ' "Kuhle Wampe oder Wem gehört die Welt"—eine exemplarische Analyse', in Helmut Korte (ed), *Film und Realität in der Weimarer Republik: Mit Analysen der Filme 'Kuhle Wampe' und 'Mutter Krausens Fahrt ins Glück'* (Munich, 1978), 169–212.

Heidelberger-Leonard, Irene, *Jean Améry. Revolte in der Resignation: Biographie* (Stuttgart, 2004).

Henke, Klaus-Dietmar, *Die amerikanische Besetzung Deutschlands* (Munich, 1995).

Herbert, Ulrich, *Fremdarbeiter: Politik und Praxis des 'Ausländer-Einsatzes' in der Kriegswirtschaft des Dritten Reiches* (Bonn, 1985).

—— Karin Orth and Christoph Dieckmann (eds), *Die nationalsozialistischen Konzentrationslager—Entwicklung und Struktur* (Göttingen, 1998).

Herf, Jeffrey, *The Jewish Enemy: Nazi propaganda during World War II and the Holocaust* (Cambridge, MA, 2006).

Hirte, Chris, *Erich Mühsam: "Ihr seht mich nicht feige"* (East-Berlin, 1985).

Hoffmann, Peter, *Widerstand, Staatsstreich, Attentat: Der Kampf der Opposition gegen Hitler* (2nd edn, Munich, 1970).

Höhne, Heinz, *Der Orden unter dem Totenkopf: Die Geschichte der SS* (Gütersloh, 1967).

Hüttenberger, Peter, *Die Gauleiter: Studie zum Wandel des Machtgefüges in der NSDAP* (Stuttgart, 1969).

Hüttenberger, Peter, 'Heimtückefälle vor dem Sondergericht München, 1933–1939', in Martin Broszat, Elke Fröhlich and Anton Grossmann (eds),

*Bayern in der NS-Zeit: Herrschaft und Gesellschaft im Konflikt* (7 vols, Munich, 1981), IV, 435–526.

Jahn, Peter, ' "Russenfurcht" und Antibolschewismus: Zur Entstehung und Wirkung von Feindbildern', in idem and Reinhard Rürup (eds), *Erobern und Vernichten: Der Krieg gegen die Sowjetunion 1941–1945* (Berlin, 1991), 47–64.

Jay, Martin, 'Against consolation: Walter Benjamin and the refusal to mourn', in Jay Winter and Emmanuel Sivan (eds), *War and Remembrance in the Twentieth Century* (Cambridge, 1999), 221–39.

Jellonnek, Burkhard, *Homosexuelle unter dem Hakenkreuz: Die Verfolgung von Homosexuellen im Dritten Reich* (Paderborn, 1990).

Joachimsthaler, Anton, *Hitlers Ende: Legenden und Dokumente* (Munich, 1995).

\_\_\_\_ *Hitlers Liste: Ein Dokument persönlicher Beziehungen* (Munich, 2003).

Johnson, Eric A, 'Cities don't cause crime: Urban-rural differences in late nineteenth- and early twentieth-century German criminality', in *Social Science History*, 16 (1992), 129–76.

\_\_\_\_ and Karl-Heinz Reuband, *What We Knew: Terror, mass murder, and everyday life in Nazi Germany* (Cambridge, Mass., 2005).

\_\_\_\_ *Nazi Terror: The Gestapo, Jews and ordinary Germans* (New York, 2000).

\_\_\_\_ *Urbanization and Crime: Germany 1871–1914* (Cambridge, 1995).

Joshi, Vandana, *Gender and Power in the Third Reich: Female denouncers and the Gestapo (1933–1945)* (London, 2003).

Kaiser, Jochen-Christoph, *Sozialer Protestantismus im 20. Jahrhundert: Beiträge zur Geschichte der Inneren Mission 1914–1945* (Munich, 1989).

Kaplan, Marion, *Between Dignity and Despair: Jewish life in Nazi Germany* (New York, 1998).

\_\_\_\_ 'Jewish daily life in wartime Germany', in David Bankier (ed), *Probing the Depths of German Antisemitism: German society and the persecution of the Jews, 1933–1941* (New York, 2000), 395–412.

Kater, Michael, *Doctors under Hitler* (Chapel Hill, 1989).

\_\_\_\_ *Hitler Youth* (Cambridge, Mass., 2004).

Kershaw, Ian, *Hitler (Profiles in Power)* (London, 2001 [1991]).

\_\_\_\_ *Hitler, 1889–1936. Hubris* (London, 1998).

\_\_\_\_ *Hitler, 1936–1945. Nemesis* (London 2000).

\_\_\_\_ *Popular Opinion and Political Dissent in the Third Reich. Bavaria, 1933–1945* (Oxford, 1983).

\_\_\_\_ *The 'Hitler Myth': Image and reality in the Third Reich* (Oxford, 1987).

\_\_\_\_ *The Nazi Dictatorship: Problems and perspectives of interpretation* (4th edn, London, 2000 [1985]).

\_\_\_\_ ' "Working towards the Führer": Reflections on the nature of the Hitler dictatorship', in *Contemporary European History*, 2 (1993), 103–18.

Kettenacker, Lothar (ed), *Ein Volk von Opfern? Die neue Debatte um den Bombenkrieg 1940–45* (Berlin 2003).

Kirwin, Gerald, 'Waiting for retaliation: A study in Nazi propaganda, behaviour and German civilian morale', in *Journal of Contemporary History*, 16 (1981), 565–83.

Klee, Ernst, *'Euthanasie' im NS-Staat: Die 'Vernichtung lebensunwerten Lebens'* (Frankfurt am Main, 1985).

Komo, Günter, *'Für Volk und Vaterland': Die Militärpsychiatrie in den Weltkriegen* (Münster, 1992).

Koszyk, Kurt, *Deutsche Presse 1914–1945: Geschichte der deutschen Presse* (3 vols, Berlin, 1972).

Kuczynski, Jürgen, *Geschichte des Alltags des Deutschen Volkes: Studien* (East-Berlin, 1982).

Kühn, Volker (ed), *Deutschlands Erwachen: Kabarett unterm Hakenkreuz 1933–1945* (Weinheim, 1989).

Kundrus, Birthe, 'Forbidden company: Romantic relationships between Germans and foreigners, 1939 to 1945', in Dagmar Herzog (ed), *Sexuality and German Fascism* (New York, 2005), 201–22.

Kushner, Howard I, *Self-Destruction in the Promised Land: A psychocultural biology of American suicide* (New Brunswick, NJ, 1989).

—— 'Women and suicide in historical perspective', in *Signs: Journal of Women in Culture and Society*, 10 (1985), 537–52.

Kwiet, Konrad and Helmut Eschwege, *Selbstbehauptung und Widerstand: Deutsche Juden im Kampf um Existenz und Menschenwürde 1933–1945* (Hamburg, 1984).

Landeshauptstadt Düsseldorf (ed), *Verfolgung und Widerstand in Düsseldorf, 1933–1945* (Düsseldorf, 1990).

Laslett, Peter, *The World We Have Lost* (2nd edn, London, 1971).

Lederer, David, 'Selbstmord im frühneuzeitlichen Deutschland: Klischee und Geschichte', in *Psychotherapie*, 4 (1999), 206–12.

Leenars, Antoon A, *Suicide Notes: Predictive clues and patterns* (New York, 1988).

Lerner, Paul, *Hysterical Men: War, psychiatry and the politics of trauma in Germany, 1890–1930* (Ithaca, 2003).

Lieberman, Lisa, *Leaving You: The cultural meaning of suicide* (Chicago, 2003).

Lind, Vera, *Selbstmord in der frühen Neuzeit: Diskurs, Lebenswelt und kultureller Wandel am Beispiel der Herzogtümer Schleswig und Holstein* (Göttingen, 1999).

Lindenberger, Thomas and Alf Lüdtke (eds), *Physische Gewalt: Studien zur Geschichte der Neuzeit* (Frankfurt am Main, 1995).

Longerich, Peter, *Die braunen Bataillone: Geschichte der SA* (Munich, 1989).

—— *Politik der Vernichtung: Eine Gesamtdarstellung der nationalsozialistischen Judenverfolgung* (Munich, 1998).

—— *'Davon haben wir nichts gewußt': Die Deutschen und die Judenverfolgung 1933–1945* (Munich, 2006).

Lorenz, Ina, 'Das Leben der Hamburger Juden im Zeichen der "Endlösung" (1942–1945)', in Arno Herzig and Ina Lorenz (eds), *Verdrängung und Vernichtung der Juden unter dem Nationalsozialismus* (Hamburg, 1992), 207–47.

Lotfi, Gabriele, *KZ der Gestapo: Arbeitserziehungslager im Dritten Reich* (Stuttgart, 2000).

Lukes, Steven, *Emile Durkheim: His life and work. A historical and critical study* (Harmondsworth, 1975).

MacDonald, Michael and Terence R Murphy, *Sleepless Souls: Suicide in early modern England* (Oxford, 1990).

Maris, Ronald W and Alan L Berman, Morton M Silverman, *Comprehensive Textbook of Suicidology* (New York, 2000).

Martin, Bernd, 'Die deutsche Kapitulation: Versuch einer Bilanz des Zweiten Weltkrieges', in *Freiburger Universitätsblätter* 34, 130 (1995), 45–70.

Mason, Timothy W, 'Introduction to the English edition', in idem, *Social Policy in the Third Reich: The working class and the 'national community'* (Oxford, 1993), 1–18.

—— *Sozialpolitik im Dritten Reich: Arbeiterklasse und Volksgemeinschaft* (Opladen, 1977).

McLeod, Hugh, *European Religion in the Age of the Great Cities: 1830–1930* (London, 1995).

McMeekin, Sean, *The Red Millionaire: A political biography of Willi Münzenberg, Moscow's secret propaganda Tsar in the West* (New Haven, 2003).

Melis, Damian van, *Entnazifizierung in Mecklenburg-Vorpommern: Herrschaft und Verwaltung 1945–1948* (Munich, 1999).

Mergel, Thomas, *Parlamentarische Kultur in der Weimarer Republik: Politische Kommunikation, symbolische Politik und Öffentlichkeit im Reichstag* (Düsseldorf, 2002).

Merkl, Peter H., *Political Violence under the Swastika: 581 early Nazis* (Princeton, 1975).

Merridale, Catherine, *Ivan's War: Life and death in the Red Army* (London, 2005).

Merson, Allan, *Communist Resistance in Nazi Germany* (London, 1985).

Messerschmidt, Manfred, *Die Wehrmachtsjustiz 1933–1945* (Paderborn, 2005).

Meyer, Beate, 'The mixed marriage: A guarantee of survival or a reflection of German society during the Nazi regime?', in Bankier (ed), *Probing the Depths of German Antisemitism*, 54–77.

Minois, Georges, *History of Suicide: Voluntary death in Western culture* (Baltimore, 1999).

Moeller, Robert G, *War Stories: The search for a usable past in the Federal Republic of Germany* (Berkeley, 2001).

Mommsen, Hans, 'Die Rückkehr zu den Ursprüngen—Betrachtungen zur inneren Auflösung des Dritten Reiches nach der Niederlage von Stalingrad', in Michael Grüttner, Rüdiger Hachtmann and Heinz-Gerhard Haupt (eds), *Geschichte und Emanzipation: Festschrift für Reinhard Rürup* (Frankfurt am Main, 1999), 418–34.

—— 'Social views and constitutional plans of the resistance', in Hermann Graml (ed), *The German Resistance to Hitler* (London, 1970), 55–147.

Morrissey, Susan K, 'Drinking to death: Suicide, vodka and religious burial in Russia', in *Past and Present*, 186 (2005), 117–46.

—— 'Suicide and civilization in late Imperial Russia', in *Jahrbücher für Geschichte Osteuropas*, 43 (1995), 201–17.

—— *Suicide and the Body Politic in Imperial Russia* (Cambridge, 2006).

Mosse, George L, *Fallen Soldiers: Reshaping the memory of the World Wars* (New York, 1990).

Münkler, Herfried, *Machtzerfall: Die letzten Tage des Dritten Reiches dargestellt am Beispiel der hessischen Kreisstadt Friedberg* (Berlin 1985).

Murray, Alexander, *Suicide in the Middle Ages* (2 vols, Oxford, 1998–2000).

Naimark, Norman M, *Fires of Hatred: Ethnic cleansing in twentieth-century Europe* (Cambridge, Mass, 2001).

—— *The Russians in Germany: A history of the Soviet zone of occupation, 1945–1949* (Cambridge, Mass, 1997 [1995]).

Nedoschill, Jan C, 'Suizide deutscher Soldaten im Zweiten Weltkrieg', in *Österreichische Zeitschrift für Soziologie*, 23 (1998), 60–81.

O'Donnell, Ian, Richard Farmer, and Jose Catalan, 'Suicide notes', in *British Journal of Psychiatry*, 163 (1993), 45–8.

Overy, Richard, *Interrogations: The Nazi elite in Allied hands 1945* (London, 2001).

Petzina, Dietmar, Werner Abelshauser and Anselm Faust (eds), *Sozialgeschichtliches Arbeitsbuch Band III: Materialien zur Statistik des Deutschen Reiches 1914–1945* (Munich, 1978).

Pinguet, Maurice, *Voluntary Death in Japan* (Cambridge 1993).

Pinnow, Kenneth M, 'Violence against the collective self and the problem of social integration in early Bolshevik Russia', in *Kritika*, 4 (2003), 653–77.

Preller, Ludwig, *Sozialpolitik in der Weimarer Republik* (Düsseldorf, 1978 [1949]).

Pretzel, Andreas and Gabriele Roßbach (eds), *Wegen der zu erwartenden hohen Strafe: Homosexuellenverfolgung in Berlin 1933–1945* (Berlin, 2000).

Pretzel, Andreas, 'Ich wünsche meinem schlimmsten Feind nicht, daß er das durchmacht, was ich da durchgemacht habe: Vorfälle im Konzentrationslager Sachsenhausen vor Gericht in Berlin', in idem and Gabriele Roßbach (eds), *Wegen der zu erwartenden hohen Strafe: Homosexuellenverfolgung in Berlin 1933–1945* (Berlin, 2000), 119–68.

Preuschoff, Klaus-Jürgen, *Suizidales Verhalten in deutschen Streitkräften* (Regensburg, 1988).

Proctor, Robert, *The Nazi War on Cancer* (Princeton, 1999).

Przyrembel, Alexandra, *'Rassenschande': Reinheitsmythos und Vernichtungslegitimation im Nationalsozialismus* (Göttingen, 2003).

Rebentisch, Dieter, 'Frankfurt am Main in der Weimarer Republik und im Dritten Reich', in Frankfurter Historische Kommission (ed), *Frankfurt am Main: Die Geschichte der Stadt in neun Beiträgen* (Sigmaringen, 1991), 423–519.

Redfield Jamison, Kay, *Night Falls Fast: Understanding suicide* (New York, 1999).

Retterstøl, Nils, *Suicide: A European perspective* (Cambridge, 1993).

Robinsohn, Hans, *Justiz als politische Verfolgung: Die Rechtsprechung in 'Rassenschandefällen' beim Landgericht Hamburg 1936–1943* (Stuttgart, 1977).

Rosenhaft, Eve, *Beating the Fascists? The German communists and political violence, 1929–1933* (Cambridge, 1983).

Rosenkranz, Herbert, *Verfolgung und Selbstbehauptung: Die Juden in Österreich, 1938–1945* (Vienna, 1978).

Rost, Karl-Ludwig, '"Euthanasie"-Filme im NS-Staat: Sozial- und filmhistorische Hintergründe einer Verführung zum Töten', in *Zeitgeschichte*, 28 (2001), 214–27.

Roßbach, Gabriele, 'Sie sahen das Zwecklose ihres Leugnens ein: Verhöre bei Gestapo und Kripo', in Andreas Pretzel and Gabriele Roßbach (eds), *Wegen der zu erwartenden hohen Strafe*, 74–98.

Sander, Helke und Barbara Johr, *BeFreier und Befreite: Krieg, Vergewaltigung, Kinder* (Munich, 1992).

Schleiermacher, Sabine, *Sozialethik im Spannungsfeld von Sozial- und Rassenhygiene: Der Mediziner Hans Harmsen im Centralausschuß für die Innere Mission* (Husum, 1998).

Schmuhl, Hans-Walter, *Rassenhygiene, Nationalsozialismus, Euthanasie: Von der Verhütung zur Vernichtung 'lebensunwerten Lebens'* (Göttingen, 1987).

Schott, Herbert, 'Die ersten drei Deportationen mainfränkischer Juden 1941/42', in Albrecht Liess (ed), *Wege in die Vernichtung: Die Deportation der Juden aus Mainfranken 1941–1943* (Munich, 2003), 73–166.

Sereny, Gitta, *Albert Speer: His battle with truth* (New York, 1995).

Sofsky, Wolfgang, *Die Ordnung des Terrors: Das Konzentrationslager* (Frankfurt am Main, 1993).

Spicer, Kevin P, *Resisting the Third Reich: The Catholic clergy in Hitler's Berlin* (DeKalb, Ill, 2004).

Stargardt, Nicholas, 'Victims of bombing and retaliation', in *German Historical Institute London Bulletin*, 16 (November 2004), 57–70.

_____ *Witnesses of War: Children's lives under the Nazis* (London, 2005).

Steinbach, Peter and Johannes Tuchel (eds), *Lexikon des Widerstandes, 1933–1945* (Munich, 1998).

Streit, Christian, *Keine Kameraden: Die Wehrmacht und die sowjetischen Kriegsgefangenen 1941–1945* (Stuttgart, 1978).

Stürickow, Regina, *Der Kommissar vom Alexanderplatz* (Berlin, 1998).

Swett, Pamela E, *Neighbours and Enemies: The culture of radicalism in Berlin, 1929–1933* (Cambridge, 2004).

Szodrynski, Joachim, 'Die "Heimatfront" zwischen Stalingrad und Kriegsende', in Forschungsstelle für Zeitgeschichte (ed), *Hamburg im Dritten Reich*, 633–85.

Tooze, J. Adam, *Statistics and the German State, 1900–1945: The making of modern economic knowledge* (Cambridge, 2001).

Tosh, John, 'What should historians do with masculinity? Reflections on nineteenth-century Britain', in *History Workshop Journal*, 38 (1994), 179–202.

Trevor-Roper, Hugh R, *The Last Days of Hitler* (London, 1947).

Wachsmann, Nikolaus, *Hitler's Prisons: Legal terror in Nazi Germany* (New Haven, 2004).

Wagner, Patrick, *Volksgemeinschaft ohne Verbrecher: Konzeption und Praxis der Kriminalpolizei in der Zeit der Weimarer Republik und des Nationalsozialismus* (Hamburg, 1996).

Wegner, Bernd, 'Hitler, der Zweite Weltkrieg und die Choreographie des Untergangs', in *Geschichte und Gesellschaft*, 26 (2000), 493–518.

Weidenhaupt, Hugo, *Kleine Geschichte der Stadt Düsseldorf* (Düsseldorf, 1993).

Weinberg, Gerhard L, 'Unexplored questions about the German military in World War II', in *Journal of Military History*, 62 (1998), 371–80.

Weitz, Eric D, *Creating German Communism, 1890–1990: From popular protests to socialist state* (Princeton, 1997).

Welch, David, *Propaganda and the German Cinema* (Oxford, 1983).

——— *The Third Reich: Politics and propaganda* (London, 1993).

Wette, Wolfram, 'Das Rußland-Bild in der NS-Propaganda: Ein Problemaufriß', in Hans-Erich Volkmann, *Das Rußlandbild im Dritten Reich* (Cologne, 1994), 55–78.

Whalen, Robert Weldon, *Bitter Wounds: German victims of the Great War, 1914–1939* (Ithaca, 1984).

Wildt, Michael, 'Violence against Jews in Germany, 1933–1939', in Bankier (ed), *Probing the Depths of German Antisemitism*, 181–212.

Wilke, Gerhard, 'The sins of the fathers: Village society and social control in the Weimar Republic', in Richard J Evans (ed), *The German Peasantry: Conflict and community in rural society from the eighteenth to the twentieth centuries* (London, 1986), 174–204.

Winkler, Heinrich August, *Der Weg in die Katastrophe: Arbeiter und Arbeiterbewegung in der Weimarer Republik 1930 bis 1933* (Bonn, 1989).

Wüllenweber, Hans, *Sondergerichte im Dritten Reich: Vergessene Verbrechen der Justiz* (Frankfurt am Main, 1990).

Zibell, Stephanie, 'Der Gauleiter Jakob Sprenger und sein Streben nach staatlicher Macht im Gau Hessen-Nassau', in *Zeitschrift für Geschichtswissenschaft*, 49 (2001), 389–408.

Zur Nieden, Susanne, *Alltag im Ausnahmezustand: Frauentagebücher im zerstörten Deutschland 1943–1945* (Berlin, 1993).

## IV UNPUBLISHED THESES

Damus, Wolfgang, 'Der Selbstmord unter besonderer Berücksichtigung der Juden' (unpublished med diss, University of Vienna, 1942).

Elder, Sace, 'Murder scenes: Criminal violence in the public culture and private lives of Weimar Berlin' (unpublished PhD thesis, University of Illinois at Urbana-Champaign, 2002).

Fulda, Bernhard, 'Press and politics in Berlin, 1924–1930' (unpublished PhD thesis, University of Cambridge, 2003).

Münster, Albrecht Graf zu, 'Ursachen des Selbstmordes in Deutschland: Eine zusammenfassende Darstellung' (unpublished med diss, University of Berlin, 1940).

Schatzmann, Jürg, 'Richard Semon (1859–1918) und seine Mnemotheorie' (unpublished med diss, University of Zurich, 1968).

Schenk McCord, Janet, 'A study of the suicides of eight Holocaust survivors/writers' (unpublished PhD thesis, Boston University, 1995).

Senff, Adolf, 'Analyse von 1000 Selbstmordfällen unter besonderer Berücksichtigung bevölkerungspolitischer und versicherungspolitischer Belange' (unpublished phil diss, University of Berlin, 1936).

# Index

Printed in the USA/Agawam, MA
April 25, 2023

809009.130